GAMES from LONG AGO & FAR AWAY

THOMAS J. CARR

Illustrations by Deborah C. Wright

PARKER PUBLISHING COMPANY
West Nyack, New York 10994

Library of Congress Cataloging-in-Publication Data

Carr, Thomas J.
    Games from far away & long ago: ready-to-use multicultural P.E. activities for elementary
    students/Thomas J. Carr.
        p. cm.
    ISBN 0-13-031161-8
    1. Games. 2. Physical education—Study and teaching (Elementary) 3. Multicultural education—Activity
    programs. I. Title: Ready-to-use multicultural P.E. activities for elementary students. II. Title.

    GV1203.C22 2000
    372.86'044—dc21

                                                                                    00-059852

10 9 8 7 6 5 4 3 2 1

ISBN 0-13-031161-8

PARKER PUBLISHING COMPANY

www.phdirect.com/education

Dedication

This book is dedicated to my wife, Charma, who while working with English as a Second Language students and earning her Master's in ESL, has shown me the whole new world of people and cultures from around the world. Thank you.

To our two girls, Kelcie and Rachel, who are full of fun and keep me young (while getting gray hair).

Acknowledgments

I would like to thank my fellow physical education teachers who have helped me with this book by reading sections and making comments on how to make it clear for others in the field: David Lausten, Doreen Barnes, and Dennis Emerson. I also want to thank two classroom teachers who read through the games to make sure they were clear for the classroom teacher to understand and follow: Sophie Ryder and Kathy Williams.

About the Author

Thomas J. Carr (B.S. from Aquinas College, Grand Rapids, Michigan; M.S. from Virginia Commonwealth University) has taught elementary physical education for over 20 years. Mr. Carr has been on various committees for the development of curriculums and assessments. He has developed a computerized assessment for elementary students that is used in Stafford County Public Schools. To aid those who score fitness test results for the President's Challenge and the state of Virginia Wellness-Related fitness scores, Mr. Carr has produced a computerized program that indicates the level of performance by inputting the test score and age of the performer.

About This Book

Games from Long Ago and Far Away offers you games in sequential order from easiest to more complex. Games are collected according to the activity to be played, such as tag or throwing. Each game that follows the first of its kind becomes a little more challenging. In this way, you can start with a game at the beginning or the middle in a particular section—wherever your students' ability is—and build in complexity from that point.

You'll find the following special features in this book:

- Basic information about each game is given. Here you'll find the country of the game's origin, the type of game, the formation the players should begin in, what equipment is needed, and the objective of the game/activity. This information is followed by interesting and/or fun facts about the particular game/activity or the country. Share this information with your students so that they'll continue to learn about our world and, in some cases, find out why the game is played as it is in the country of origin. Understanding each other and each other's differences will provide a common bond when different cultures come together and meet in our schools.

- At the end of some games is an "Also See" listing of other related games/activities in this book. You'll also find an index of games for each section's activities. This will help you be able to quickly locate related games.

- Countries are listed along with the continent in which they are located—Africa, Asia, Australia, Europe, North America, and South America. Different regions, such as the Caribbean Islands, Central America, Far East, Middle East, and Oceania, are also listed for better geographic identification.

- Many of these games/activities can be played in the classroom with some modifications. (One possible modification when needing to use a ball, for example, is to use a light foam ball.) These games are marked in the index on the opening page of each Section with an asterisk (*).

Why play games and activities from long ago and far away? Although most of these games have survived the test of time, many are still in danger of becoming forgotten and extinct because they are no longer played. Games offer a glimpse of other cultures—both past and present. It would be very sad indeed if your students were deprived the fun and enjoyment of these games and activities.

I hope this book whets both yours and your students' appetites to explore these multicultural games from long ago and far away!

Thomas J. Carr

Contents

Section 3: Hopscotch · 43

Section 4: Jacks · 79

Section 5: Races and Relays • 109

Section 6: Sports • 167

Section 7: Toss-Throw-Catch • 209

Section 8: Tag · 261

One Tagger—One Runner • 263

One Tagger—Many Runners • 291

We wish to acknowledge the following sources for permitting us to adapt certain activities from their books:

Games Children Play Around the World by Ruth Oakley (Tarrytown, NY: Marshall Cavendish Corp., 1989)

<u>Ball Games:</u> Call Ball 7-10; Donkey 7-7; Folding Arms 7-6; Hole Ball 7-23; Hurley Burley 8-74; Les Boules 6-9; Monday, Tuesday 7-11; Pass and Catch 7-3; Pitch Ball 7-26; Salazar's Obelisks 7-37; Skittles 6-2

<u>Chasing Games:</u> Badger the Sun 8-26; Blackberry 8-51; Blind Man's Bluff 1-20; Cat and Lynx 8-24; Cat and Mouse 8-10, 8-15; Catch Old Mrs. Winter and Throw Her in the River 8-70; Clapstick Blind Man's Bluff 1-18; Gathering Stars 8-53; A Gecko and a Stag Beetle 8-71; Gorelki 8-30; King Caesar 8-48

<u>Games of Strength and Skill:</u> Bunny Hop 5-5; Rooster 2-1; War Canoes 5-48

<u>Games with Ropes and String:</u> A-Fishing 8-65; Crick-Crack Crocodile 2-17; Fukuwarai 1-21; Ptarmigans and Ducks 2-11; Saxons and Dragons 2-13; Tug of War—England 2-10; Tug of War—Japan 2-12

<u>Sticks, Stones and Shells:</u> Chuck Stones 7-35; Herqr Relay Race 5-22; Nekki 7-39; O Krotalias 1-8; Throwing Sticks 7-33

Handbook of American Indian Games by Allen Macfarlan and Paulette Macfarlan (Mineola, NY: Dover Publications, Inc., 1989)

Ball Relay 5-34; Ball Toss Race 5-39; Bear Race 5-3; Breath-Hold Tag 8-37; Crab Race 5-4; Cross Country Relay 5-33; Fish Trap 8-66; Frog Race 5-8; Indian Foot Race 5-17; Indian Kickball 5-40; Kick Stick Races 5-42; Lance Head 5-37; Menomini Foot Race 5-13; Obstacle Run 5-32; Rattler 1-7; Stealing Sticks 8-76; Stick Relay 5-35; Tender the Fire 1-13; Twin Tag 8-57; There! 1-12

Section 1
Blindfold Activities

In *Blind Man's Bluff,* which dates back to Ancient Greece to a game called *Brazen Fly*, a player's eyes are covered (blinded) with a piece of cloth. This player then tries to find other players within the playing area. In medieval times, men wore shirts with hoods attached; to play the game, the hoods were taken off, turned around, and pulled over to cover the face. This blinded player then tried to catch other players, who would have had their hoods removed and knotted so as to strike the blinded player to get his attention.

In this unit of Blindfold Activities, *Blind Man's Bluff* (also known as *Blind Man's Buff*) is but one activity (played in various ways) in which blindfolds are used. Many activities involve the sense of listening and following the sound.

In this section you'll find 22 different blindfold games from 10 different countries/regions of the world located in 4 different continents.

Africa

Hunter and Gazelle (1-9)—Kalahari Desert in Botswana

Hunting Game (1-11)—Kalahari Desert in Botswana

Europe

Baton Maudit (The Cursed Stick) (1-3)*— Belgium

Blind Fly (1-14)—Italy

Blind Man's Bluff (1-20)—Ancient Greece

How Many Miles to London? (1-2)—Great Britain

Les Grelots (Bells) (1-4)—France

O Krotalias (Rattlesnake) (1-8)—Greece

Sherlock and Watson (1-1)*—Britain

Swap Chairs by the Numbers (1-17)—France

Far East (Asia)

Clapstick Blind Man's Bluff (1-16)—Taiwan

Clapstick Blind Man's Bluff (1-18)—Hong Kong

Fukuwarai (1-21)*—Japan

Ojiisan–Obaasan (1-6)—Japan

North America

Hoodsman Blind (1-15)—Colonial America

Jingling Match (1-5)—Colonial America

Moose Hunt (1-10)*—Plains/Woodlands/Southwest/Northwest Coast Native Americans

Pin the Tail on the Donkey (1-22)*—United States

Rattler (1-7)—Plains/Northwest Coast/Southwest Native Americans

Still Water, Still Water, Stop (1-19)—Colonial America

Tender the Fire (1-13)*—Plains/Northwest Coast/Woodlands Native Americans

There! (1-12)*—Plains/Woodlands/Northwest Coast Native Americans

*Games that may be played in the classroom.

1-1. Sherlock and Watson

Country: Great Britain (Europe)

Type of Game: Blindfold

Formation: Players stand in a single circle or are spread out.

Equipment: Blindfold

Objective: Sherlock locates and tags Watson.

This game is named after the famous literary detective Sherlock Holmes and his helper, Dr. Watson, by the English author Sir Arthur Conan Doyle.

Directions: One player is chosen to be Sherlock Holmes, who is taken into the circle and blindfolded. Once blindfolded, the leader chooses a circle player to be Dr. Watson. On the signal to begin, Sherlock calls out "Watson!" Watson answers "Sherlock!" Following the sound of the voice, Sherlock travels (carefully) towards the voice.

At any time, Sherlock can call out "Watson" and Watson has to reply. When Sherlock locates Watson and touches her/him, the game is over. Watson becomes the new Sherlock and a new Watson is picked when Sherlock is blindfolded.

If Sherlock locates a wrong player three times before finding the real Watson, the game is over and a new Sherlock and a new Watson are picked.

Adaptation: If Sherlock becomes adept at locating Watson with little difficulty, the leader can spin Sherlock around three times after the first call from Sherlock and Watson's reply.

Variation: Players are scattered throughout the area. When Sherlock comes to a player, Sherlock asks if that person is Watson. If the answer is correct, Sherlock wins. If not, Sherlock keeps searching. If Sherlock is incorrect in three tries, Watson wins. Sherlock may find a player and not ask if he/she is Watson. This does not count against Sherlock as a guess; but be careful, Sherlock, you might just let Watson get away!

1-2. How Many Miles to London?

Country: Great Britain (Europe)

Type of Game: Blindfold

Formation: Players stand behind a starting line. IT stands to the side and is blindfolded.

Equipment: Starting line; blindfold

Objective: The players follow IT's directions, then IT follows her/his own directions to find the others.

This is a challenging game of giving directions and then following the same directions in order to end in the same spot.

Directions: Standing in a line, the players are given directions for moving forward, backward, sideways (right or left), and how many steps to take. After 5–10 separate directions, the players freeze in that space.

IT is taken to the starting line. Following the same directions, IT tries to find the other players. When IT thinks he/she is close enough to the others, IT tries to touch one. Players sway, bob, and weave out of the way, but may not move their feet. When IT does find a player, he/she must try to identify the player in order to exchange places.

1-3. Baton Maudit (The Cursed Stick)

Country: Belgium (Europe)

Type of Game: Blindfold

Formation: Players sit in a single circle (about 3 feet apart). IT sits blindfolded in the center.

Equipment: Blindfold, stick, towel, or rolled-up newspaper

Objective: The players try not to get caught holding the stick when IT calls for the passing to stop.

Slightly larger than the state of Maryland at 11,798 square miles, Belgium is found in northern Europe bordering the countries of France, Luxembourg, Germany, and the Netherlands.

Directions: Players start by sitting in a circle. IT sits in the center of the circle blindfolded so as not to see where the stick is. The stick is passed around the circle from player to player. When IT whistles or calls out "Stop!" the stick freezes with the player who has it. (At no time should the stick be thrown.)

The player who has the stick when IT whistles must pay a simple penalty, such as hopping around the circle on one foot, before play begins again.

1-4. Les Grelots (Bells)

Country: France (Europe)

Type of Game: Blindfold

Formation: All players are scattered throughout the play area. All players but one are blindfolded. This lone player (IT) has bells tied to both ankles.

Equipment: Blindfolds; bells

Objective: The blindfolded players try to find the player with the bells.

Located in western Europe, France is between the Atlantic Ocean and the Mediterranean Sea. France is four-fifths the size of the state of Texas at 220,668 square miles.

Directions: Listening for the bells on the ankles of IT, the blindfolded players carefully try to find and tag IT before anyone else. As IT moves, the bells ring to help the other players locate the whereabouts of the IT player. IT may not do anything to silence the bells as he/she moves about.

Also See: *Jingling Match* (1-5)

   Ojiisan–Obaasan (1-6)

1-5. Jingling Match

Country: Colonial America (North America)

Type of Game: Blindfold

Formation: Blindfolded players are scattered. Jingler is not blindfolded in the playing area.

Equipment: Blindfolds; bells

Objective: The blindfolded players try to catch the jingler.

Also called Jingles, Blind Tag, Bell and Cat, *and* Catch–Fairy. *This game was played at medieval fairs in England.*

Directions: The Jingler rings a bell in each hand as the game is being played. The blindfolded players follow the ringing to try to be first to tag the Jingler. The first player who tags the Jingler becomes the new Jingler for the next game. The bells need to be rung the whole time the game is going on, even if the Jingler is standing still.

Variation: The bells may stop ringing when the Jingler does not move. Limit this to 5-second rest periods when the Jingler is not moving and the bells are silent.

Safety: When playing in an enclosed area, one or two players should be available to stop blindfolded players from running into walls or other obstacles.

Also See: *Les Grelots* (1-4)

              Ojiisan–Obaasan (1-6)

1-6. Ojiisan-Obaasan

Country: Japan (Far East, Asia)

Type of Game: Blindfold

Formation: Children form large single circle, with two players standing inside. One inside player is blindfolded (IT); the other is not blindfolded, and holds a bell.

Equipment: Blindfold; bell

Objective: The blindfolded player tries to locate and touch the bell ringer.

Traditionally played with one boy (ojiisan) and one girl (obaasan) inside the circle.

Directions: One boy and one girl stand inside the circle of players. The boy (ojiisan) is blindfolded while the girl (obaasan) is not. The boy (IT) is spun around three times before he is allowed to try to find the girl. To help IT find her, the boy calls out "obaasan, obaasan" twice and the girl must ring the bell she is carrying. This helps IT locate her as he follows the ringing sound and tries to tag her.

The bells are rung every time IT calls "obaasan." Then the girl can move to another place inside the circle.

When the girl is tagged, she becomes blindfolded (IT) and another boy enters the circle for her to try to locate and tag. The boy is to ring the bell each time IT calls out "ojiisan, ojiisan."

Variation: For higher skilled players, both players are blindfolded. The first calls out "obaasan, obaasan" (for a girl) or "ojiisan, ojiisan" (for a boy) and that player has to ring the bell. The bell ringer listens to the location of the voice in order to move away.

Also See: *Les Grelots* (1-4)

Jingling Match (1-5)

1-7. Rattler

Country: Plains/Northwest Coast/Southwest Native Americans, United States (North America)

Type of Game: Blindfold

Formation: Children form large single circle with two players inside, both blindfolded. One player holds a tin can with pebbles inside.

Equipment: Blindfolds; tin can with pebbles inside

Objective: The Hunter tries to locate and tag the Rattler.

This activity is used to develop listening skills and the ability to locate the direction from which the sound is coming.

Directions: Both participants are blindfolded and separated inside the circle of players. One blindfolded player is the Hunter, the other is the Rattler. On the signal from the leader, the Rattler begins rattling the can for 2–3 seconds. The Hunter tries to follow the sound in an effort to tag the Rattler. By the time the Hunter gets where the sound came from, the Rattler has moved.

Every 10 seconds or so, the Rattler must shake the can again (always loud enough to be heard) to give the Hunter a new clue as to her/his position. To help disguise her/his actual location, the Rattler can shake the can high overhead, low to the ground, or far to the right or left.

If either player is in a position where she/he would be in danger or be leaving the circle, the leader shouts "Stop!" and repositions the players before allowing either to move again.

Once the Rattler is located, the Hunter becomes the Rattler and a new Hunter is chosen from the circle of players.

Adaptation: When a player's ability to track the Rattler becomes quite developed, a softer, quieter rattle may be used.

Also See: *O Krotalias* (1-8)

1-8. O Krotalias (Rattlesnake)

Country: Greece (Europe)

Type of Game: Blindfold

Formation: Players are scattered. One holds a small box with stones called the Krotalias (rattlesnake). All other players are scattered and blindfolded.

Equipment: Blindfolds; box with pebbles

Objective: The blindfolded players try to locate and tag the Rattlesnake.

The population of the city of Athens, Greece grew sixfold between the years 1945 and 1995. Cars have been banned from the city's center because of the intense air pollution threatening the classical monuments.

Directions: The blindfolded players are scattered throughout the playing area. One player, who is not blindfolded, holds the box containing the pebbles. During the game and as this player moves around, the box is continually being shaken to create a rattling sound. The blindfolded players try to follow the rattling sound and be the first to tag the Rattler.

Also See: *Rattler (1-7)*

1-9. Hunter and Gazelle

Country: Kalahari Desert in Botswana (Africa)

Type of Game: Blindfold

Formation: Hunter and Gazelle are both blindfolded inside a playing area. The Gazelle has a pair of clapsticks. A chair, box, or other obstacle is in the center of the play area to represent a bush.

Equipment: Blindfolds; clapsticks; chair, box, or other obstacle

Objective: The Hunter tries to catch the Gazelle.

The first white men to cross the Kalahari Desert in Botswana are believed to be David Livingstone and W.C. Oswell in 1849.

Directions: The Hunter and Gazelle are both blindfolded inside the playing area. An obstacle is placed between the Hunter and Gazelle around which both have to navigate.

The Gazelle hits together a set of clapsticks every 5–10 seconds to give the Hunter clues to the Gazelle's location. If the Hunter catches the Gazelle, the Hunter becomes the new Gazelle. If time expires before the Gazelle is tagged, new players replace both the Hunter and the Gazelle.

1-10. Moose Hunt

Country: Plains/Woodlands/Southwest/Northwest Coast Native Americans, United States (North America)

Type of Game: Blindfold

Formation: One partner is blindfolded (Hunter); the other (Moose) is not.

Equipment: Blindfold; play area where footsteps and other sounds can be heard when moving; obstacles (chairs, boxes, etc.)

Objective: The Hunter tries to follow the Moose through the area, avoiding running into obstacles.

This activity develops the ability of moving silently and listening for the slightest noise to help track and locate.

Directions: Standing about seven feet from the Hunter, the Moose begins walking away. Moving in various ways—zigzag, stopping, stepping sideways or other varied movements—the Moose tries to confuse the Hunter.

Variation: Provide an obstacle course for the Moose and Hunter to follow. The Moose's movements lead the Hunter through the course only by walking so the Hunter can hear where the course leads.

Also See: *Hunting Game* (1-11)

1-11. Hunting Game

Country: Kalahari Desert in Botswana (Africa)

Type of Game: Blindfold

Formation: Players form single circle. Two players (Hunter and Springbok) are blindfolded inside the circle.

Equipment: Blindfolds

Objective: The Hunter tries to tag the Springbok.

African children have played this game for centuries to learn how to track silently, listening for sound clues to find their prey—in this case, a springbok, which is a graceful gazelle.

Directions: Standing inside the circle, the Hunter and Springbok are blindfolded and spun around to disorient them. The leader then tells them to begin.

As silently as they can, both players move around inside the circle, the Hunter listening for clues as to the whereabouts of the Springbok in order to tag her/him; and the Springbok listening for clues as to the whereabouts of the Hunter in order to avoid her/him.

If the Springbok is able to avoid being tagged during a set period of time, the Springbok wins and becomes the next Hunter. If the Hunter tags the Springbok, a new Hunter and new Springbok are chosen for the next game.

Also See: *Moose Hunt* (1-10)

1-12. There!

Country: Plains/Woodlands/Northwest Coast Native Americans, United States (North America)

Type of Game: Blindfold

Formation: Players stand in a single circle with one player (Chief) sitting in the center, blindfolded.

Equipment: Blindfold

Objective: Circle players try to tag the Chief without letting the Chief tag them back.

This easy activity is used to develop the ability in young Native Americans to hear the slightest sound and detect the direction from where it comes.

Directions: The Chief sits blindfolded in the center of a 50-foot circle. The other players stand outside this circle. The leader of the activity points to a circle player to quietly advance towards the Chief.

Listening for sound clues of an advancing player, the Chief is to point in the direction of the sound and call out "There!" to stop an advancing player. If correct, that player sits down quietly in that spot. If incorrect, the leader responds "Not there" and the invading player may continue.

If an invading player is able to lightly tag the Chief before being detected, the invader becomes the new Chief. The Chief may also reach out in the direction of the sound and try to tag the invader before being tagged her-/himself.

Invaders are warned not to rush in quickly towards the Chief. This is a game of quiet, stealth-like movements. The first player to successfully touch the Chief wins the right to be the next Chief. If no player touches the Chief, the one sitting closest is the next Chief.

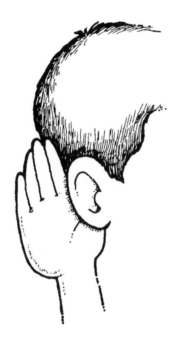

1-13. Tender the Fire

Country: Plains/Northwest Coast/Woodlands Native Americans, United States (North America)

Type of Game: Blindfold

Formation: One player (Chief) is blindfolded and kneels near a pile of firewood. The other players (Wood Gatherers) stand about 30 feet away.

Equipment: 1 stick for each Wood Gatherer

Objective: The Chief tries to listen for and stop the Wood Gatherers from sneaking firewood from his pile.

Although not so important in today's Indian village, protecting one's heat source (firewood) is an important job not to be taken lightly.

Directions: In order to keep the woodpile from being taken, the Chief listens for the advancement of the Wood Gatherers. Standing away from the pile of wood and the Chief, one Wood Gatherer announces "Wood Gatherers, we need wood" and points to one Wood Gatherer to lead the activity. This player quietly comes forward and tries to take one piece of wood. The Chief listens for the advancement of the Wood Gatherer and has her/his hands ready to move about the wood when she/he feels it is in danger.

Alert Chiefs will wait and reach out when she/he feels the Wood Gatherer is reaching for the wood. Taking only one piece of wood at a time, the Wood Gatherer then takes it back to where the Wood Gatherers stand and waits for another turn.

1-14. Blind Fly

Country: Italy (Europe)

Type of Game: Blindfold

Formation: Children form a single circle with IT blindfolded inside.

Equipment: Blindfold

Objective: IT tries to tag a player and identify her/him.

During the fourteenth century, players would make whips to lightly whip IT in order to gain IT's attention.

Directions: One player is chosen to be IT. This player goes into the center of the circle and is blindfolded. A helper turns IT around three times before returning to the circle.

As IT is being turned around, the circle players recite this chant:

> *"Blind fly, blind fly*
> *Sure you can't see?*
> *Turn round three times,*
> *And try to catch me."*
>
> *"Turn east, turn west,*
> *Catch as you can,*
> *Did you think you caught me?*
> *Blind fly, blind fly!"*

Following the end of the chant, the circle players enter into the circle and try to touch IT to draw her/his attention. IT tries to tag a circle player. A circle player tagged by IT exchanges places with IT for the next game.

Variation: Circle players are seated and are numbered off. A leader calls out two numbers. These circle players exchange places by going through the circle avoiding IT. If IT tags one of these players, they exchange places. If neither player is tagged, two new numbers are called.

Also See: *Hoodsman Blind (1-15)*

   Blind Man's Bluff (1-20)

1-15. Hoodsman Blind

Country: Colonial America (North America)

Type of Game: Blindfold

Formation: Players are scattered.

Equipment: Hoods or blindfolds

Objective: IT (blindfolded player) tries to tag the other players.

This is Blind Man's Bluff *of the Middle Ages.*

Directions: Players move around IT, challenging IT to try to tag them. Once IT tags a player, that player must stand still as IT tries to identify the tagged player by gently feeling the player's face, hair, and shoulder area. If identified in one to three guesses, the two players change places.

Players taunt IT by chanting:

> *"Blind man, blind man*
> *Sure you can't see?*
> *Turn round three times,*
> *And try to catch me.*
>
> *"Turn east, turn west,*
> *Catch as you can,*
> *Did you think you caught me?*
> *Blind man, blind man!"*

Variations:

- IT can be allowed to ask the caught player questions. Although not allowed to ask what the player's name is, the player must answer a nonidentifying question disguising her/his voice.

- If IT cannot identify two caught players, IT chooses a player to become the new IT for the next game.

Also See: *Blind Fly* (1-14)

                Blind Man's Bluff (1-20)

1-16. Clapstick Blind Man's Bluff

Country: Taiwan (Far East, Asia)

Type of Game: Blindfold

Formation: Two or three home bases are set up 10–15 yards apart. Players are divided between these bases. IT stands in the center of the play area, blindfolded.

Equipment: Blindfold; set of clapsticks for one player in each home base; handkerchief

Objective: IT tries to tag a player while he/she changes places. Noisemakers need not make the same sound.

Shaped like a tobacco leaf, the main island of Taiwan is 240 miles long (north to south) and, at the widest point, about 90 miles wide (east to west).

Directions: Noisemakers are given to one player in each home base. IT, blindfolded, stands in the center of the play area and holds the handkerchief. As players move from one base to another, they must make noise with the noisemakers. As they reach the new base, the noisemaker is handed to a new player. The noisemakers must be in constant movement.

IT tries to tag a moving player with the handkerchief. A tagged player becomes the new IT.

1-17. Swap Chairs by the Numbers

Country: France (Europe)

Type of Game: Blindfold

Formation: Children sit in chairs in a single circle. IT is blindfolded in the center of the circle. Players count off and remember their numbers.

Equipment: Blindfold; one less chair than number of players

Objective: IT calls two numbers; as these players change places, IT tries to either tag one of them or take a vacated seat.

This game is a form of Blind Man's Bluff *played in France.*

Directions: All players but one sit in a chair in the circle. These players count off starting from one so that everyone has a number.

The one player not sitting in a chair (IT) stands in the center of the circle and is blindfolded. When ready, IT calls out two numbers of players sitting down. These two players try silently to change places as IT tries to either tag one of them or take one of the vacant seats as her/his own.

A player tagged or the player left without a seat becomes the new IT for the next game. IT may need to call several sets of numbers before successfully tagging someone or capturing a chair for her-/himself. IT also needs to remember which numbers were already called so she/he doesn't call them again.

1-18. Clapstick Blind Man's Bluff

Country: Hong Kong (Far East, Asia)

Type of Game: Blindfold

Formation: Players are scattered. IT (blindfolded player) stands in the center of the playing area.

Equipment: Blindfold; noisemaker for each player

Objective: IT tries to tag a player.

This game is part of the New Year's celebration in Hong Kong.

Directions: As the players move throughout the area making noise with the noisemakers, IT tries to tag one of the players. A player tagged by IT becomes the new IT.

1-19. Still Water, Still Water, Stop

Country: Colonial America (North America)

Type of Game: Blindfold

Formation: Players are scattered.

Equipment: Blindfold

Objective: IT (blindfolded player) tries to locate and identify a player.

There were no toy factories in Colonial America. If the children had toys, they were handmade. Dolls were made from corn husks. Spinning tops were whittled from wood and used leftover string to spin the top.

Directions: IT, blindfolded, stands near the center of the playing area. The other players stand nearby. The following questions and answers are called out:

PLAYERS: *"How many horses does your father have?"*

IT: *"Three."*

PLAYERS: *"What colors are they?"*

IT: *"Black, white, and gray."*

PLAYERS: *"Turn around three times and catch whom you may."*

IT is turned around with the help of another player as the other players run away, but stay within the playing area. When IT feels no one touching her/him anymore, IT calls out "Still water, still water, stop!" The other players must stop where they are.

Moving throughout the area, IT tries to touch any player. Players may move three steps if IT comes close to them; after their three steps, the players cannot move their feet anymore. However, they may dodge, duck, or stoop down to avoid being tagged.

When IT does tag a player, IT must try to identify her/him in three or fewer guesses. Clues are obtained by gently feeling the height, hair, face, and shoulders of the player found. If correctly identified, this player is the new IT. If not, IT searches for a new player.

1-20. Blind Man's Bluff

Country: Ancient Greece (Europe)

Type of Game: Blindfold

Formation: Players form a single circle holding hands. IT stands in the center, blindfolded.

Equipment: Blindfold

Objective: IT tries to identify a circle player.

Blind Man's Bluff *dates back to Ancient Greece when it was known as* Brazen Fly.

Directions: The circle players, while holding hands, walk around IT who is in the center. IT claps her/his hands three times to stop the circle. IT points to a circle player and asks that player to make a sound of an animal. Disguising her/his voice, the circle player creates an animal sound. IT has only one chance to identify the circle player. If correct, IT and the circle player exchange places. If incorrect, the circle player steps into the circle.

Still blindfolded, IT tries to tag the circle player who is allowed to move around inside the circle, but must not leave it. When tagged, the circle player stands still, allowing IT to try to identify this player by carefully touching the face, hair, and shoulders of the circle player for clues to her/his identify. Again, IT has only one guess. If identified, IT becomes a circle player and the circle player becomes the new IT. If incorrect, IT remains IT for the next game.

Variations:

- Asking the circle player to create a noise, IT has only one guess to the player's identity.

- IT sits in the circle of players. Players sit in a single circle. Pointing to a circle player, that player is asked to create a certain sound (bark like a dog, meow like a cat, etc.). IT tries to identify the circle player in three guesses. After each guess, the circle player is asked to make a different sound.

Also See: *Blind Fly* (1-14)

Hoodsman Blind (1-15)

1-21. Fukuwarai

Country: Japan (Far East, Asia)

Type of Game: Blindfold

Formation: Players stand waiting their turns. Outline of a face is taped to a wall.

Equipment: Outline of a face; paper face parts (eyes, nose, ears, etc.); adhesive; blindfold

Objective: Players take turns trying to put parts of the face in the correct place while blindfolded.

This is Japan's version of Pin the Tail on the Donkey.

Directions: One player at a time is blindfolded and given a facial feature. Spun around three times, the player is positioned several feet away from the face outline and released by the spinner. Using both hands to find the paper face, the blindfolded player tries to place the facial feature in the correct place.

Variation: Each player has a partner. The partner without the blindfold can give up to three clues to help the blindfolded player place the facial feature in the correct place.

Also See: *Pin the Tail on the Donkey* (1-22)

1-22. Pin the Tail on the Donkey

Country: United States (North America)

Type of Game: Blindfold

Formation: Donkey outline is attached to a wall. Blindfolded player stands 3–4 feet away holding a paper tail.

Equipment: Outline of a donkey; tail with some form of fastener; blindfold

Objective: The blindfolded player tries to stick the tail on the proper part of the donkey outline while blindfolded.

Pin the Tail on the Donkey *is traditionally a party game for all ages.*

Directions: The blindfolded player stands 3–4 feet away from the donkey when blindfolded. Once prepared and unable to see, the blindfolded player is spun around three times and directed towards the donkey. Once the wall and donkey outline are located, the player attaches the donkey tail to the part of the donkey where she/he feels it belongs.

The player's initials are written where the tail is attached before the next player takes her/his turn. When all have had a turn, the player whose initials are closest to the proper place is the winner.

Variation: A second player helps the blindfolded player by giving up to three clues as to how to change direction in order to get closer to the proper place on the donkey.

Also See: *Fukuwarai (1-21)*

Section 2
Strength Builders

Strength builders are used to test players' strength and skills. Activities in this section help develop a player's strength as an individual or as a member of a team. A player's balance is also developed.

Adult supervision during these activities is necessary to prevent injuries or accidents. When games of this nature are played, the likelihood of an accident is increased due to their competitive nature. Adult supervisors need to make sure that the players are evenly matched to each other's abilities and strengths.

In this section you will find 19 games from 15 different countries and 7 continents/regions.

Africa

Crick Crack Crocodile (2-17)—Gambia

Asia

Insuknawr (2-19)—India
Kirip (Nicrobarese Wrestling) (2-7)—India
Porok—Pamin Sinam (2-3)—India
Square Pull (2-18)—Russia

Australia

Hoppo Bumpo (2-2)—Australia

Caribbean Islands

Rooster (2-1)—Puerto Rico

Europe

Red Rover (2-8)—Scotland
Saxons and Dragons (2-13)—Great Britain
Stork Fight (2-5)—Europe
Tug-of-War (2-10)—Great Britain

Middle East

Tug-of-War (2-16)—Egypt

Far East (Asia)

Tug o' War (2-15)—Korea
Tug-of-War (2-12)—Japan

North America

Indian Wrestling (2-6)—Native Americans
Ptarmigans and Ducks (2-11)—(Eskimo) Canada/United States
Rooks (2-14)—Colonial America

South America

Chicken Fight (2-4)—Brazil
Shove Winter Out (2-9)—Tierra del Fuego Islands

2-1. Rooster

Country: Puerto Rico (Caribbean Islands)

Type of Game: Strength builder—Balance

Formation: All players stand inside a marked circle. Each player places a 3-foot stick behind the knees, squats down, wraps the arms under the stick, and clasps her/his hands in front of the shins.

Equipment: 3-foot sticks; marked boundaries

Objective: Players try to knock the other players off balance while maintaining theirs.

Puerto Rico is an island that lies between the Atlantic Ocean on its northern shores and the Caribbean Sea on its southern shores. Puerto Rico is the eastern most portion of the West Indies called the Greater Antilles. Cuba, Hispaniola, and Jamaica are also within this group of islands. Puerto Rico is 3,435 square miles in size.

Directions: On the signal "Go!" the players try to knock the other players off balance so they will either fall over or release their hands to stop themselves from falling over. In either case, those players are eliminated. The last player still on her/his feet is the winner.

2-2. Hoppo Bumpo

Country: Australia

Type of Game: Strength builder—Balance

Formation: Players stand inside a marked playing area. Standing on one foot, each player holds the other foot in back with the opposite hand.

Equipment: Marked playing area

Objective: Players try to bump the other players off balance.

Settlers first came to Australia in 1788. These were convicts, soldiers, and government officials from Britain.

Directions: On the signal "Go!" the players hop on one foot trying to bump the other players off balance while trying to maintain their own balance. Players are eliminated when either the held foot is released, the player's foot touches the ground, or excessive roughness is used to get other players to fall.

Also See: *Chicken Fight* (2-4)

   Porok—Pamin Sinam (2-3)

2-3. Porok—Pamin Sinam

Country: India (Asia)

Type of Game: Strength builder—Balance

Formation: Two players stand inside a circle. Each player holds one foot in the opposite hand behind the other leg; the other hand is placed on the opposite shoulder.

Equipment: 6–8-foot circle

Objective: Players try to knock or bump the other player out of the circle, or cause to become off balance to fall, or cause to put the second foot down.

Sport in India has paralleled that of Ancient Greece, stretching back to 975 B.C. The zest for chariot racing and wrestling was common in both countries.

Directions: Balancing on one foot, each player hops inside the circle in an attempt to either knock the other player out of the circle, to cause the player to become off balance to fall down, or to release the other foot from the hand.

Also See: *Chicken Fight* (2-4)

        Hoppo Bumpo (2-2)

2-4. Chicken Fight

Country: Brazil (South America)

Type of Game: Strength builder—Balance

Formation: Two players stand in a hula hoop on one foot. Each player has a handkerchief hanging out of a back pocket.

Equipment: Hula hoops; handkerchiefs or flags

Objective: Players try to grab the other player's handkerchief while protecting their own.

After deposing emperor Dom Pedro II in 1889 and proclaiming Brazil a republic, Brazil was called the "United States of Brazil." In 1967 the country was renamed the Federative Republic of Brazil.

Directions: On the signal "Go!" each player in each hula hoop tries to grasp the opponent's flag while protecting her/his own. A player is eliminated when either her/his flag is pulled out, the raised foot touches the floor, or the player steps out of the hula hoop. If a player falls but does not drop the raised foot or touch out of the hula hoop, that player may get back up and continue.

Safety: Warn players to be careful when reaching or blocking to not bump heads.

Also See: *Hoppo Bumpo* (2-2)

        Porok—Pamin Sinam (2-3)

2-5. Stork Fight

Country: (Europe)

Type of Game: Strength builder—Balance

Formation: Partners have their left ankles tied together (about 6–8 inches apart) with a soft cloth. The players stand on their right feet, holding the tied left feet in the air.

Equipment: Soft playing surface; soft cloths

Objective: Players try to force the other player to put her/his left foot down without letting their left foot touch.

Europe, including the European part of Russia, ranks sixth in size of all continents; only Australia is smaller. Europe is not a distinct and separate body of land; rather, it shares the same landmass as Asia. Europe and Asia are separate continents due to historical rather than geographic reasons.

Directions: On the signal "Go!" each partner tries to force the other to put the left foot to the ground without touching her/his own left foot to the ground. When a player falls down but the left foot does not touch, the fallen player is not yet out and may continue after getting back up.

Adaptation: If tying the feet is not an option, have the players hold the left foot behind their back, but watch closely for a toe touch to the ground.

Also See: *Hoppo Bumpo (2-2)*

2-6. Indian Wrestling

Country: Native Americans, United States (North America)

Type of Game: Strength builder—Balance

Formation: Partners face each other with their right feet forward and touching the outside edge of each other's foot. The left foot is placed behind in a position of power and balance. Partners reach forward and grasp their right hands.

Equipment: None

Objective: Players try to force the other to move a foot or put a hand to the ground.

Native American Indians can also refer to Indians of Central and South America.

Directions: On the signal "Go!" the players push and pull with the right hands in an effort to force the other player to either lose balance and put the left hand down to the floor, or fall, or move either foot from its starting position.

Variation: Players may move the back foot during the time of competition. Players are eliminated when any other part of the body (other than the feet) touches the floor.

2-7. Kirip (Nicrobarese Wrestling)

Country: India (Asia)

Type of Game: Strength builder—Wrestling

Formation: Standing inside a circle, same gender and equal-ability partners reach the right arm under the opponent's left arm and grasp their hands behind the opponent's back (hugging each other). Heads are placed close together and held there to prevent head bumping during the match.

Equipment: 6–8-foot circle

Objective: Players try to force the opponent to step out of the circle.

The Nicrobarese tribe of India perform this wrestling activity in an attempt to touch the opponent's back to the ground for victory.

Directions: Without loosening the grip around the opponent, players attempt to force each other to step out of the circle. The first player who steps out loses that round. If a player loses her/his balance and falls or goes to one knee inside the circle, one point is declared on that player. Players are reset to begin again.

If after a one-minute time period no player has stepped out of the circle, the player with the lower number of points is declared the winner.

Any time a player is forced to step out of the circle, victory is declared for the opponent at that moment.

Editor's Note: Due to the physical contact and closeness of this activity, a careful match up of competitors is very necessary. Players should be matched up according to gender, size, and ability.

Beginning players should place hands on opponents' shoulders. Without moving their hands, players try to push each other off balance to face out of the circle, or to push the opponent so she or he steps out of the circle.

2-8. Red Rover

Country: Scotland (Europe)

Type of Game: Strength builder—Team

Formation: Two teams stand in opposite parallel lines and hold hands.

Equipment: Parallel lines 10 yards apart

Objective: A named player tries to break through the other team's chain.

Begun as Jockey Rover *in the late nineteenth century, this game later became better known as* Red Rover. *This is a physical game that can get quite rough.*

Directions: Standing on opposite parallel lines, players hold hands to form a chain. The captain of Team 1 calls out to Team 2: *"Red Rover, Red Rover, please send (name of player) over."*

The named player from Team 2 runs to Team 1 and tries to pass through Team 1's chain between two players. If successful, the player returns to Team 2. If unsuccessful, the player becomes part of Team 1. Time limits may be necessary to determine the amount of time a player has to break through the other team's chain.

Variations:

- When a player successfully breaks through the opponent's chain, that player returns to her/his team with a player from the other team.

- Teams do not hold hands. When trying to prevent advancing players from passing through, only the two players who the advancing player tries to pass between are allowed to try to stop her/him. Chain players may use open hands to keep the advancing player from passing through. The advancing player can use hands to pass between players, but also may duck down, spin, or wiggle through.

Safety: At no time should any player grab a person or clothing. Care needs to be taken to not bump heads.

2-9. Shove Winter Out

Country: Indians of Tierra del Fuego (South America)

Type of Game: Strength builder—Team

Formation: Half the players stand inside a circle (Winter); the other half, outside the circle (Summer).

Equipment: 12–15-foot circle; markings (vests, pinnies, etc.) to identify Winter and Summer players

Objective: The Summer players try to push the Winter players out of the circle.

Tierra del Fuego is a series of islands at the southern tip of South America. It was discovered in 1520 by Magellan and named the Land of Fire because of the Indians' majestic fires. Tierra del Fuego is also the name of the largest island (18,800 square miles) that is in both Chile and Argentina.

Directions: On the signal "Go!" the Summer players enter the circle and—using only their backs and shoulders—try to push out the Winter players. Winter players who are forced out of the circle reenter as Summer players to try to force out other Winter players. When all Winter players are eliminated, the roles are reversed for the next game.

Safety: Be careful not to bump heads.

2-10. Tug-of-War

Country: Great Britain (Europe)

Type of Game: Strength builder—Tug-of-war

Formation: Two teams face each other at opposite ends of a sturdy tug-of-war rope. Markers are placed 12–15 feet behind the last person on each team.

Equipment: Tug-of-war rope; 2 markers

Objective: Each team tries to pull the other team so the last player steps past the marker behind her/his team.

Scotland was united with England when James VI of Scotland was crowned James I, King of England, in 1603.

Directions: On the signal "Go!" each team pulls on the rope in an effort to pull the other team away from its marker and the last player can step behind her/his team's marker. The first team that does so wins.

Safety: No player should release the rope until "Stop!" has been called, unless a player has fallen and is about to be stepped on.

Also See: *Saxons and Dragons* (2-13)

2-11. Ptarmigans and Ducks

Country: Eskimo Indians, Canada/United States (North America)

Type of Game: Strength builder—Tug-of-war

Formation: Teams are divided by birthdays. Fall and Winter birthdays form the Winter team; Spring and Summer birthdays form the Summer team. Teams face each other while holding opposite ends of the tug-of-war rope. A cone is placed under the center of the rope.

Equipment: Tug-of-war rope having a mark six feet from the center toward each end (the front team player of each team must be behind this mark); cone

Objective: Each team tries to pull the rope so the other team's rope marker passes the cone in the center.

Ptarmigans are hearty birds that stay in the north the whole year. Ducks are in the north for only the warm summer months. This activity is to decide how harsh the winter will be. If Ptarmigans win, the winter will be harsh. If Ducks win, the winter will be mild. Other Native American Indians play this game and call it "Winter and Summer."

Directions: Each team stands holding its end of the rope. On the signal "Go!" each team pulls on the rope in an effort to pull the other team's marker past the center cone. The team that does so is the winner.

Also See: *Saxons and Dragons* (2-13)

   Tug-of-War (2-10)

   Tug-of-War (2-12)

   Tug o' War (2-15)

2-12. Tug-of-War

Country: Japan (Far East, Asia)

Type of Game: Strength builder—Tug-of-war

Formation: Two teams face each other at opposite ends of a tug-of-war rope.

Equipment: Tug-of-war rope; center line marked on the ground between teams

Objective: Each team tries to pull the other team to its side of the center line.

Villagers of Japan use woven straw ropes. These contests are to guarantee good harvests.

Directions: On the signal "Go!" each team attempts to pull the other team across the center line.

Also See: *Saxons and Dragons* (2-13)

           Tug-of-War (2-10)

           Tug o' War (2-15)

2-13. Saxons and Dragons

Country: Great Britain (Europe)

Type of Game: Strength builder—Tug-of-war

Formation: Two teams face each other at opposite ends of a tug-of-war rope. The center of the rope is tied to a stake that is driven into the ground at a center line.

Equipment: Tug-of-war rope; stake; center line

Objective: Each team tries to pull the stake out of the ground and pull the other team past the center line.

England was added to the Roman Empire in 43 A.D. Legions of Romans left England in 410 A.D.—and then Jutes, Anglos, and Saxons from German lands entered England.

Directions: One team is called the Saxons; the other team, the Dragons. On the signal "Go!" each team pulls the rope, trying to pull out the stake and pull the other team across the center line. The team to do so wins.

Also See: *Tug-of-War (2-10)*

Tug-of-War (2-12)

Tug o' War (2-15)

2-14. Rooks

Country: Colonial America (North America)

Type of Game: Strength builder—Tug-of-war

Formation: Partners each squat down on separate platforms 10 feet apart. Each player holds an end of a sturdy rope. The playing area should be covered with mats.

Equipment: 2 slightly raised 18" x 18" platforms; tug-of-war rope

Objective: Each partner tries to unbalance the opponent to fall off the platform.

In colonial days this activity was played in water, mud, or a pigsty.

Directions: On the signal "Go!" opponents pull the rope to try to unbalance the other player so that she/he will fall off the platform. Pulling on the rope and then reducing the tension by letting the rope slip a little can topple the other player onto the mats. No player should totally release the rope.

2-15. Tug o' War

Country: Korea (Far East, Asia)

Type of Game: Strength builder—Tug-of-war

Formation: Two teams each stand in a single-file line grasping the waist of the player in front of her/him. The first player from each team reaches across a center line to grasp the hands of the other team's front player.

Equipment: Center line

Objective: Each team tries to pull the entire other team across the center line onto its side of the line.

This tug-of-war activity requires no rope. When lining up players in line, be sure to have your strongest players at the front of the line.

Directions: On the signal "Go!" each team begins pulling in an attempt to pull the other team entirely across the center line for the win.

Also See: *Tug-of-War (2-16)*

2-16. Tug-of-War

Country: Egypt (Middle East, Africa)

Type of Game: Strength builder—Tug-of-war

Formation: Form teams of three players each. Teams face each other in single-file formation with the first players standing at the center line. Each player reaches across to grasp the hands of the facing first player.

Equipment: Center line

Objective: Each team tries to pull the other team across the center line.

In lining up players, the stronger players should be near the front, the weaker near the back of the lines.

Directions: On the signal "Go!" each team begins pulling backwards, trying to pull the other team across the center line. The first team to do so wins.

Also See: *Tug o' War (2-15)*

2-17. Crick Crack Crocodile

Country: Gambia (Africa)

Type of Game: Strength builder—Tug-of-war

Formation: Form three teams: two teams are at opposite ends of the tug-of-war rope ready to pull; the third team (Crocodiles) is at the center of the rope. This center section is the Crocodile, and where the Crocodile team holds onto the tug-of-war rope. Posts are driven into the ground 10 feet behind the last player of each pulling team.

Equipment: Tug-of-war rope marked off in three sections: the two ends for pulling are made of rope (a loop is tied at each end of the rope) and the center is a pole with the ropes connected at the ends.

Objective: Each team tries to pull the other team and the Crocodiles towards the post so that that team's loop will slip over and onto the post.

Gambia is found at the western tip of Africa on the Atlantic coast. Only 4,127 square miles in size, Gambia is smaller than the state of Connecticut.

Directions: On the signal "Go!" both pulling teams try to pull the rope to the post behind the team and drop the loop over the post. The Crocodile team in the center does not pull for either team; it will be the next competitor against the winner.

Alternative: An alternative tug-of-war rope can be used where a long single tug-of-war rope is marked into thirds. A loop is tied at the ends of the rope.

Also See: *Tug-of-War (2-10)*

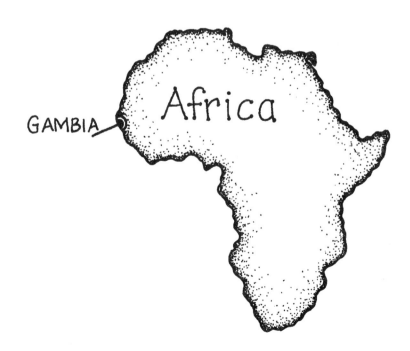

GAMBIA
Africa

2-18. Square Pull

Country: Russia (Europe)

Type of Game: Strength builder—Tug-of-war

Formation: Form four teams. Each team holds one end of two ropes tied at the centers to form an X. Cones are set up equal distant from the center behind the last player of each team.

Equipment: 2 tug-of-war ropes tied at the centers; cones

Objective: Each team tries to pull the rope so the last player on the team can grab his/her team's cone while still holding the rope.

The Ural Mountains stretch for 1,250 miles south from the Arctic Ocean, forming the boundary between Europe and Asia. This mountain range is through the country of Russia, but forms no significant boundary for Russia itself other than separating European Russia from Asiatic Russia—for geographical reasons only.

Directions: With all four teams ready to pull, the signal "Go!" is given. Each team pulls in an attempt for the last person on its team to hold onto the rope with one hand and grasp the team's cone with the other. The first team to do so wins.

Variations:

- The last player is allowed to kick over the cone.
- A handkerchief is set on top of the cone and is grabbed by the last person in line.

2-19. Insuknawr

Country: India (Asia)

Type of Game: Strength builder—Rod pushing

Formation: Players stand holding opposite ends of a sturdy pole.

Equipment: Sturdy 8–10-foot poles 3–4 inches in diameter; 12–14-foot circles

Objective: Each player tries to push the other player out of the circle.

Played in the state of Mizoram, India, Insuknawr *is declared a Mizo National Game!*

Directions: Each player holds her/his end of the pole under one armpit so 4–6 inches stick out behind the shoulder. The center of the pole is lined up in the center of the circle.

On the signal "Go!" both players begin pushing the pole in an attempt to push the other player out of the circle. If neither player has stepped out after one minute, "Stop!" is called and a short rest is taken before beginning a second round. Play continues for up to three rounds if there is no winner.

At the end of the third round, a tiebreaker is played with a time limit. The first player to step out of the circle or fall down is the loser. Players are not allowed to pull the pole or allow it to slip in her/his grasp in order to throw the opponent off balance.

Section 3
Hopscotch

Hopscotch is an ancient activity involving hopping or jumping through a designed pattern. (At the Forum in Rome, a hopscotch pattern is drawn in the cement floor!) Many hopscotch games involve the tossing of a marker that may be anything ranging from a stone to a piece of broken pottery.

Not all hopscotch patterns involve numbers being placed in each section of the pattern. The patterns for hopscotch are as varied as the players who participate in the activity.

Here you'll find 31 different hopscotch activities from 17 countries and 7 different continents/regions of the world.

Africa

Ta Galagala (3-27)—Nigeria

Asia

Chilly (3-8)—India
Klassika (3-10)—Moldova

Caribbean Islands

Jumby (3-18)—Trinidad and Tobago
Pele (3-23)—Aruba

Central America (North America)

La Rayuela (3-21)—Honduras
Peregrin (3-24)—El Salvador

Europe

Campana (3-13)—Italy
Escargot/La Marelle Ronde (3-2)—France
German Hopscotch (3-15)—Germany
Giuoco del Mondo (3-16)—Italy
Hop Round (3-17)—Great Britain
Hop the Beds (3-26)—Great Britain
Hopscotch (3-4)—Great Britain
Klassa (3-19)—Poland
Kritz (3-20)—former Czechoslovakia
Paradies Hüpfen (3-22)—Germany
Round Hopscotch (3-1)—Great Britain

Far East (Asia)

Chinese Hopscotch (3-9)—China
Gat Fei Gei (Airplane) (3-14)—China
Hopscotch (3-7)—Korea

North America

Alaskan Hopscotch (3-12)—United States
Boxes (3-30)—United States
Home (3-29)—United States
Hop Scotch (3-5)—Colonial America
One-Way Hopscotch (3-31)—United States
Potsy (3-25)—United States
Pottsie (3-6)—United States
Texan Hopscotch (3-28)—United States

South America

La Pollerita (3-3)—Bolivia
La Thunkuna (3-11)—Bolivia

3-1. Round Hopscotch

Country: Great Britain (Europe)

Type of Game: Hopscotch

Formation: Stand at entry of pattern.

Equipment: Hopscotch pattern without numbers; chalk

Objective: The player tries to hop on one foot to the center of the pattern and back.

England, Scotland, Wales, and Northern Ireland are the countries that make up the United Kingdom and Northern Ireland.

Directions: The first player stands outside the first section. Choosing which foot to jump on, she/he begins hopping on only that foot, working towards the center "Rest" section. Once in this section the player can stand on both feet for a rest. When coming back out, the player retraces her/his path, hopping in each section in the pattern. Players able to hop into and back out from the center without making a mistake (touching a line, putting the second foot down, or missing a section) may put her/his initials in any box not already claimed. ("Rest" section is claimed for everyone.) Now the next player may take her/his turn.

Sections having initials written in are available to only that person as another "Rest" section. All other players need to hop over this/those sections into an open one or one of their own. Players hopping into sections claimed by others lose the rest of her/his turn, but may continue the next time it is her/his turn.

The player with the most sections claimed at the end is the winner.

Also See: *Escargot/La Marelle Ronde (3-2)*

La Pollerita (3-3)

3-2. Escargot/La Marelle Ronde

Country: France (Europe)

Type of Game: Hopscotch

Formation: Player stands at entry to pattern.

Equipment: Hopscotch pattern with markings; chalk

Objective: The player tries to hop on one foot to the center of the pattern and back.

France is known for fine wine and fine dining. One food dish associated with France is escargot (snails).

Directions: This hopscotch pattern is shaped like a snail shell. (See Illustration 1.) Each player must decide which foot she/he will use for each turn. The first player hops through the whole pattern, hopping in each section only once until reaching the center space. Once in the center, the second foot can be put down for a brief rest. The player now hops back out with the same foot—one section at a time—to the beginning and hops out. If successfully completed without a mistake (without putting the second foot down or landing on a line), the player repeats the pattern again with the same foot. If successful the second time, the player places her/his initials in any space available. (The center is claimed for all players.) This initialed section is another resting section for only that player. All other players must hop over this section while going through the pattern.

When all spaces are occupied with initials, or it is impossible for anyone to complete the pattern, the game is over. The player owning the greatest number of sections wins.

Also See: *Round Hopscotch* (3-1)

La Pollerita (3-3)

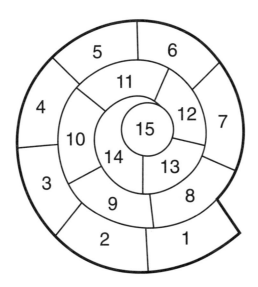

Illustration 1: *Escargot/La Marelle Ronde*

3-3. La Pollerita

Country: Bolivia (South America)

Type of Game: Hopscotch

Formation: Player stands at entry to pattern.

Equipment: Hopscotch pattern; stone (or puck)

Objective: The player tries to hop on one foot through the pattern while kicking the stone (with hopping foot) into each section.

Bolivia is 424,165 square miles, about the size of Texas and California combined. Neighboring countries to Bolivia are Peru, Chile, Argentina, Paraguay, and Brazil.

Directions: A spiral-designed pattern is drawn with sections marked off. (See Illustration 1.) Names or numbers are not used in the pattern.

The stone (or puck) is placed at the beginning of the pattern. The player kicks the stone into each square while hopping on the kicking foot. Once the stone reaches the center "Rest" section, it is kicked back out through the pattern to the beginning.

Players who step on a line, put the second foot down in a section other than the center "Rest" section, or kick the puck out of the proper section, lose their turn. Players begin their next turn at the beginning.

If two spirals are available, races between players/teams may be held to see who can complete the pattern first.

Also See: *Round Hopscotch (3-1)*

Escargot/La Marelle Ronde (3-3)

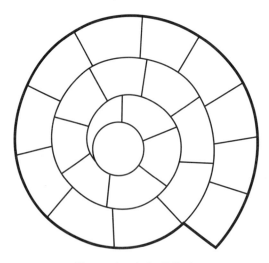

Illustration 1: *La Pollerita*

3-4. Hopscotch

Country: Great Britain (Europe)

Type of Game: Hopscotch

Formation: Player stands at entry to pattern.

Equipment: Hopscotch pattern; stone

Objective: The player tries to hop through the pattern while kicking the stone from section to section.

Influenced by the Gulf Stream, England's weather is moderate with mild winters and cool summers. Winter temperatures range from 37° to 45° F. in January, to 59° to 64° F. in the summer.

Directions: The player tosses the stone into square 1. (See Illustration 1.) Hopping on one foot into that square, the stone is kicked out over the base line with the *other foot* before hopping back out. The stone is now tossed into square 2. The player hops into square 1, then into square 2, and kicks the stone out of the pattern past the base line before hopping back out reversing the order. This continues through square 10.

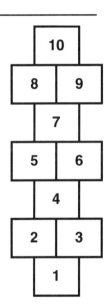

Illustration 1: *Hopscotch*

In hopscotch patterns using side-by-side squares (see Illustration 2), players land on both feet, one foot in each square. The foot in the square with the stone then kicks out the stone.

A player's turn is over when the second foot touches where it shouldn't, the player touches a line, the stone lands on a line or a wrong square, or the stone does not pass the base line on the kick-out.

Players who lose a turn begin their next turn where they left off.

Adaptation: Advanced players may be required to repeat the sequences a second time—in reverse—in order to win.

9	10
7	8
5	6
3	4
1	2

Illustration 2: *Hopscotch*

3-5. Hop Scotch

Country: Colonial America (North America)

Type of Game: Hopscotch

Formation: Player stands at entry to pattern with stone held between his/her feet.

Equipment: Hopscotch pattern; stone

Objective: The player tries to jump through the pattern without dropping the stone.

These two hopscotch games were brought to Colonial America from England. The patterns and methods date back to medieval England.

Directions for Game One: The first game has six 12" x 12" squares forming two parallel rows. (See Illustration 1.) The player begins at square 1 by jumping with both feet, holding a stone between her/his feet. The player jumps from one square to the next and then out when she/he reaches square 6. More experienced players must travel through the pattern without dropping the stone, stepping on a line, or shuffling their feet; and must make only one jump in each square.

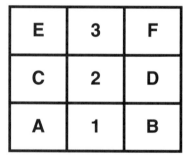

Illustration 1: *Hop Scotch*

After completing the pattern without a mistake, the player reenters the pattern by jumping over square 1 into square 2. The player jumps into each of the following squares and then out at square 6. Each subsequent round begins at the next number until the jumper enters at and exits from square 6.

Directions for Game Two: The second hopscotch game is played without a stone. Nine 15" x 15" squares are drawn to form a large square (Illustration 2), with letters and numbers as shown.

The first player stands at the base line and jumps into square 1 with both feet. Then jumping straight up, the player lands to straddle square 1, placing one foot in square A and the other in square B. Jumping again, the player lands with both feet in square 1 before jumping backwards out of the pattern. If the jumper is able to complete this sequence, she/he continues. This time the player jumps over the first row of squares to land with both feet in square 2. The player straddle jumps to land in squares C and D, jumps back into square 2, and then jumps backwards into square 1 with both feet before jumping out. This is repeated a third time, but the player must jump into square 3, straddle into E and F, jump back into 3, jump backwards into 2, then backwards to square 1, and then out. All jumps are made from a standing start, with feet together, never from a step or a run.

Illustration 2: *Hop Scotch*

If the player successfully completes this sequence, she/he stands on the B–D–F side and repeats the process. This continues all around the square, entering from each side.

If the player successfully completes her/his jumps without a mistake (missing a square or stepping on a line), she/he wins. If a miss is made, the next player begins where the previous player failed. The winner is the player who is able to finish the fourfold jumping sequence.

More advanced players may be required to go through the entire sequence without a miss to be declared the winner.

3-6. Pottsie

Country: United States (North America)

Type of Game: Hopscotch

Formation: Player stands at entry to pattern.

Equipment: Hopscotch pattern; ball

Objective: The player tries to hop through the pattern and bounce the ball while correctly adding to the list in each category.

The United States is divided into 50 separate states and the District of Columbia. Forty-nine states are all part of the continental North America, with Alaska separated from the "lower" 48 states by part of Canada. Hawaii, the 50th state, is comprised of islands in the Pacific Ocean 2,397 miles off the coast of California.

Directions: This hopscotch pattern consists of two columns of three or four rows. Each section is approximately 2 feet wide and 1-1/2 feet deep. Each box has a name of a category from which a list may be made. (See Illustration 1.) Possible categories are foods, numbers, letters, countries, calendar (months, days), presidents, colors, states, etc. Any classroom subject could have its own list of categories about which the players could give information.

Foods	Numbers
Letters	Countries
Calendar	Presidents
Colors	States

Illustration 1: *Pottsie*

The player begins by hopping on one foot into the first square. While standing on one foot, the player bounces the ball one time while naming one item that fits the category. The player now hops into the second box and repeats the ball bounce, naming an item for this category. This continues for the remaining sections. When the first player has completed her/his turn, the second player begins. As the following players go through the pattern, they are to name different items in each category from those already named.

Players remain in the game as long as they complete the pattern each turn without making a mistake. Mistakes include touching the nonhopping foot to the ground when in the pattern, hopping or bouncing the ball on a line, repeating an item already named, losing control of the ball, or bouncing the ball twice in the same section.

As players have more turns, they become eliminated faster. The last player left is the winner.

Variation: A player stands on one foot outside the bottom left section and kicks a stone into the first section. The following player must name one item that fits the category. The player on one foot continues through the pattern to the end.

3-7. Hopscotch

Country: Korea (Far East, Asia)

Type of Game: Hopscotch

Formation: Player stands at entry to pattern.

Equipment: Hopscotch pattern; stone

Objective: The player tries to go through the pattern without a miss.

Like children in many other countries, Korean children use different patterns for the hopscotch games, not just the one shown here.

Directions: Standing at the base line, the player tosses a stone into square 1. (See Illustration 1.) The player, without stepping on a line, hops on one foot into square 1 and tries to keep the other foot from touching the ground. While standing on the hopping foot, the player must kick the stone into square 3 (passing square 2) without kicking it out of the pattern. (Players who hop on a line, touch the second foot to the ground, or kick the stone out of the pattern lose their turn.)

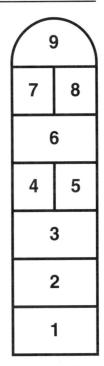

Illustration 1: *Hopscotch*

The player then hops into square 3 and kicks the stone into square 6, past squares 4 and 5. The player hops into squares 4 and 5, landing with one foot in each. Following a short rest, the player jumps into square 6, lands on the hopping foot, and kicks the stone past squares 7 and 8 into square 9. The player then jumps into squares 7 and 8 for another rest, standing on both feet. The player finally jumps into square 9, lands on one foot, bends forward to pick up the stone, and hops out of the pattern without a mistake.

If a player completes the round without a mistake, she/he scores a win for her/his turn.

The other players, in turn, then have their opportunity at the hopscotch pattern.

On a player's second turn (after having successfully completed the pattern on the first), she/he begins by tossing the stone into square 2 and repeats the process. Players who made a mistake on their first or previous turn must repeat the pattern that was missed.

3-8. Chilly

Country: India (Asia)

Type of Game: Hopscotch

Formation: Player stands at entry to pattern.

Equipment: Hopscotch pattern; stone

Objective: The player tries to go through the pattern correctly while kicking the stone.

India is 1,266,595 square miles in size, equal to about one-third the size of the United States in area. Geographically India covers all of the Indian Peninsula and portions of the Asian mainland.

Children of India draw hopscotch patterns either in the dirt using a stick or on pavement/sidewalks using chalk or soft stone. Three patterns are typically used using no names or numbers in the squares.

Directions for Game One: The player stands at the base line and tosses the stone into the first square. (See Illustration 1.) Hopping into the first square, the player begins to kick the stone into one square at a time with the hopping foot. The stone is kicked out of the pattern at the end. The player then tosses the stone into the second square from the base line. Hopping over the first square into the second, the player kicks the stone into the last square before kicking it out. The stone now is tossed into the third square. Hopping directly into the third square, the player kicks the stone out of the pattern. (If the player or the stone touches a line or touches the ground with the second foot, her/his turn is over and the next player goes.)

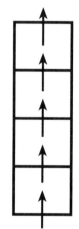

Illustration 1: *Chilly*

Once a player has successfully completed the pattern, the player begins again but must face away from the pattern to toss the stone over a shoulder or head to land in a square. Then, facing the squares, the player hops into the square where the stone landed and finishes the pattern.

Directions for Game Two: Beginning at the lower left square, the player tosses the stone into the first square. (See Illustration 2.) As in Game One, the player hops from square to square, kicking the stone into the next square ahead. Once through the pattern the first time, the stone is tossed into the second square. The player hops over the first square and into the second, kicking the stone again from square to square while traveling through the pattern. Once successfully through the pattern, the player repeats the pattern for the next (third) square.

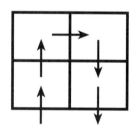

Illustration 2: *Chilly*

Always remember to hop directly into the square where the stone is tossed.

Directions for Game Three: Beginning again at the bottom left square, the player tosses the stone into the first square. Jumping into each consecutive square, the player must kick the stone into the square before hopping into it. Once through the pattern, the stone is then tossed into the next square, where the player begins kicking and hopping through the pattern again.

Each time a player goes through the pattern successfully, the stone begins in the next consecutive square and the player must hop past the earlier squares of the pattern. Like that of Game One, play begins in each square only once.

If a player misses during a turn, she/he begins the next turn from where the miss occurred.

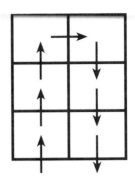

Illustration 3: *Chilly*

3-9. Chinese Hopscotch

Country: China (Far East, Asia)

Type of Game: Hopscotch

Formation: Player stands at entry to pattern.

Equipment: Hopscotch pattern; stone

Objective: The player tries to perform the activity correctly throughout the whole pattern.

The Great Wall of China stretches from the Gansu (Kansu) province to the Yellow Sea, a distance of 1,500 miles!

Directions: Standing at the base line by square 1, the player tosses the stone into square 1. (See Illustration 1.) The player hops into square 1 and kicks the stone out of the pattern with the hopping foot. The player returns to the base line and now tosses the stone into square 2. Hopping directly into square 2, the player kicks the stone into square 1 and then out of the pattern, following the stone through the pattern. This pattern of play continues until the player has successfully begun in all eight squares.

A player loses a turn if she/he tosses a stone that lands on a line or outside the proper square, or if she/he touches a line or brings the second foot down. The player's next turn begins from that point.

4	5
3	6
2	7
1	8

Illustration 1:
Chinese Hopscotch

3-10. Klassika

Country: Moldova (Asia)

Type of Game: Hopscotch

Formation: Player stands at entry to pattern.

Equipment: Hopscotch pattern; stone

Objective: The player tries to go through the pattern properly without a miss.

Moldova is a former republic of the Union of Soviet Socialist Republics [USSR] located between Romania and the Ukraine.

Directions for Game One: The player tosses the stone into square 1. (See Illustration 1.) Hopping on only one foot, the player kicks the stone with the nonhopping foot into each square in number order to square 7, then back to square 1 and out of the pattern.

The player now tosses the stone into square 2. The player jumps over square 1 into square 2, landing on the hopping foot. The stone is kicked through the pattern again as performed for square 1. This is repeated for squares 3 and 4. When the stone is tossed into squares 5, 6, and 7, the player jumps into squares 3 and 4 before hopping into squares 5, 6, and 7.

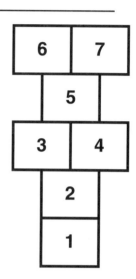

Illustration 1: *Klassika (Game One)*

Directions for Game Two ("Ten Classes"): This hopscotch game begins as in Game One, with the player tossing the stone into square 1 and hopping into that square. (See Illustration 2.) The player kicks the stone with the nonhopping foot into square 2 and through the rest of the sequential squares to square 10, and then out of the pattern.

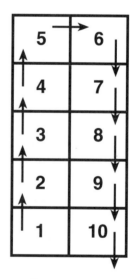

Illustration 2:
Klassika (Game Two: "Ten Classes")

In order to win, a player must complete the pattern and the following two "exams":

- **Exam One:** Toss the stone into square 1. (See Illustration 3.) Hop into square 1 and kick the stone with the nonhopping foot diagonally into square 9. Hop into square 9 and kick the stone into square 3. This zigzag pattern goes to the top of the diagram using the odd numbers. On the return to the base line, the stone and player travel through the even-numbered squares before kicking the stone out of the pattern. This "exam" is performed only once if the player goes through the pattern, keeping the stone in the proper squares and off the lines while staying off the lines her-/himself and on the hopping foot only.

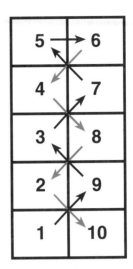

Illustration 3:
Klassika ("Exam One")

- **Exam Two:** The stone is tossed into square 1 before the player hops into the same square. (See Illustration 4.) With the nonhopping foot, the stone is kicked into square 3. Hop into square 2 and then into square 3. Kick the stone into square 5. Hop into square 4 before hopping into square 5. Kick the stone into square 6 before hopping into square 8. Continue kicking the stone two squares ahead while hopping into each square. From square 10 the stone is kicked out of the pattern, followed by the player.

The first successful player to complete the "ten classes" and both "exams" wins.

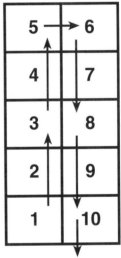

Illustration 4:
Klassika ("Exam Two")

3-11. La Thunkuna

Country: Bolivia (South America)

Type of Game: Hopscotch

Formation: Player stands at entry to pattern.

Equipment: Hopscotch pattern; stone

Objective: The player tries to perform the pattern correctly and kick the stone out of the pattern on the return trip.

The squares in La Thunkuna are named the days of the week, Heaven, and World.

Illustration 1: *La Thunkuna*

Directions: The player stands at the base line and tosses the stone into Lunes (Monday). (See Illustration 1.) The player then hops into Martes (Tuesday), passing over Lunes, turns around, hops into Lunes, and kicks the stone out past the base line. If the player hops on a line or touches the floor with the nonhopping foot, or if the stone lands on a line or out of the correct square, this player loses her/his turn.

The player continues by tossing the stone into Martes, hopping into Lunes and then into Miercoles (Wednesday). Turning around, the player hops into Martes, kicks the stone out of the pattern past the base line on one kick, and hops out of the pattern. This continues through the rest of the pattern. Make sure the player hops over the square that has the stone in it.

When the stone is tossed into Jueves (Thursday), the player hops into both Viernes (Friday) and Sabado (Saturday), landing with one foot in each section. She/he hops once more into Dominico (Sunday) and kicks the stone back over the base line as performed before.

The next toss is into Dominico (Sunday) and then El Cielo (Heaven). The player lands with both feet when jumping into El Mundo (World). The player performs a jump turn, jumps into El Cielo, and kicks the stone out with the nonhopping foot as before. If the stone lands on a wrong space on a toss or a kick, the player's turn is over. The player begins the next turn where she/he left off.

The first person to finish wins.

Also See: *German Hopscotch (3-15)*

3-12. Alaskan Hopscotch

Country: United States (North America)

Type of Game: Hopscotch

Formation: Player stands at entry to pattern.

Equipment: Hopscotch pattern has no names or numbers put inside; 2" x 2" stones (referred to as "Man")

Objective: The player tries to hop through the pattern without making a mistake.

Summer in Alaska allows the children time to go outside and play hopscotch. Warmer days and longer periods of sunlight melt the snow to provide places on which to draw hopscotch patterns.

Directions: Each player tosses her/his MAN into the square nearest the side pocket, with the closest stone (not touching a line) going first. (See Illustration 1.) Deciding which foot to hop on, the first player begins. With all the MEN still in the first square, the first player jumps, landing on one foot in the next square. Without stepping on a line or putting the other foot down (in a single box), the jumper jumps through the pattern and back. The jumper stands on one foot in the square next to where the MEN are, picks up her/his MAN, and hops over the square and out of the pattern. (Boxes that are side by side are played by normal rules—one foot in each.) Before the next player begins, the first player tosses her/his MAN into the next square.

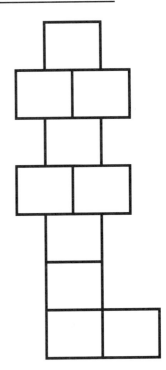

Illustration 1:
Alaskan Hopscotch

Without stepping into a square that contains a player's MAN, the next player hops into the third square. When jumping into the pattern beyond the squares where players' MEN are located, the player cannot have a walking or running start. The side pocket may be used to step into by a player to help make a diagonal leap into a distant square otherwise unreachable.

A MAN that lands on a line or outside a square causes that player to lose her/his turn.

Once a player has completed the whole pattern, she/he must hop through the pattern one more time and recite the alphabet along the way.

3-13. Campana

Country: Italy (Europe)

Type of Game: Hopscotch

Formation: Player stands at entry to pattern.

Equipment: Hopscotch pattern with numbers; stone

Objective: The player tries to go through the pattern without making a mistake.

Italy is a boot-shaped peninsula located in the Mediterranean Sea. The sunny climate and mild weather allow the children many months to play outdoors.

Directions: The first player stands near square 1. (See Illustration 1.) Tossing the stone into the square, the player jumps over square 1 to land on one foot in square 2. Without changing feet, stepping on a line, or putting the second foot down, the player jumps through the pattern and back, following the number sequence. Stopping in square 2, the player picks up the stone and hops out of the pattern. At squares that are side by side and touching, the jumper puts one foot in each square and jumps to the next one in sequence. The jumper repeats the above, tossing the stone into the next box each round until a mistake is made.

If the stone lands out of the correct box or on a line, the player's turn is over. A player's next turn following a mistake begins at the point where the mistake was made.

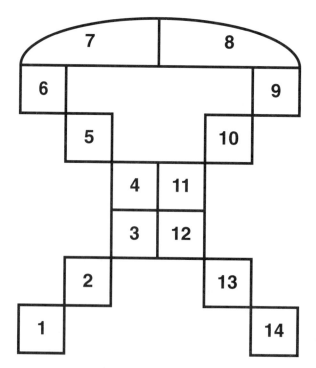

Illustration 1: *Campana*

3-14. Gat Fei Gei (Airplane)

Country: China (Far East, Asia)

Type of Game: Hopscotch

Formation: Player stands at entry to pattern.

Equipment: Hopscotch pattern; stone; chalk

Objective: The player tries to hop through the pattern, kicking the stone from square to square.

This hopscotch game originated in China, but is played around the world in Chinese communities. Gat Fei Gei means "one foot jumping flying machine" or "airplane" because the shape of the pattern resembles that of an airplane.

Directions: Like most other hopscotch games, the player lands with both feet, one in each square, in squares that are touching side by side (4–5 and 7–8). When hopping into only one square, the same foot is always used.

Standing at the base line of square 1 the player tosses her/his stone into the Pig's Head. (See Illustration 1.) Hopping through the pattern, the player stops in squares 7–8. Jumping and turning around, the player again stands in 7 and 8 facing away from the Pig's Head. Reaching behind or between the legs, the player picks up the stone before hopping back out of the pattern. The turn is over if a line is touched, a hand touches outside the Pig's Head when reaching for the stone, or the stone lands on a line or out of the space.

If successful, the first player now can claim square 1 as her/his own by putting her/his name or initials in the square. No other player may hop into this square except for the owner, who uses this square for a rest stop on both feet.

The remaining players in turn follow in the same way. A player who hops into her/his own square must land on both feet or be "burned." A square that is "burned" becomes free for some other players to own.

Generous owners may mark off a corner of a square that allows other players to hop into this area of the square. The area marked off needs to be large enough for it to be available for all players to use.

After all boxes are owned, the Pig's Head can be divided into four parts to be competed for as in the rest of the airplane.

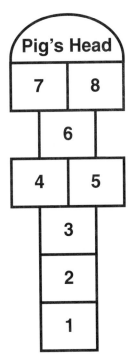

Illustration 1: *Gat Fei Gei*

3-15. German Hopscotch

Country: Germany (Europe)

Type of Game: Hopscotch

Formation: Player stands at entry to pattern.

Equipment: Hopscotch pattern; stone; chalk

Objective: The player tries to complete the pattern without mistakes.

The country was divided after World War II (1939–1945) into the Federal Republic of Germany (FRG, also known as West Germany) which had a western influence, and the German Democratic Republic (GDR or East Germany) which had a communist influence from the Union of Soviet Socialist Republics (USSR). On October 3, 1990 the German Democratic Republic reunited with the Federal Republic of Germany to unify Germany into one country once again.

Directions: The player stands at the base line of the pattern facing away. Tossing the stone over the shoulder, the player claims the square or section of the pattern as her/his "House" and marks it with her/his initials. In order to own the House, the player must hop on one foot successfully through the proper sequence. If the player steps on a line, puts the other foot down, or hops out of sequence, the House is "up for sale." Once a House is owned, tossed stones landing in an owned House means a loss of turn. Each player in turn has a chance to own unclaimed Houses.

Players may hop only into unclaimed Houses or Houses they already own. Hopping into someone else's House is "trespassing" and the end of that player's turn.

The winner is the last player left or the player with the most Houses if everyone else is eliminated when all have had equal turns.

Variation: Children draw a hopscotch pattern with the days of the week or numbers written inside. (See illustrations 1 and 2.) This will help them learn the days of the week as well as their numbers. As they progress, you may want to change the days of the week to months and to use larger numbers than those shown in the illustration.

Also See: *La Thunkuna* (3-11)

	Sunday	
Friday	Thursday	Saturday
	Wednesday	
	Tuesday	
	Monday	

Illustration 1: *German Hopscotch*

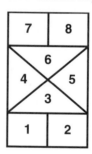

Illustration 2: *German Hopscotch*

3-16. Giuoco del Mondo

Country: Italy (Europe)

Type of Game: Hopscotch

Formation: Player stands at entry to pattern.

Equipment: Hopscotch pattern; stone

Objective: The player tries to complete the pattern without making a mistake.

Before 1861 Italy consisted of many separate states. In 1861 these states were united under Victor Emmanuel II, then King of Sardinia and who was crowned King of Italy. Although united, these states keep a strong regional identity in today's 20 administrative regions throughout Italy.

Directions: The first player tosses a stone into square 1 while standing three feet away behind the tossing line. (See Illustration 1.) If the stone lands inside square 1 without touching a line, the player jumps into that square, landing on her/his hopping foot. Continuing through the pattern to the Rest section, the player lands with both feet in side-by-side squares (2–3 and 5–6), but hops over the blank ovals.

When in the Rest section, the player jumps and turns around to return back towards square 1. Stopping in the square(s) before reaching the stone, the stone is picked up before completing the pattern. The second player then begins her/his turn.

When successful, players toss the stone into the next square on their next turn. When unsuccessful, the square is repeated. Play continues through square 7.

The tossed stone must land completely in the correct square. If it lands in a wrong square or on a line, that player loses a turn. A stone landing in the blank oval between 4–6 is also the loss of a turn. If the stone lands in the blank oval between 7 and Rest, the player must begin again at square 1 following the loss of that turn.

Unlike other hopscotch games, players do hop into the squares where their stone lands on their way to the Rest section.

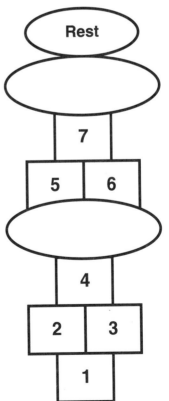

Illustration 1: *Giuoco del Mondo*

3-17. Hop Round

Country: Great Britain (Europe)
Type of Game: Hopscotch
Formation: Player stands at entry to pattern.
Equipment: Hopscotch pattern; 5 stones per player; chalk
Objective: The player tries to hop through the pattern without making a mistake.

It is believed this form of hopscotch was brought to England with the Roman soldiers as they invaded this part of the world. This pattern is also found inlaid in the floors of the Roman Forum.

Directions: Each player has five stones to use. The players need to decide upon a winning score before play begins. The first player tosses her/his stones into the hopscotch pattern. (See Illustration 1.) The sum of the numbers where the stones land is the player's score, if successful. Hopping on one foot, the player hops through the pattern in sequence, picking up the stones while traveling through. Hopping on a line causes the player's turn to end as does putting the other foot down, resulting in a "0" score. Stones landing on a line do not score.

If all stones are picked up and the player successfully completes the pattern, the player earns the score of the stones but also puts her/his initials in one section of the outer circle or "tire." Following players must hop over claimed sections while enroute during their turn. The first player to reach the designated score wins the game.

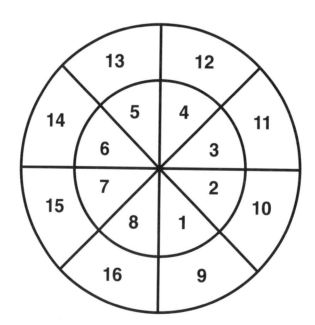

Illustration 1: *Hop Round*

3-18. Jumby

Country: Republic of Trinidad and Tobago (Caribbean Islands)

Type of Game: Hopscotch

Formation: Player stands at entry to pattern.

Equipment: Hopscotch pattern; stone

Objective: The player tries to be the first to complete the pattern.

Trinidad and Tobago are two islands forming one country called the Republic of Trinidad and Tobago, the size of the state of Delaware at 1,980 square miles. The island of Trinidad is in the Atlantic Ocean off the eastern coast of Venezuela, the Republic's closest neighbor.

Directions: The first player tosses the stone into square 1. (See Illustration 1.) Hopping over square 1 into square 2, the player proceeds through the pattern and back again. When a player comes to side-by-side squares, she/he lands with both feet, one in each square. At the end of the pattern, the player performs a jump-turn, landing on both feet and facing towards the start of the pattern. The player returns through the pattern, stops in square 2, picks up the stone, hops into square 1, and hops out.

The stone is now tossed into square 2 and the player repeats the pattern hopping over square 2. The player always must hop over the square that contains the stone. If a player makes a mistake—stone lands in a wrong square or on a line, the player puts second foot down where she/he shouldn't, or the player touches a line—the player must start at the first square the next time it's her/his turn.

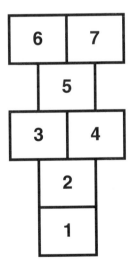

Illustration 1: *Jumby*

3-19. Klassa

Country: Poland (Europe)

Type of Game: Hopscotch

Formation: Player stands at entry to pattern.

Equipment: Hopscotch pattern; stone

Objective: The player tries to go through the hopscotch pattern without a mistake.

Poland is in central Europe, bordered on the north by the Baltic Sea and Russia. Other neighboring countries are Lithuania, Belerus, and the Ukraine (to the east), Czech Republic and Slovakia (to the south), and Germany (to the west.)

Directions for Game One: The jumper tosses the stone into square 1. (See Illustration 1.) The player jumps with both feet into square 1 and picks up the stone. The player continues through the pattern to square 7 and then back to square 1, tossing the stone into each square and jumping with both feet together in each square.

The first player to complete the pattern without making a mistake—tossing the stone in a wrong square or touching a line—wins. All players get the same number of turns for ties.

Directions for Game Two: The player hops on one foot in single squares and lands with one foot in each square when two squares are side by side (3–4 and 6–7). (See Illustration 1.) In squares 6 and 7, the player performs a jump-turn to face the start for the return trip. The rest of the game is performed as described in Game One.

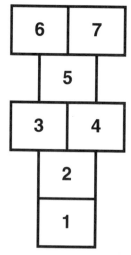

Illustration 1: *Klassa*

3-20. Kritz

Country: former Czechoslovakia (Europe)

Type of Game: Hopscotch

Formation: Player stands at entry to pattern.

Equipment: Hopscotch pattern; stone

Objective: The player tries to hop through the pattern without a mistake.

On January 1, 1993 Czechoslovakia was split into two separate countries called Czech Republic and Slovakia.

Directions: The stone is tossed into square 1. (See Illustration 1.) The player hops on one foot into square 1, picks up the stone, and hops back out. The stone is tossed into square 2. The player hops into square 1, then into square 2 to pick up the stone and hop back out through square 1. The player continues by tossing the stone into each numbered square consecutively and hopping in each square consecutively without missing a square both in or out.

When a player has completed all ten squares without a miss, she/he must try to toss the stone into Raj (Paradise) to win. If the stone lands in Beklo (Hell), the player begins the game again by tossing the stone into square 1.

A player loses her/his turn if the stone doesn't land inside the lines of the proper square, or if she/he touches a line or touches the other foot to the ground.

(Hell)	Beklo	Raj	(Paradise)
	9	10	
	7	8	
	5	6	
	3	4	
	1	2	

Illustration 1: *Kritz*

3-21. La Rayuela

Country: Honduras (Central America, North America)
Type of Game: Hopscotch
Formation: Player stands at entry to pattern.
Equipment: Hopscotch pattern; stone (*teho*)
Objective: The player tries to hop through the pattern without a mistake.

The Honduran word teho *means "puck" and comes from the Spanish word* teja *meaning "tile." Hondurans toss broken roofing tile as hopscotch markers.*

Directions: The player stands outside the pattern and tosses the *teho* into the first box named *primera*. (See Illustration 1.) The player then hops on one foot through the pattern and back again. When the player reaches the *casa* (home) square, the player can land on both feet, but must hop on only one foot in all other squares. In reaching the *primera* (first) square, the player picks up the *teho* before hopping out of the pattern.

The *teho* is tossed into the *segundo* (second) square and the player hops through the pattern, stopping at the *segundo* square on the way back, and picks up the *teho* before hopping into square *primera* and out. The player repeats when tossing into the *terecero* (third) square.

The last square to toss into is the *casa* (home) square. If the *teho* lands in either *brazo* (brave) square or in *cabeza* (head) square, the player's turn is over.

The player's turn is over if the *teho* lands in a wrong square or on a line, if a player puts down the wrong foot, steps on a line, or fails to pick up the *teho*.

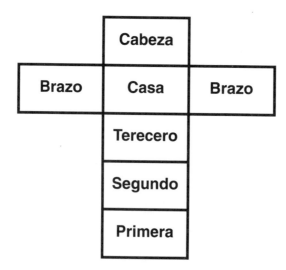

Illustration 1: *La Rayuela*

3-22. Paradies Hüpfen

Country: Germany (Europe)

Type of Game: Hopscotch

Formation: Player stands at entry to pattern.

Equipment: Hopscotch pattern; stone

Objective: The player tries to hop through the pattern without a mistake.

The Berlin Wall was constructed in 1961, separating the east and west sides of the city. The wall prevented East Berliners from going into West Berlin. East Berlin was aligned with communist Russia while West Berlin was aligned with the United States and its allies. The Berlin Wall was dismantled in 1990, reuniting Berlin into one city under Germany's new government.

In *Paradies Hüpfen* (also known as *Himmel Und Hölle*) the players try to move from *Erde* (earth) through *Hölle* (hell) and into *Himmel* (heaven). Players do not hop in the F spaces (F for *fegevuer* or purgatory) or into *Hölle*. If the stone lands in the P space (P is for paradise), the player cannot talk or laugh for the rest of the game.

Directions: The player stands in *Erde* (earth) and tosses the stone into square 1. (See Illustration 1.) Hopping into square 1, the player picks up the stone and hops back to *Erde*. The stone is then tossed into square 2. The player hops in square 1 and square 2, picks up the stone, and tosses it back into *Erde* before hopping back to *Erde* through square 1. This process continues to square 9. For side-by-side boxes (4–5 and 7–8) the player lands on both feet, one in each square.

After successfully tossing and hopping in squares 1–9, the player tosses the stone into *Himmel*, hops through the pattern, picks up the stone, and carries it back to *Erde*. Players must remember to not hop into *Hölle*. If the stone lands in either F section they may skip doing the trick (described later).

The player continues the process by tossing into square 9 and each square back down to 1. In each square, the stone is tossed back into *Erde* before hopping back to *Erde* each time.

If the stone lands in a wrong square or on a line, the player's turn is over and begins again on the next turn at the point of the mistake. If a stone lands in *Hölle*, the player's turn ends and must begin from the beginning on the next turn.

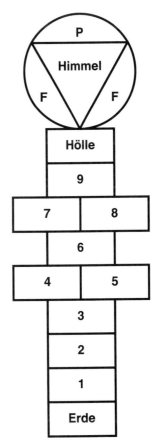

Illustration 1: *Paradies Hüpfen*

When the pattern is completed, the player must perform a trick to win:

- Move the stone with the nonhopping foot from square to square to *Himmel* and then back to *Erde*.

- Balance the stone on the nonhopping foot through all the squares without having it fall off. The player is out if the stone drops.

- Balance the stone on the head while hopping through the pattern.

- Balance the stone on the knee while hopping through the pattern.

3-23. Pele

Country: Aruba (Caribbean Islands)

Type of Game: Hopscotch

Formation: Player stands at entry to pattern.

Equipment: Hopscotch pattern; stone

Objective: The player tries to hop through the pattern without a mistake.

Located in the Caribbean Sea just north of Venezuela, the island of Aruba gained its independence from the Netherlands Antilles on January 1, 1986 and is an autonomous member of the Netherlands.

Directions: The player tosses the stone into square 1 and hops over square 1 into square 2 and through the rest of the pattern. (See Illustration 1.) When in squares 6–7, the player does a jump-turn to turn around and hop back towards square 1. In side-by-side squares (3–4 and 6–7) the player lands with one foot in each square.

When the player hops back to square 2, she/he balances on the hopping foot and picks up the stone before hopping over square 1 and out. Players are not to hop into squares where their stone lands—even after it is picked up.

Play continues by tossing the stone into square 2 and repeating the whole sequence again.

A player's turn is over if the stone lands out of the intended square, on a line, or a player touches the second foot down in a square intended for only one foot.

When the stone is in square 3, 4, 6, or 7, the neighbor square is treated like a single box. The player must not step into the square where the stone is sitting. If the stone is in square 3, for example, the player stands on one foot in square 4 to pick it up.

If the player steps on a line, she/he loses a turn, but the stone is not cleared from the pattern; the following players must not hop or jump into that square during their turn. The player who owns the stone continues her/his turn the next time with the stone already in place.

The first player to complete the entire pattern wins.

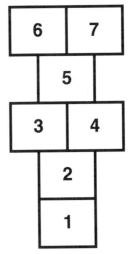

Illustration 1: *Pele*

3-24. Peregrin

Country: El Salvador (Central America, North America)
Type of Game: Hopscotch
Formation: Player stands at entry to pattern.
Equipment: Hopscotch pattern; stone (*tisto*); chalk
Objective: The player tries to hop through the pattern without a mistake.

Located on the western side of Central America, El Salvador's land neighbors—Guatemala and Honduras—block El Salvador from the Caribbean Sea, the only Central American country not to touch these waters.

Directions: El Salvadorian children's name for the stone to toss is *tisto*. The player tosses the *tisto* into the first square. (See Illustration 1.) The player hops over this square and lands in the second. Balancing on the hopping foot, the player picks up the *tisto*, hops over the first square again, and out of the pattern.

The *tisto* is tossed into the second square and the player hops into the first square, over the second, and into the first set of *ala* (wing) squares. In these side-by-side squares the player is allowed to land on both feet as long as the feet are in separate squares. The player jump-turns, picks up the *tisto*, jumps over the second square into the first and out of the pattern. This progression goes through the rest of the pattern.

When tossing the *tisto* into the *ala's*, the player tosses it first into the left *ala*, followed by the right *ala*. Players must also remember to never jump into a square where the *tisto* is located.

When a player's *tisto* is in the last section, *El Mundo* (world), the player jumps into *El Mundo* landing on two feet, performs a jump-turn to face the return direction, picks up the *tisto*, hops/jumps out in each square, and finally out.

The first player to finish the sequence can draw a *bimba* (big stomach) in the first square. No other player may hop into that square and no other player may draw a *bimba* in a square that already has one.

When the first two squares have *bimba's*, the next player must jump into the two *ala's* and land on both feet.

The greatest number of *bimba's* by one player at the end of the game wins.

A player's turn ends when the *tisto* is in a wrong square or touches a line, or when a player touches a line, touches the second foot down when she/he shouldn't, or puts a hand on the ground to maintain balance.

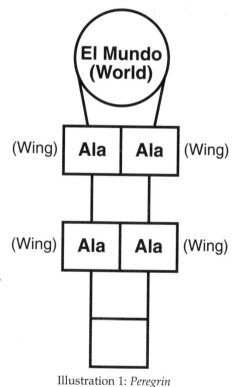

Illustration 1: *Peregrin*

3-25. Potsy

Country: United States (North America)

Type of Game: Hopscotch

Formation: Player stands at entry to pattern.

Equipment: Hopscotch pattern; stone; chalk

Objective: The player tries to hop through the pattern without a mistake.

With a geographic area of 3,618,770 square miles (50 states and the District of Columbia), the United States is only about 55% the size of Russia (the largest country in the world).

Directions: The player tosses the stone into the first square. (See Illustration 1.) Hopping over square 1 into square 2 and through the rest of the pattern, the player returns to square 2. Balancing on the hopping foot, the stone is picked up before hopping into square 1 and out of the pattern. The stone is tossed into square 2. The player hops into square 1, then into square 3, avoiding square 2 until the return. This process continues by tossing in each square in turn. The square in which the stone rests is always jumped over until the return trip when the stone is picked up.

In side-by-side squares (1–2, 4–5, and 7–8) the player hops and lands with one foot in each square at the same time—unless the stone is in one of the squares.

When the player reaches the 7–8 squares, she/he jump-turns and lands facing the opposite direction with feet in opposite squares. Players who complete the whole pattern without making a mistake write an initial in any square not already having a player's initial. Only that player whose initial is in the square is allowed to hop into that square. (Some regions allow players to stand with both feet in squares containing their initials.)

A player's turn ends when the stone lands in a wrong square, on a line, or the player touches a line or places two feet down when only one is allowed to touch.

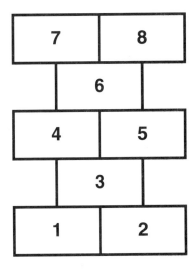

Illustration 1: *Potsy*

3-26. Hop the Beds

Country: Great Britain (Europe)

Type of Game: Hopscotch

Formation: Player stands at entry to pattern.

Equipment: Hopscotch pattern; stone

Objective: The player tries to hop through the pattern without a mistake.

In Hop the Beds (*also known as* Scotch-Hoppers) *the squares are referred to as beds.*

Directions: The first player stands by the base line and tosses a stone into the first bed. (See Illustration 1.) Hopping and jumping through the pattern, the player goes to bed 10 and back to bed 1, picks up the stone, and hops out. The only time a player is allowed to put both feet down is in beds 2–3, 5–6, and 8–9 while straddling the blank bed. The player hops on only one foot in single beds.

Each player goes through the pattern before the next player takes her/his turn.

When players complete the pattern without making a mistake, the stone is tossed into the next numbered bed. Mistakes are when the stone lands in the wrong bed, on a line, or the player touches a line, puts a hand down for balance, or touches the second foot to the ground when in a single bed.

The winner is the first player to complete the pattern tossing into all ten beds.

Illustration 1: *Hop the Beds*

3-27. Ta Galagala

Country: Nigeria (Africa)
Type of Game: Hopscotch
Formation: Player stands at entry to pattern.
Equipment: Hopscotch pattern; stone (*kwalo*)
Objective: The player tries to hop through the pattern without making a mistake.

Traditionally played in soft ground, eight kurtus *(circles) are drawn on the ground. The* kurtus *are close together, but do not touch. Nothing is written inside the circles. Although* Ta Galagala *has no real meaning in the Hausa language, adults say the name is "what keeps the children from going to the far"—or simpler yet, what the children do to keep from doing their work.*

Directions: The stone is called *kwalo*. The players stand at the single *kurtu* end and try to toss the *kwalo* into the first *kurtu*. (See Illustration 1.) If the *kwalo* does not land inside, another player can place it in for the tosser so the player does not miss a turn.

Hopping over the *kurtu* that contains the *kwalo*, the player hops into the single *kurtus* and then jumps, landing with one foot in each side-by-side *kurtu*. The player then jump-turns to face the base line, clapping once while in the air. Hopping and jumping back through the pattern, the player jumps over the first *kurtu* and out of the pattern before reaching back to get the *kwalo*. The player must not jump into a *kurtu* that contains the *kwalo*.

The *kwalo* is now tossed into the succeeding *kurtus* and the process of hopping down and back is repeated, always remembering to hop over the *kwalo* each time and picking it up on the way back after hopping past the *kurtu* a second time.

When the *kwalo* has been tossed into each *kurta* and retrieved, one last toss is made just beyond the last two *kurtas*. The player hops through the pattern to *kurtas* 7 and 8 (as if they were numbered) and jump-turns to face the beginning. The player reaches between her/his legs to pick up the *kwalo*, and hops back through the pattern and out.

Players stepping on or outside a circle line or tossing the *kwalo* in a wrong *kurtu* lose their turn and begin at that place on their next turn.

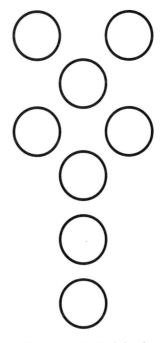

Illustration 1: *Ta Galagala*

3-28. Texan Hopscotch

Country: United States (North America)

Type of Game: Hopscotch

Formation: Player stands at entry to pattern.

Equipment: Hopscotch pattern; stone

Objective: The player tries to hop through the pattern without making a mistake.

Texas is the largest continental state at 266,807 square miles. Found in the south central part of the United States, Texas borders Mexico to its south and the Gulf of Mexico to the southeast.

Directions: The player stands at the base line and tosses the stone into square 1. (See Illustration 1.) Hopping on one foot in single squares and jumping with both feet into side-by-side (1–2, 5–6, 9–10) squares (one foot in each), the player hops and jumps through the pattern and back. When the player reaches the square where the stone is located, she/he picks up the stone and continues out of the pattern. When the player jumps into squares 9 and 10, a jump-turn is made to return to the beginning.

The stone is tossed into each square in sequence and the player jumps through the pattern for each number.

A player's turn ends if the stone lands in a wrong square, lands on a line, or the player steps on a line or puts the nonhopping foot down in a single square.

The first player to finish all ten throws wins the game.

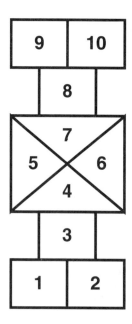

Illustration 1: *Texas Hopscotch*

3-29. Home

Country: United States (North America)

Type of Game: Hopscotch

Formation: Player stands at entry to pattern.

Equipment: Hopscotch pattern; stone

Objective: The player tries to be the first to complete the hopscotch pattern.

Home to over 270 million people, the United States borders Canada to its north, and Mexico and the Gulf of Mexico to its south. The U.S. touches the Pacific Ocean on the west coast and the Atlantic Ocean on the east coast.

Directions: Standing at the base line, the player tosses the stone into square 1. (See Illustration 1.) Without stepping into square 1, the player hops into square 8. Alternating the feet on each hop, the player hops into square 2, then squares 7, 3, 6, 4, and 5 before hopping into HOME and landing on both feet. Turning around with a jump-turn, the player's return trip begins in square 5, then squares 4, 6, 3, 7, 2, 8, and 1. While standing in square 1 on one foot, the player picks up the stone before hopping out. If successfully completed, the player tosses the stone into square 2. After each successful trip, the player tosses the stone into the next number and tries to complete the pattern without a mistake.

Illustration 1: *Home*

If a player steps on a line or touches both feet to the ground anywhere but in HOME, her/his turn is over. If the stone is tossed in a wrong square or on a line, the turn is lost before it begins.

On the trip towards HOME the player does not hop in the square where the stone is located. On the return trip the player must hop into the square on one foot while picking up the stone before finishing the pattern and exiting.

Once the stone has been tossed into all eight squares, the player then closes her/his eyes and tosses the stone to land in HOME. If the stone lands in HOME without touching a line, the player jumps with the left foot in the left square, and the right foot in the right square to HOME, picks up the stone while at HOME, and jumps back. *This is performed with the eyes closed.* If successful without touching any lines, the player has won the game.

Variation: The player stands on the base line of a different pattern and tosses the stone into square 1. (See Illustration 2.) Jumping into the pattern and landing with one foot in square 1 and the other foot in square 2, the player hops and jumps to square 12. Performing a jump-turn, the player returns through the pattern to the beginning, picking up the stone on the return trip. If successfully completed without touching a line or putting the second foot down in a single square, the player tosses the stone into square 2 and repeats the pattern. Play continues until the stone is successfully tossed into all 12 squares.

The player to complete all 12 rounds first wins. Any player who makes a mistake that ends a turn begins her/his next turn at the number where the mistake was made.

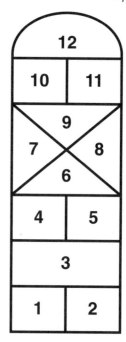

Illustration 2: *Home* (variation)

Additional <u>Home</u> Patterns: Illustrations 3 through 8 show a variety of other patterns you can use for the hopscotch game of *Home*.

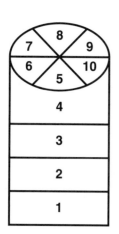

Illustration 3: *Home* (variation)

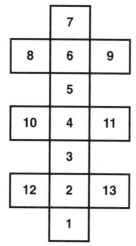

Illustration 4: *Home* (variation)

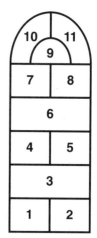

Illustration 5: *Home* (variation)

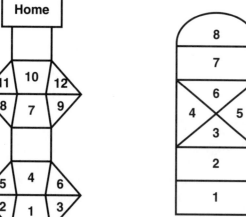

Illustration 6: *Home* (variation)

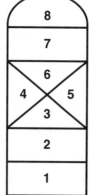

Illustration 7: *Home* (variation)

Illustration 8: *Home* (variation)

3-30. Boxes

Country: Unites States (North America)

Type of Game: Hopscotch

Formation: Player stands at entry to pattern.

Equipment: Hopscotch pattern; stone; chalk

Objective: The player tries to be the first to complete the pattern with the highest number of boxes.

Any hopscotch pattern that uses single and side-by-side squares can be used. Numbers or names in the squares are not necessary.

Directions: The first player stands at the base line and tosses the stone into the first square. (See the sample pattern in Illustration 1.) Hopping over this square, the player hops/jumps through the pattern to the end, jump-turns, and returns to the square(s) just before the square containing the stone. The player picks up the stone, hops into that square, and then hops out of the pattern. The player places one foot in each box that are side by side.

If successful without touching a line, falling over, or hopping into the square containing the stone, the player writes her/his initials in *any square* of her/his choosing. The remaining players then take their turns in order. Any square with a player's initials can only be used by that player. All other players must hop or jump over that square to the next open square or to one with their initials if that is the next available square. Players who toss a stone that lands on a line or into a wrong square, or into a square with another player's initials misses her/his turn.

When it is no longer possible for players to get to the far end because of squares not available, an extra box can be drawn with broken or dotted lines. No player can claim this box as his or her own. When all boxes are claimed, the player with the highest number of boxes is the winner.

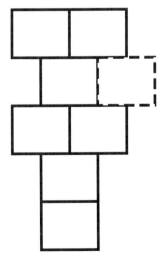

Illustration 1: *Boxes* (sample pattern)

3-31. One-Way Hopscotch

Country: United States (North America)

Type of Game: Hopscotch

Formation: Player stands at entry to pattern.

Equipment: Hopscotch pattern with 5 single squares; beanbag

Objective: The player tries to successfully complete the pattern first.

The United States has a total of 3,700 coastal miles on the eastern-southeastern coastline (Atlantic Ocean and Gulf of Mexico); 1,300 coastal miles on the western coastline (California, Oregon, and Washington); and 6,700 coastal miles around Alaska (Pacific Ocean and Arctic Ocean.)

Directions: A series of single squares are drawn in a straight line, and names or numbers are given to the squares. (See Illustration 1.) The marker should be soft and flexible, such as a beanbag.

The first player tosses the beanbag into the first square and hops into that square. The player picks up the beanbag, balances it on the back of her/his hand, and proceeds to hop through the rest of the squares without dropping the beanbag. At no time may the player use any other body part to help control or trap the beanbag to keep it from falling. If successful, the player hops out of the pattern at the other end.

Each player has one turn before the first player has a second turn. On the player's second turn (if the first was successful) the beanbag is tossed into the second square. Hopping into the first square and then the second, the player picks up the beanbag, places it on her/his head, and proceeds to the far end of the pattern and out. All other players do the same in turn. Players who made a mistake in the first round (tossing in the first square) must repeat the first square in turn.

On the player's third turn, the beanbag is tossed into the third square. When the player hops into this square, the beanbag is placed on top of the nonhopping foot and the player continues out the pattern.

The player places the beanbag on one shoulder for her/his fourth turn, and on her/his forehead with the head tilted back for the fifth turn.

The winner is the player who can complete the sequence in the fewest number of turns. If a beanbag falls off during the hopping or a line is stepped on, the player must repeat that square. If the beanbag lands on a line or in a wrong square, the player loses that turn without hopping.

Adaptation: For advanced players, use the same diagram. This time, however, the player tosses the beanbag into the first square, hops on one foot in each square, and returns to the first square. Picking up the beanbag, the player balances it on the back of her/his hand through each square to the far end and back to the base line without dropping the beanbag or hopping on a line. This is then repeated for all the other squares in the same manner.

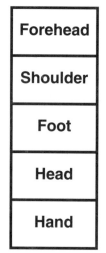

Illustration 1: *One-Way Hopscotch* (sample)

Section 4
Jacks

Jacks is an ancient game that utilized stones, pebbles—even sheep knuckles—before the development of the steel jack and ball used today. Through the years the name has evolved from *Knucklebones* (for sheep knuckles) to *Five Stones* (for using five stones for tossing, catching, and picking up) to *Jacks* (the modern 3/4-inch six-spike jacks used with a rubber ball). Early *Jacks*-type games involved catching the stones on the back of the hand as part of the game itself.

Some cultures use chopsticks or short sticks in place of the above-mentioned materials.

In this section you'll find 25 different *Jacks* games plus 31 variations from 20 different countries and 7 continents/regions. *Note:* All of these *Jacks* games may be played in the classroom, or in gym for those who cannot participate in regular P.E. activities due to illness, injury, and so forth.

Africa

Gariir (4-9)—Somalia

Iguni (4-8)—Zimbabwe

Nuwakha Nchuwa (Tossing Stones) (4-12)—Malawi

Asia

Abhadhö (4-20)—Tibet

Jackstones (4-2)—Pakistan

Australia

Jacks (4-5)—Australia

Caribbean Islands

Trier (4-4)—Trinidad and Tobago

Europe

Knucklebones (4-22)—Ancient Greece

Far East (Asia)

Catching Seven Pieces (4-14)—China

Chopsticks Jacks (4-18)—Laos

Five Stones (4-16)—Singapore

Jacks (4-17)—Korea

Kong Keui (Laying Eggs, Sitting Eggs, Hatching Eggs) (4-6)—South Korea

Kulit K'Rang (4-10)—Indonesia

Maakgep (4-7)—Thailand

Otedama (4-15)—Japan

Pick-up Sticks (4-19)—Laos

Middle East

Hamesh Avamin (4-23)—Israel

North America

Ball and Jack (4-25)—United States

Five Stones (4-21)—Colonial America

Jacks (4-24)—(Texas) United States

Kimo (4-11)—(Hawaii) United States

Turn-Around Game (4-3)—Native Americans

Oceania

Huripapa (4-1)—New Zealand

South America

Cinco Marias (4-13)—Brazil

4-1. Huripapa

Country: New Zealand (Oceania)

Type of Game: Jacks with stones

Formation: Players sit in a circle on the floor facing the playing area.

Equipment: 5 stones

Objective: The player tries to perform all challenges, ending with collecting all five on the last turn.

Maori are the first inhabitants of New Zealand, but now are a minority of the population. Influences from explorers and sailors have shaped the games played by the Maori people.

Directions: Four stones are placed in a straight line like steps of a ladder. The fifth stone is tossed into the air. Before catching the tossed stone, the player finger-jumps the first stone. This is performed by touching the ground before the first stone, jumping over the stone, and touching between the first and second stones before catching the tossed stone.

On the next toss the player finger-jumps the second stone. This is repeated for the rest of the stones.

In the *second round,* the player jumps the first two on the first toss. On the second toss, the player finger-jumps the third and fourth stones.

In the *third round,* the player jumps the first three stones on the first toss and the last stone on the second toss. In the *fourth round,* the player finger-jumps all four stones before catching the stone.

Variation (Polly Put the Kettle On): All stones are tossed to the ground. One is chosen to toss into the air as the others are moved. On the first three tosses one stone is moved at a time to form a triangle. On the fourth toss the fourth stone is placed on top of the three stones to form the "kettle on top of the burner."

4-2. Jackstones

Country: Pakistan (Asia)

Type of Game: Jacks with stones

Formation: A circle is drawn with two lines at 90° angles of each other crossing at the center of the circle. (See Illustration 1.) Each player places her/his colored marker where the line meets the circle.

Equipment: 12-inch circle with cross lines meeting at the center; 5 stones plus a colored marker for each player

Objective: The player tries to have her/his marker reach the center first.

This game differs from other jacks-type games because the stones are caught on the back of the hand each turn, instead of picked up when the stone is tossed.

Directions: Taking turns, each player tosses her/his five stones in the air and catches as many as possible on the back of both hands. The player catching the most stones goes first.

The first player again tosses her/his five stones into the air and catches as many as possible on the back of both hands. The player moves her/his marker one finger width for each stone caught on the back of the hands. The player's turn is over if no stones are caught. The player's turn ends and she/he misses her/his next turn if three stones are caught.

If one, two, or four stones are caught, that many finger widths are placed together on the line next to the marker going towards the center where the lines cross. (Remember, it's finger widths, not finger lengths.) When a player catches all five stones, she/he tosses them into the air from the back of the hands and tries to catch them in the palm of the tossing hand. If all five are caught again, the player moves her/his marker a palm width instead of the width of five fingers. If any stone is dropped, the marker moves the number of finger widths equaling the number of stones caught in the palm.

Players having successful catches (one, two, four, or five stones) toss again until catching none or three on the back of the hand ends her/his turn or the marker reaches the middle where the lines intersect for the win.

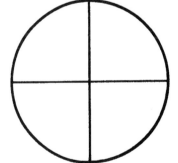

Variations:

- Players catch the stones on the back of only one hand.
- Have increment marks on the crossing lines. Players advance by these increments instead of finger widths.

Also See: *Turn-Around Game* (4-3)

Trier (4-4)

Jacks (4-5)

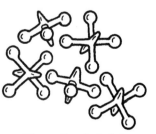

Illustration 1: *Jackstones*

4-3. Turn-Around Game

Country: Native Americans, United States (North America)

Type of Game: Jacks with chopsticks

Formation: Players sit or stand holding the sticks in one hand.

Equipment: 20–40 6-inch chopstick-size sticks

Objective: The player tries to toss and catch the sticks on the backs of the hands and then back to the palm of the tossing hand.

Sticks falling to the ground in this game are out of play and not used until the next game.

Directions: The player holds all sticks in one hand. Tossing the sticks into the air, the player tries to catch as many sticks as possible on the backs of both hands. Any sticks on the backs of the hands are tossed back to the palm of the tossing hand.

If an odd number of sticks are caught, the player takes one stick as a counter and tosses the rest of the sticks to catch on the back of both hands again. The player then tosses them up to catch in the palm of the tossing hand once more.

This continues until either all sticks are gone or an even number of sticks are caught in the palm of the tossing hand. The next player begins her/his turn with the sticks still in play. The player who catches the last stick wins the other players' sticks and play begins again with all sticks (except the counters).

Adaptation: Younger players may use both hands to catch the sticks in the palms.

Also See: *Jackstones* (4-2)

4-4. Trier

Country: Republic of Trinadad and Tobago (Caribbean Islands)

Type of Game: Jacks with stones

Formation: Players sit in a circle on the floor facing the playing area.

Equipment: 5 stones

Objective: The player tries to score the highest number of points by the end of the game.

Traces of this game can be found in other jacks-type games of Africa, India, China, and Europe.

Directions: Players use only one hand throughout the game. Tossing all five stones into the air, the player attempts to catch as many stones on the back of the tossing hand as she/he can. Then, tossing the stones from the back of the hand, the player tries to catch them again in the palm of the same hand. If no stone is dropped from the back of the hand to the palm, the number of stones caught in the palm is the player's score. If a stone is dropped, no score is made.

This is repeated for two more rounds. The highest score wins.

Variation: Players may play to a predetermined score, such as 20, 30, 40, perhaps 50 or 100!

Also See: *Jackstones* (4-2)

4-5. Jacks

Country: Australia

Type of Game: Jacks with stones

Formation: Players sit in a circle on the floor facing the playing area.

Equipment: 5 stones

Objective: The player tries to complete the series of challenges on as few turns as possible.

Oceania is found in the Pacific Ocean off the southeast coast of Asia. It consists of thousands of islands that include New Zealand, the island groups of Melanesia, Micronesia and Polynesia, and sometimes Australia.

Directions: Each player in turn takes all five stones in her/his tossing hand. Tossing the stones in the air, the player tries to catch all the stones on the back of her/his tossing hand. The stones caught on the back of the hand are tossed from this position and caught again in the palm of the tossing hand. The player catching the highest number of stones after both tosses begins.

ONES: Players toss all five stones in the air to begin her/his turn trying to catch all five on the back of the tossing hand. If all are caught, the player goes directly to the Twos. If stones are dropped, the player tosses four of the five stones to the ground, spreading them out. The one stone not tossed to the ground is tossed into the air. The player picks up one stone from those on the ground before catching the tossed stone. This is all done with the same hand. The other three stones on the ground are picked up one at a time in the same manner.

A player's turn is over when the tossed stone is missed or dropped, a picked up stone is dropped, or the wrong number of stones is picked up.

When the player completes picking up all the stones on the ground, one at a time, she/he proceeds to the Twos.

TWOS: This is played like the Ones except the player picks up two stones on each toss of the stone.

THREES: This is played like the Twos except the player picks up three stones on the first toss and the remaining single stone on the second toss.

FOURS: The player picks up all stones on one toss.

Also See: *Jackstones* (4-2)

 Maakgep (4-7)

 Jacks (4-17)

 Abhadhö (4-20)

 Five Stones (4-21)

 Knucklebones (4-22)

 Hamesh Avamin (4-23)

4-6. Kong Keui
(Laying Eggs, Sitting Eggs, Hatching Eggs)

Country: South Korea (Far East, Asia)

Type of Game: Jacks with stones

Formation: Players sit in a circle on the floor facing the playing area.

Equipment: 5 stones

Objective: The player tries to be the first to "hatch" the eggs.

Each round increases the challenge for the player. The rounds are called "al-natpki" (laying the eggs), "al-hpoum-ki" (sitting the eggs), and "al-kka-ki" (hatching the eggs).

Directions:

AL-NATPKI (Laying the Eggs): The player tosses four stones to the ground. The fifth stone is tossed into the air. Before catching the tossed stone, the player picks up one stone from the ground with the same hand. After catching the tossed stone, the picked-up stone is placed to the side. The other three stones are picked up one at a time.

AL-HPOUM-KI (Sitting the Eggs): The nonplaying hand is placed palm side down to the ground with the pinkie on the ground, and the thumb and palm off the ground to create a space under the palm for the stones to go.

    After spreading the four stones on the ground again, the player tosses the fifth stone into the air, pushes one of the stones on the ground under the palm of the other hand, and catches the stone before it falls to the ground. This is repeated for the remaining three stones.

AL-KKA-KI (Hatching the Eggs): The player spreads out three stones on the ground. The fourth stone is held by the pinkie of the tossing/catching hand.

    The player tosses the fifth stone into the air, being careful not to let go of the fourth stone. While the fifth stone is in the air, the player taps the fourth stone to one of the three stones on the ground. This is repeated for the remaining two stones.

    The first player to successfully complete all three rounds is the winner.

Variation: As in other jacks-type games, this may be performed in twos, threes, and fours.

Adaptation: After completing each level but before going to the next, more skilled players might perform the same level a second time using the opposite hand.

4-7. Maakgep

Country: Thailand (Far East, Asia)

Type of Game: Jacks with stones

Formation: Players sit in a circle on the floor facing the playing area.

Equipment: 5 stones

Objective: The player tries to be the first player to score 20 points.

The country of Siam changed its name in 1939 to Thailand, which means land of the free. Thailand has never been a European colony.

Directions: The player tosses the five stones to the ground. The player selects one stone and, using one hand, tosses this stone in the air while another stone is picked up from the ground before the player catches the tossed stone. If successful, the picked-up stone is set aside on the ground. The tossing stone is tossed again and another stone is picked from the ground before the player catches the tossed stone. This continues for the last two stones.

When all four stones are picked up from the ground, the player holds them in the tossing hand along with the fifth stone. The player tosses into the air and catches as many as possible on the back of the tossing hand. The number of stones caught is this player's score.

Each player in turn attempts to pick up the stones and to score points before the first player begins the second round. Players failing to complete the first round repeat picking up one stone at a time the next time it is their turn.

Players who successfully complete the first round move to the *second round*, where they attempt to pick up two stones at a time and still catch the tossed stone. All five stones are tossed and caught on the back of the hand for a score.

In the *third round*, players must pick up three stones on the first toss and the single stone on the second.

The *fourth round* consists of one toss to pick up all four stones from the ground.

If players have reached the end of the fourth round and no player has yet scored 20 points, the *fifth round* consists of picking up one stone at a time. This process continues until a player has reached 20 points.

Variation: While balancing the tossing stone on the back of the tossing hand, the player picks up a stone from the ground. The balanced stone is lightly tossed up off the back of the hand and then caught in the palm of the tossing hand along with the stone picked up from the ground.

The game continues as explained above until a player reaches 20 points.

Also See: *Jacks* (4-5)

Jacks (4-17)

Abhadhö (4-20)

Five Stones (4-21)

Knucklebones (4-22)

Hamesh Avamin (4-23)

4-8. Iguni

Country: Zimbabwe (Africa)

Type of Game: Jacks with stones

Formation: Eleven stones are placed around a 2- to 3-inch wide hole. The player holds the twelfth stone. All players sit around this hole.

Equipment: 2- to 3-inch wide hole; 12 rounded stones

Objective: The player tries to be the first to successfully complete all three rounds.

Known as Rhodesia when it was a British colony, Zimbabwe gained independence in 1980.

Directions: The player tosses the twelfth stone into the air and knocks one stone into the hole before catching the tossed stone. This is repeated until all eleven stones are knocked into the hole one at a time. The *first round* is completed when all eleven stones are in the hole and the twelfth stone is tossed one more time, allowing the player to remove all the stones from the hole before catching the stone.

The *second round* is played as the first, but two stones are knocked into the hole for each toss of the twelfth stone. One stone is left and is picked up and placed inside the hole last.

This procedure is repeated for the total of eleven rounds. The number of the round equals the number of stones to be knocked into the hole on each toss. The odd remaining stones are always picked up and placed in the hole instead of being knocked in. Any time a player is unsuccessful, the turn is over and must be repeated on her/his next turn.

Also See: *Gariir* (4-9)

4-9. Gariir

Country: Somalia (Africa)

Type of Game: Jacks with stones

Formation: Twelve stones are placed in a hole just large enough to hold them. Players sit around this hole.

Equipment: 12 stones; hole

Objective: The player tries to be the first to finish three rounds.

Somalia is slightly smaller than the state of Texas in size at 246,300 square miles. Located at the eastern horn of Africa on the shores of the Indian Ocean and Gulf of Aden, its land neighbors are Djibouti, Ethiopia, and Kenya.

Directions: The first player picks one stone from the hole. This stone should be identifiable from the other stones so all know that this is the one to toss.

Using only one hand, the player tosses the stone into the air and picks out one stone from the hole before catching the tossed stone. If more than one stone is picked up, the player holds all stones, tosses the tossing stone once more, and replaces the appropriate number of stones to the pile, keeping one stone in the hand and catching the tossed stone. Any failure to retain one stone in the hand or catch the tossed stone ends the player's turn. The player removes one stone at a time until all are out of the hole.

In the *second round*, the player removes two stones at a time until only one remains. The single stone is removed last.

The *third round* requires three stones to be removed on each toss of the stone. Two stones will remain at the end and are to be removed last.

The first player to successfully get through all three rounds is the winner.

Players who fail at some point to complete a required pick up or catch repeats the same level the next time it is their turn.

Also See: *Iguni* (4-8)

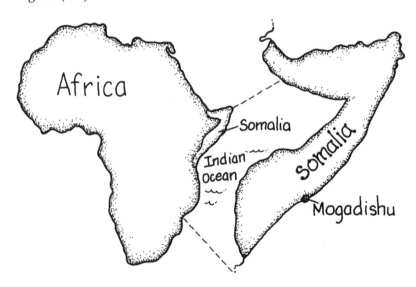

4-10. Kulit K'Rang

Country: Indonesia (Far East, Asia)

Type of Game: Jacks with small shells

Formation: Players sit on the floor in a circle facing the center. In front of each player are 15 small shells. In the center of the circle is a bowl with 5 shells from each player.

Equipment: Bowl; 20 small shells per player.

Objective: The player tries to be the last person to have at least one shell left.

Indonesia is 735,268 square miles spread out over 17,000 islands. Located along the Equator, Indonesia's closest neighbors are Malaysia and Papua New Guinea. The island of Java is one of the most densely populated areas of the world at 1,500 people per square mile.

Directions: Five shells from each player are placed in the center bowl. Each player in turn places one small shell on the back of her/his hand. Tossing it into the air from the back of the hand, the player picks up another shell from the pile in front of her/him and catches the tossed shell in the palm of the tossing hand. If either shell is dropped, one shell is placed in the bowl in the center.

The player having the most shells left after one player has lost all her/his shells is the winner.

Ways to Play: The game can be done in many different ways. Here are three suggestions:

- Each player may continue her/his turn until a shell is dropped.
- The last player to have a shell left is the winner.
- Each player tosses and picks up a predetermined number of times each turn. A shell is placed in the center bowl each time a miss is made.

Variation: Each player puts five shells into the center bowl. The player picks one shell from the bowl for each successful toss and catch. The player places one shell into the bowl for each failed toss and catch.

Also See: *Kimo* (4-11)

4-11. Kimo

Country: Hawaii, United States (North America)

Type of Game: Jacks with pebbles

Formation: Two players sit on the ground facing each other. One hundred pebbles are placed in a pile between them.

Equipment: 100 pebbles

Objective: The player tries to have more pebbles at the end than her/his opponent.

Kimo *means "to bob" in Hawaiian. The tossed stone is called the* kimo.

Directions: The first player tosses her/his *kimo* into the air and picks up one pebble from the pile in the middle before catching the *kimo*. If successful, the player continues. If a pebble is not picked up, or is dropped or the *kimo* is missed, the player's turn ends.

   If the first player misses a pick up or a catch during her/his first turn, the second player begins her/his turn. When all 100 pebbles have been picked up, the player with more pebbles is the winner.

Variation: Players alternate turns. When all the pebbles are taken from the center pile, the player with more pebbles is the winner.

Also See: *Kulit K'Rang* (4-10)

   Nuwakha Nchuwa (Tossing Stones) (4-12)

4-12. Nuwakha Nchuwa
(Tossing Stones)

Country: Malawi (Africa)

Type of Game: Jacks with stones

Formation: Players sit on the floor in a circle, with 100–200 stones placed in the center of a 2- to 3-foot circle.

Equipment: 100–200 stones; 2- to 3-foot circle

Objective: The player tries to have the most stones at the end of the game.

Malawi is 45,747 square miles, the size of Pennsylvania. Located in southeast Africa, its border neighbors are Zambia, Mozambique, and Tanzania.

Directions: Using only one hand, each player in turn tosses the tossing stone ten times. On the *first toss* only one stone from the pile may be picked up. On the *second toss* one or two stones may be picked up. On the *third toss,* up to three stones. On *tosses four and five,* up to four and five stones may be picked up. On *tosses six through ten,* up to five stones may be picked up on each toss.

On turns that the tossing stone is not caught or more than the allowed number of stones are picked up, the player replaces the stones into the center pile of stones. After all players have had ten tosses, the player with the most stones is the winner.

Also See: *Kimo* (4-11)

4-13. Cinco Marias

Country: Brazil (South America)

Type of Game: Jacks with stones

Equipment: 5 stones

Objective: The player tries to complete the series of challenges and collect all five stones on the last turn.

Brazil shares borders with all South American countries except Chile and Ecuador.

Directions: The player scatters all five stones on the ground. One stone is picked to toss. Tossing this stone in the air, the player picks up a stone from the ground before catching the tossed stone. All this is performed with the same hand. The player continues until all four stones are picked up.

If the player drops a stone or fails to pick up the correct number, that player's turn is over and the next player begins. When a player gets another turn, she/he resumes at the same level where the mistake was made.

In rounds two, three, and four, the player picks up two, three, and four stones, respectively, on each toss of the stone. The first player to successfully pick up all four stones on one toss is the winner.

Variation (A Visit to Mama's House): The player forms a "doorway" by placing the thumb and fingertips on the ground with the palm up high. The game is played as above except instead of picking up the stones, the player pushes them through the doorway (Mama's front door).

4-14. Catching Seven Pieces

Country: China (Far East, Asia)

Type of Game: Jacks with filled bags

Formation: Players sit in a circle facing the playing area.

Equipment: 7 small square bags filled with sand or rice.

Objective: The player tries to collect all seven bags in the hand without dropping one.

The bags for this game need to be small so the players can hold all seven in one hand at the same time without dropping any.

Directions: The first player drops all seven bags onto the playing surface. If two or more bags are touching, these are redropped. One bag is chosen to toss. Using only one hand, the player tosses the one bag in the air, picks up a bag from the ground, and catches the tossed bag before it hits the ground. If successful, the player tosses the bag again and picks up another bag.

In this game of Jacks, the picked-up bags are kept in the playing hand until all seven bags are picked up.

A player's turn is over if the tossed bag is dropped, a bag is not picked up, a second bag is moved during a pick up, or a bag in the hand is dropped.

Play continues until all players have had a turn and one player has collected all seven bags without a mistake.

Also See: *Otedama* (4-15)

Five Stones (4-16)

Jacks (4-17)

4-15. Otedama

Country: Japan (Far East, Asia)

Type of Game: Jacks with filled bags

Formation: Players sit in a circle facing the playing area.

Equipment: 9 small bags filled with sand or rice (one bag is identified as the "parent" bag to toss).

Objective: The player tries to toss the parent bag and pick up the correct number of bags from the ground.

The player says the number of bags to be picked up each time the parent bag is tossed.

Directions: The player tosses all nine bags into the air. As the bags fall to the playing surface, the player must catch only the parent bag, letting the others fall to the surface. If done correctly, the player begins. If not, it's the next player's turn.

In *round one,* the parent bag is tossed and the player says "one" as she/he picks up one bag from the surface before catching the parent bag. This is repeated until all eight bags are picked up from the floor. A mistake costs the player the remaining part of her/his turn and the next player begins.

In *round two,* the parent bag is tossed and the player calls out "two" while picking up two bags before catching the parent bag.

In *round three,* three bags are picked up on each toss and "three" is called. Two bags remain, so on the final toss in this round the player must call "two" as she/he picks up the last two bags.

Round four consists of two tosses and picking up (and saying) "four" each time. The first player to complete all four rounds is the winner.

Variation: If the player's hands are big enough or the bags small enough, repeat the above sequence having *rounds five through eight.*

Also See: *Catching Seven Pieces* (4-14)

   Five Stones (4-16)

4-16. Five Stones

Country: Singapore (Far East, Asia)

Type of Game: Jacks with filled bags called "stones"

Formation: Players sit on the ground in a circle facing the playing area.

Equipment: 5 triangular-shaped cloth bags filled with rice, sand, or seeds (these bags are called "stones")

Objective: The player tries to go through the series of challenges, ending with collecting all five stones on the last turn.

Singapore has a pleasant summer climate all year because it is only 87 miles north of the Equator.

Directions: The player tosses all five stones to the ground. One stone is chosen to toss. Using only one hand, the one stone is tossed in the air as a second stone is picked up, catching the tossed stone before it lands on the ground. This is repeated until all stones are picked up.

Once all four stones are picked up successfully, all five are tossed to the ground again and one is picked to toss. This time two stones are picked up on the next two tosses. The stones are thrown to the ground again. Three stones are picked up on the next toss, one on the second. Throwing all five stones once more, one is chosen to toss and the other four are picked up on one toss of the stone.

Once all four stones are picked up on one toss and the tossed stone caught, the tossed stone is tossed once more as the four stones are placed on the ground. The player tosses the lone stone once more and picks up the four off the ground a second time.

Variations:

- With all five stones in hand, the player tosses all to the ground. This time two are chosen to pick up. Toss one of the two stones and exchange the one in hand with one on the ground. This is repeated until all are exchanged.

  The player now tosses the two stones into the air. She/he catches one in the nontossing hand, and picks one stone with the tossing hand before catching the tossed stone. Keep the stone caught in the nonthrowing hand. Repeat until all stones are picked up—three in the nonthrowing hand, two in the throwing hand. Toss the two in the throwing hand, and catch one in each hand. Toss the single stone one more time, and transfer the four stones into the throwing hand before catching the tossed stone.

- The player places four stones to look like this: 0 00 0. Toss the fifth stone and pick up the two center stones. Toss the fifth stone again and pick up the remaining two before catching the tossed stone.

Also See: *Catching Seven Pieces* (4-14)

                 Otedama (4-15)

4-17. Jacks

Country: Korea (Far East, Asia)

Type of Game: Jacks with no ball

Formation: Players sit in a circle facing the playing area.

Equipment: Pebbles or stones called "Jacks."

Objective: The player tries to pick up a Jack before catching the tossed Jack without disturbing other Jacks on the ground.

Japan ruled South Korea, then known as Chosun, from 1910–1945. Seoul, South Korea hosted the 1988 Summer Olympic Games.

Directions: Using only one hand, the first player tosses one Jack in the air, and picks up a Jack from those on the ground before catching the tossed Jack. If performed correctly, the player continues. If, however, a Jack is not picked up, another Jack is bumped or moved, or the tossed Jack is not caught, the player's turn ends and the next player begins her/his turn.

At the end of a player's turn, the number of Jacks are counted before the Jacks are put back into the play area for the next player. The player having the highest number of Jacks collected during her/his turn is the winner.

Variation: Play more than one round. During each subsequent round, players need to add another Jack to the number to be picked up. In *round two*, for example, players need to pick up two Jacks at a time; in round three, three Jacks at a time; etc.

If a player's turn has not ended before the Jacks are depleted, the collected Jacks are spread out again so the player may continue. Be sure to keep track of the total number of Jacks collected by each player.

Also See: *Jacks* (4-5)

                Maakgep (4-7)

                Catching Seven Pieces (4-14)

                Abhadhö (4-20)

                Five Stones (4-21)

                Knucklebones (4-22)

                Hamesh Avamin (4-23)

4-18. Chopsticks Jacks

Country: Laos (Far East, Asia)

Type of Game: Jacks with chopsticks

Formation: Players sit in a circle facing the playing area.

Equipment: 10 chopsticks; small ball or nut

Objective: The player tries to pick up as many chopsticks—one at a time—on each turn.

Chopsticks are used in place of small stones, jacks, or small bags for this game.

Directions: The first player drops or carefully tosses the chopsticks to the playing surface. Using only one hand, the player tosses the ball into the air, picks up one chopstick, then catches the ball before it lands on the ground. If successful, the player continues; if not, the chopsticks and ball are passed to the next player.

Each player begins her/his turn by collecting the chopsticks and dropping/tossing them for her-/himself. When a player collects all ten chopsticks successfully on one turn, she/he collects them and drops/tosses them again to continue.

After all players have had one turn, the player scoring the greatest number of chopsticks is the winner.

Also See: *Pick-up Sticks* (4-19)

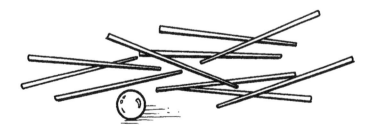

4-19. Pick-up Sticks

Country: Laos (Far East, Asia)

Type of Game: Jacks with chopsticks

Formation: Players sit in a circle facing the playing area.

Equipment: 15–30 10-inch chopsticks; ball or large nut (walnut or pecan size)

Objective: The player tries to pick up the correct number of chopsticks on each toss of the ball.

Laos is slightly larger than Utah with 91,428 square miles inside its boundaries. Although found on the Indochina Peninsula, Laos is landlocked with Myanmar (formerly Burma), China, Vietnam, Cambodia, and Thailand as neighbors.

Directions: Holding the chopsticks vertically to the playing surface, the player drops them so they bounce on end and fall scattering randomly. The player must look at the chopsticks and plan on which sticks to pick up on each toss.

Using one hand, the player tosses the ball, picks up a chopstick, and catches the ball before it lands on the playing surface. If successful, the player tosses the ball a second time. This time two chopsticks are picked up before catching the ball. On each subsequent toss of the ball, one more stick is picked up than the toss before.

If the wrong number of chopsticks are picked up, a chopstick is dropped, the ball is not caught, or the other hand is used in any way to help, the player's turn ends and the next player begins.

Variations:

- On the first five tosses, players pick up one, two, three, four, and five chopsticks. On toss six, the player picks up four chopsticks; toss seven, three chopsticks; and so forth.

- Instead of putting down the chopsticks after successfully collected, the player holds them in the playing hand while continuing to toss the ball and collect more chopsticks. After the fifth toss and five chopsticks are collected, the player tosses the ball a sixth time and places five chopsticks in the playing area. On toss seven, the player places four chopsticks down.
  This procedure continues until all chopsticks are placed back down on the playing surface.

Also See: *Chopsticks Jacks (4-18)*

4-20. Abhadhō

Country: Tibet (Asia)

Type of Game: Jacks with stones

Formation: Players sit on the floor in a circle facing the playing surface.

Equipment: 5 stones

Objective: The player tries to successfully complete all tasks.

Tibet is 470,000 square miles in size, found north of the Himalayan Mountains. Tibet is on a high plateau averaging 15,000 feet in altitude. Jiachan, at a 15,870-foot elevation, is believed to be the highest inhabited town on Earth. Tibet is not a country in itself; it has been under Chinese rule since 1951.

Directions: The player tosses all five stones to the ground. One stone is chosen to toss. Using the same hand, the stone is tossed, one more is picked up from the ground, and the stone is caught before hitting the ground. If successful, the process is repeated for the remaining three pieces.

As the stone is tossed up, the player says "Going up." As the stone begins to fall, the player says "Coming down." After each stone is individually picked up in *round one*, the stones are tossed to the ground again for round two. In *round two*, stones are picked up each time the stone is tossed.

In *round three*, stones are picked up in the first toss and one stone is picked up on the second. In *round four*, the stone is tossed only once and all four stones are picked up before the fifth stone is caught.

Variation (Bridge): The player's fingertips of the nonthrowing hand are placed on the ground. The thumb is placed away from the fingers to form a bridge for the stones to pass through.

The process is the same as for *Abhadhō*, except instead of picking up the stones on the toss, the correct number of stones are pushed under/through the bridge before catching the stone. When all the stones are under the bridge, all the stones are gathered in the tossing hand. They are all tossed into the air and caught on the back of the tossing hand. Any stones falling to the ground are picked up with the index finger and thumb while balancing the others on the back of the hand.

This is repeated for the twos, threes, and fours.

Variation (Hooks): The player's nonthrowing hand forms a bridge, but this time the fingertips are spread apart to allow stones to be pushed between the fingertips. The stones are thrown to the playing surface and one is chosen to be the one tossed. Tossing this stone, another stone is pushed between the thumb and index finger before catching the stone. The stone is tossed again and another stone is pushed between the index finger and the middle finger. This continues, putting the final two stones in the next two open spaces between fingers.

When all four stones are in place between the fingers, the player tosses the stone one more time, removes the nonthrowing hand, and picks up the four stones before catching the tossed stone.

Also See: *Jacks* (4-5)

Maakegep (4-7)

Jacks (4-17)

Five Stones (4-21)

Knucklebones (4-22)

Hamesh Avamin (4-23)

4-21. Five Stones

Country: Colonial America (North America)

Type of Game: Jacks with stones

Formation: Players sit in playing area.

Equipment: 5 stones

Objective: The player tries to toss one stone and pick up the appropriate number of stones before catching the tossed stone.

Besides stones, many colonists used sheep's knucklebones that were found in the pastures and fields.

Directions: To find the first player, the stones are tossed into the air and caught on the back of the same hand. Stones caught are set aside; stones that fell to the ground are tossed again. The first player is the one who catches all five stones on the fewest turns.

To begin the game, the player tosses four stones to the ground. The fifth stone, called the "Jack," is tossed into the air. The player picks up one stone in the tossing hand before the Jack is caught as it falls toward the ground. (This is performed with the same hand.) The player repeats this action to pick up the remaining three stones.

Any time a player moves one stone while picking up another, fails to pick up a stone, or allows the Jack to fall to the ground, that player's turn is over. The next time this player has a turn, she/he begins at the level the mistake happened.

When the player successfully finishes picking up all four stones, one at a time, she/he picks up the four stones, tosses them to the ground, and begins the second round. In *round two,* the player picks up two stones on each toss of the Jack. In the *third round,* three stones are picked up on the first toss, but one on the second. The *fourth round* consists of one toss to pick up all four stones before catching the Jack.

The winner is the player who finishes all four rounds first.

Variation (Over and Back): This game is played only as Ones. The Jack is tossed in the air and one stone is picked up before catching the Jack as it falls towards the ground. With the stone and Jack in hand, the player tosses both in the air and catches them on the back of the hand. If successful, both are tossed from the back of the hand and caught with the palm. If a stone is dropped, the player's turn ends.

The stone picked from the ground is set aside and the Jack is tossed once more and a different stone is picked up. This continues for the remaining two stones.

Variation (<u>Scutters</u>): This is a continuation of *Over and Back*. After the first stone has been picked up, tossed over, and moved from the back of the hand back to the palm, the first stone is held in the palm as the Jack is tossed again and a second stone is picked up. The Jack and the two stones are tossed and caught on the back of the hand. They are tossed again from the back of the hand and caught in the palm. This is repeated until all five stones perform a successful "over and back" on one toss.

Variation (<u>Under the Arch</u>): The player's thumb and index finger of the nonthrowing hand form an archway by placing the fingertips on the ground and holding the palm high. Played Ones through Fours, the player knocks or pushes the stones through the arch on the toss of the Jack.

Variation (<u>Horses in the Stables</u>): The player's nonthrowing hand is placed palm high, fingertips down, and spread apart. The spaces between the fingers are the stables.

Played as Ones only, the stones are placed between the doorways of the stables. The player tries to retrieve the stones one at a time as the Jack is tossed.

Variation (<u>Jump the Ditch</u>): The four stones are placed in a straight line. On the first toss of the Jack, the player picks up the first and third stones, trying not to touch the second and fourth. On the second toss of the Jack, the player picks up the second and fourth stones.

Variation (<u>Four Corners</u>): The stones are placed in the center of a square. On each toss, the player places one stone at a corner of the square. On the fifth toss, the player uses her/his tossing hand to replace the four stones into the center of the square in a pile.

Also See: *Jacks* (4-5)

Maakgep (4-7)

Jacks (4-17)

Abhadö (4-20)

Knucklebones (4-22)

Hamesh Avamin (4-23)

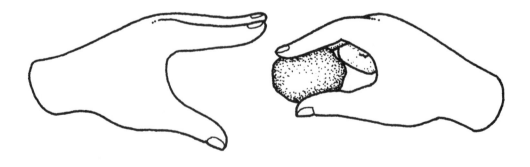

4-22. Knucklebones

Country: Ancient Greece (Europe)

Type of Game: Jacks with stones

Formation: Players sit on the ground in a circle facing the playing area.

Equipment: 5 stones (or sheep knuckles) for each player

Objective: The player tries to complete the sequence of challenges.

As in all games of Jacks, players begin with easier challenges and progress to the most difficult challenge of collecting all stones (or sheep knucklebones) on the last turn.

Directions: All players take their five stones, toss them into the air, and try to catch as many as they can on the back of the tossing hand. The player with the most goes first.

To begin, the player holds all five stones in the tossing hand. Tossing the stones into the air, the player tries to catch all five on the back of her/his hand again. If all five are caught, the player passes to the next round. If not, the player proceeds to the first round.

ROUND—ONES: Holding all five stones in hand, the player tosses them to the ground to scatter. One stone is picked up and used to toss. Tossing this stone, the player attempts to pick up one stone from the ground and catch the tossed stone before it falls to the ground. When all four are picked up, the player tosses all stones to the ground again and tries to pick up two stones on each toss.

ROUND—TWOS: On each toss of the tossing stone, the player tries to pick up two stones before catching the tossed stone. When all are picked up, the player tosses all stones to the ground and tries to pick up three.

ROUND—THREES: On the first toss of the stone, the player picks up three stones before catching the tossed stone. One stone is left to pick up on the second toss. When all four stones are in the hand successfully, all stones are tossed to the ground again and one is chosen to toss.

ROUND—FOURS: On a single toss of the tossing stone, the player tries to pick up all four stones on the ground before catching the tossed stone.

ROUND—PECKS: Tossing all five stones in the air, the player attempts to catch all five on the back of the tossing hand. The stones are tossed from the back of the hand and caught in the palm of the tossing hand. If successful in catching all five stones, the player passes this round and goes directly to *Bushel*. If zero or only one stone is caught, the player's turn is over and may continue the next time her/his turn comes. If two, three, or four stones are caught, the player may continue in this round.

If two to four stones are caught in the palm, one stone is worked towards the fingertips and held between the fingers. Other stones in the palm are trapped in the palm. The stone between the fingertips is tossed in the air and one stone from the ground is picked up before catching the tossed stone. This is repeated for all stones on the ground. The player ends this game with all stones in the tossing hand.

ROUND—BUSHEL: All five stones are held in the tossing hand. The player attempts to toss all five stones, catch them on the back of the tossing hand, and then tosses them from the back of the hand to the tossing hand's palm. If all five stones are caught in the palm, the player proceeds directly to the next round called the *Claw*. If not successful, the player needs to complete *Bushel* before proceeding.

All stones caught in the palm are tossed in the air and any dropped stone is picked up before catching all the tossed stones. This is repeated until all stones missed on the original throw are picked up.

ROUND—CLAW: The player tosses the five stones into the air and catches them on the back of the tossing hand. Tossed again, the stones are caught in the palm of the tossing hand. If all five are caught both times, the player proceeds to *Ones Under the Arch*. If any stones are dropped, the player must complete *Claw* first.

While balancing the stones caught on the back of the hand, the player picks up stones between the tips of the fingers—no more than one stone between any two fingers. When the stones are picked up, the stones on the back of the hand are tossed up and caught in the palm. The stones in the fingers are transferred to the palm.

ROUND—ONES UNDER THE ARCH: The player's nonthrowing hand forms an arch by placing the fingertips down on the ground and holding the palm high off the ground.

The stones are thrown into the playing area and one stone is picked to be tossed. The player tosses the stone into the air while knocking or pushing one on the ground through the arch.

This is repeated for the rest of the stones.

Variation (Stables): The player's nonthrowing hand forms an archway by spreading the fingers apart so stones can be pushed between each set of fingers.

Each time the stone is tossed, a stone on the ground is pushed through a different stable opening.

Variation (Toad in the Hole): The player's fingers of the nonthrowing hand form a hole by touching the fingertips of the fingers to the tip of the thumb. The pinkie side of the hand is placed on the ground.

The five stones are thrown to the ground and one is chosen to toss. The player tosses the stone into the air while picking up one ground stone and putting it into the hole before catching the tossed stone. This is repeated until all four stones are caught. The player may try to perform Twos, Threes, and Fours.

Also See: *Jacks* (4-5)

                     Maakgep (4-7)

                     Jacks (4-17)

                     Abhadhö (4-20)

                     Five Stones (4-21)

                     Hamesh Avamin (4-23)

4-23. Hamesh Avamin

Country: Israel (Middle East, Asia)

Type of Game: Jacks with cubes

Formation: Players sit on the floor in a circle facing the playing area.

Equipment: 5 cubes or stones

Objective: The player tries to go through all challenges, ending with collecting all five stones on the last turn.

Traditionally, Hamesh Avamin *is played with five gold-colored cubes.*

Directions: The five cubes are tossed to the ground and one is chosen to toss. The player tosses this cube into the air and picks up as many cubes as possible. The tossed cube is caught on the back of the tossing hand before hitting the ground. Caution should be used to make sure the cube can be caught; too many cubes in the hand at one time may make it too difficult to catch the tossed cube on the back of the hand.

In the *second round,* the player tosses two cubes when trying to pick up cubes from the ground. She/he still picks up as many cubes as possible, while still catching the cubes on the back of the hand.

Rounds three and four require three and four cubes to be tossed and the others to be picked up in the same fashion.

The first player able to complete all rounds is the winner.

Also See: *Jacks* (4-5)

Maakgep (4-7)

Jacks (4-17)

Abhadhö (4-20)

Five Stones (4-21)

Knucklebones (4-22)

4-24. Jacks

Country: Texas, United States (North America)

Type of Game: Jacks with ball

Formation: Players sit facing the playing area.

Equipment: Ball; 6 jacks

Objective: The player tries to be the first to complete all three rounds.

In the history of Texas, flags from six countries have flown over its land: Spain, France, Mexico, Texas as an independent country, the Confederate flag of the south, and the flag of the United States of America.

Directions: Allowing the ball to bounce one time before being caught during the following games enables the player to perform different stunts.

ROUND ONE, Pigs in the Pen: The jacks are tossed or dropped to the ground spreading them apart from each other. The player's nonplaying hand is placed in a cup shape with the pinkie side on the ground, thumb side up to form a "pigpen."

The player tosses the ball into the air and slides one jack into the pigpen before catching the ball after one bounce. This is continued for the remaining five jacks, one jack at a time.

When all six jacks are in the pigpen, they are picked up and spread out again. This time when the ball is tossed, the player slides two jacks at a time into the pigpen. This is followed by three at a time, four and two, five and one, and finally all six slid into the pigpen on one toss of the ball.

If a player fails to put the correct number of jacks into the pigpen or catch the ball, the player's turn is over and the next player's turn begins. When play gets back to the first player, she/he plays at the level that the mistake was made.

ROUND TWO, Counting Sheep: This is played as in round one except the pigpen is made into a fence. The pinkie side of the nonplaying hand is placed on the playing surface. The fingers are held together and straight and the hand is held horizontal to form the fence the sheep (jacks) jump over.

The player tosses the ball, picks up the correct number of jacks, and places them on the other side of the fence before catching the ball after one bounce.

ROUND THREE, Bees in the Hive: The player's nonplaying hand forms the beehive by placing the fingertips on the playing surface next to the jacks. The fingers are spread apart to create space for the jacks to slide through. The palm is held high off the surface.

The player tosses up the ball and slides the correct number of jacks into the beehive before catching the ball. After all jacks are inside the beehive, the ball is tossed again. The beehive is lifted out of the way, all six jacks are collected in the tossing hand, and the ball is caught.

The beehive is put back, jacks are scattered again, and the game continues, this time sliding two jacks in at a time. The player continues until all six jacks are slid into the beehive on one toss of the ball.

The first player to complete all six rounds is the winner.

Also See: *Ball and Jack (4-25)*

4-25. Ball and Jack

Country: United States (North America)

Type of Game: Jacks with ball

Formation: Players sit facing the playing area.

Equipment: Small bouncing ball for each player; 10 (metal or plastic) jacks for each player

Objective: The player tries to toss the ball, pick up the correct number of jacks, and catch the ball after it bounces once (not twice).

Allowing the ball to bounce provides extra time to perform the activities described and prescribed in the different rounds/games.

Directions: To find who will be the first player, each player takes all ten jacks in the tossing hand. Tossing slightly in the air, the player catches as many jacks on the back of the tossing hand as possible. The player catching the most will be first. The player catching the next highest is second, and so on.

Basic Rules: The player's turn ends when:

- The player completes all levels of the game.
- The player moves a jack when picking up a different jack.
- The player picks up the wrong number of jacks.
- The player drops a jack when catching the ball.
- The ball does not bounce or bounces more than once.
- The ball bounces on a jack.
- The player's second hand helps in any way to toss, pick up, or catch.
- The player's second hand is used in any way other than described in tricks requiring the second hand.
- The player fails to catch the ball after the first bounce.

Basic Game:

ONES: The jacks are tossed to the ground so they scatter. The ball is tossed into the air and allowed to bounce once as the player picks up one jack before catching the ball. If successful, the player repeats until all ten jacks are picked up. If a mistake is made, it becomes the second player's turn.

TWOS THROUGH TENS: In each round one more jack is picked up than the round before. In rounds where an odd number of jacks is left at the end, these remain for the final toss of the ball.

Variation (Sweeps): The jacks are scattered on the ground. The player tosses the ball and sweeps a jack toward the body with the tossing hand before catching the ball (after one bounce). Play continues as described above for the basic game.

Variation (Eggs in a Basket): The jacks are scattered on the ground. The player tosses the ball, picks up a jack, and places it in the nonthrowing hand before catching the ball (after it bounces once.) When all eggs are collected in the basket, the player attempts to pick up two eggs at a time. Again, as above, each round adds one more jack to pick up on each toss of the ball.

Variation (<u>Crack the Eggs</u>): The jacks are scattered on the ground. Performing rounds Ones through Tens, the player tosses the ball, picks up the correct number of jacks, and taps them to the ground (cracking the egg) before catching the ball. After catching the ball, the cracked eggs are transferred to the nonthrowing hand before the next toss.

Variation (<u>Scrubs</u>): The jacks are scattered on the playing surface. The player tosses the ball and the tossing hand grasps one jack. The jack is scrubbed back and forth across the playing surface before being picked up and catching the ball. This is performed for Ones through Tens.

Variation (<u>Pigs in the Pen</u>): The jacks are scattered on the playing surface. The player's nonthrowing hand is cupped and placed with the outside edge on the surface close to the jacks. The player tosses the ball and pushes one jack into the pen before catching the ball. This is performed for Ones through Tens.

Variation (<u>Pigs over the Fence</u>): The jacks are scattered on the ground. The player's nonthrowing hand is placed to the side with the fingers extended to form a fence. The ball is tossed and the player picks up one jack and places it on the other side of the fence before catching the ball. This is performed for Ones through Tens.

Variation (<u>Add a Jack</u>): The jacks are scattered on the playing surface. The ball is tossed and the player picks up one jack before the ball is caught on one bounce. The ball is tossed a second time and two jacks are picked up before catching the ball on one bounce. Each time the ball is tossed and jacks are picked up, one more jack is gathered in the hand than on the toss before.

Variation (<u>Flying Dutchman</u>): The jacks are scattered on the floor. The player tosses the ball and catches the jack after one bounce. Holding the jack and ball in the same hand, the ball is tossed once more and the jack is tossed to the other hand before catching the ball after one more bounce. Play continues through the regular sequence of play of the basic game.

Variation (<u>Bounce, No Bounce</u>): The jacks are scattered on the floor. The player tosses the ball and catches the jack after one bounce. Holding the jack and ball in the same hand, the ball is tossed once more and the jack is tossed to the other hand before catching the ball *before* it bounces. Play continues through the regular sequence of play of the basic game.

Variation (<u>Down and Up</u>): Holding the ball and jacks in the tossing hand, the player tosses the ball in the air, tosses the jacks on the playing surface, and catches the ball after one bounce. Tossing the ball one more time, the player picks up all the jacks before catching the ball after it bounces once.

Variation (<u>Around the World</u>): The jacks are scattered on the playing surface. The player tosses the ball and picks up one jack. Before catching the ball following the first bounce, the tossing hand (with the jack held inside) orbits one time around the ball before catching it before it bounces a second time. Play continues through the basic game.

Variation (<u>Double Bounce</u>): The ball is allowed to bounce twice before being caught for any of the above games.

Also See: *Jacks* (4-24)

Section 5
Races and Relays

The following races and relays are put together simply because of their link to each other. In most cases, the races can be performed as either a race or modified into a relay by having players form teams in which they take turns performing the activity. The activities are listed as either Race or Relay Race in the Type of Game description because that is how I found the activity while researching for this book.

In this section you'll find 56 games from 17 countries and 6 different continents/regions.

Africa

Blindfolded Horse Relay (5-46)—Nigeria

Bokwele (5-20)—Africa

Bottle Relay (5-51)—Uganda

War Canoes (5-48)—Nigeria

Asia

Asol–Tale Aap (Canoe Race on Sand) (5-47)—India

Lamjei (The Race) (5-12)—India

Australia

Australian Bottle Game (5-49)—Australia

Coconut Shell Game (5-1)*—(Aborigine) Australia

Fielding Race (5-16)—Australia

Hand-Tag Relay Race (5-10)—Australia

Kangaroo Jump Race (5-6)—Australia

Spinning the Plate (5-27)*—Australia

Tag Relay with Bouncing Ball (5-11)—Australia

Europe

Bunny Hop (5-5)—Great Britain

Corkscrew (5-38)—Great Britain

Dzien Dobry (Good Morning) (5-23)—Poland

Handshake Race (5-24)—Sweden

Herqr Relay Race (Arrow Relay Race) (5-22)—Scandinavia

Leapfrog (5-9)—Europe

Nut Relay (5-50)*—Europe

Plate, Potato, Broom Relay (5-53)—Germany

Thread the Needle (5-55)—Great Britain

Three-Legged Race (5-45)—Europe

Tunnel Relay (5-2)—Belgium

Far East

Chung Tou Teh Tou (Plant Beans, Reap Beans) (5-14)—Hong Kong

Harvest Race (5-15)—China

Lame Chicken (5-7)—China

Memutar Pinggan (Plate Spinning) (5-29)*—Malaysia

North America

Ball Relay (5-34)—Northwest Coast/Plains Native Americans

Ball Toss Race (5-39)—Plains/Southwest Native Americans

Bear Race (5-3)—Northwest Coast Native Americans

Crab Race (5-4)—Northwest Coast Native Americans

Cross-Country Relay (5-33)—Northwest Coast/Plains/Woodlands Native Americans

Double Relay (5-36)—Northwest Coast/Plains Native Americans

Feather Racing (5-52)—United States

Frog Race (5-8)—Northwest Coast Native Americans

Indian Foot Race (5-17)—Plains Native Americans

Indian Kickball (5-40)—Hopi, United States/Tarthumara, Mexico Native Americans

North America *(continued)*

Kaipsak (Spinning Tops) (5-28)—Inuit Native Americans

Kick Stick Races (5-42)—Zuni Native Americans

Kickball Races (5-41)—Southwest Native Americans

Kiwa Trail (Twisted Trail) (5-31)—Northwest Coast/Woodlands Native Americans

Lance Head (5-37)—Plains Native Americans

Menomini Foot Race (5-13)—Menomini Native Americans

Obstacle Run (5-32)—Northwest Coast/Woodlands Native Americans

Run for Your Supper (5-25)—United States

Spinning Tops (5-30)—United States

Stick Relay (5-35)—Northwest Coast/Plains Native Americans

Stick vs. Foot (5-43)—Apache Native Americans

Tadpole Relay (5-56)—United States

Tipi Race (5-18)—Plains Native Americans

Toss a Ring Race (5-44)—Northern Mexico/Southwest United States Native Americans

Oceania

Ver Ver Aras Lama (5-21)—New Guinea

South America

Balon en el Aire (Ball in the Air) (5-54)—Argentina

Circular Race in Zigzag (5-26)—Bolivia

Juego De Panuelo (Handkerchief Game) (5-19)—Bolivia

*Games that may be played in the classroom.

5-1. Coconut Shell Game

Country: Australia (Aborigine)

Type of Game: Relay Race

Formation: Each team creates a single circle. Beanbags are placed at the feet of the first player.

Equipment: 7 beanbags or shells if available per team

Objective: The team tries to pass the beanbags around the circle as quickly as possible.

Australia is the sixth largest nation, almost the size of the continental United States, and the least populated continent except for Antarctica. Being an island nation, Australia has a tremendous amount of shoreline to gather shells to play this game.

Directions: One player in each circle is declared the leader. The beanbags are placed at the feet of the leader. On the signal "Go!" the first beanbag is picked up by the leader and passed to the next person to the left. When the beanbag is passed to the last person of the circle, it is placed on the floor at her/his feet.

While players can have only one beanbag in her/his hands at a time, more than one can be traveling around the circle at a time. When all beanbags are at the feet of the last player, the team is finished. The first team finished wins.

Variations:

- When all beanbags are at the feet of the last player, one beanbag is picked up and passed back around the circle in the reverse direction to the leader of the circle, who places the beanbags on the floor at her/his feet. Again, each player can have only one beanbag in her/his hands at a time, but more than one can be in motion around the circle at any given time. The first team with the beanbags returned to the leader wins.

- The beanbags are picked up and passed one at a time to the second player who places them at her/his feet until she/he has all the beanbags. The second player then hands the beanbags to the third player who places them at her/his feet until all are collected. This continues until the beanbags are at the feet of the last player.

- The beanbags are picked up and passed using the right hand only; the left hand only.

5-2. Tunnel Relay

Country: Belgium (Europe)

Type of Game: Relay Race

Formation: Each team stands in single file one yard apart with feet in straddle position. The front player of each line holds the ball.

Equipment: 1 ball per team

Objective: The team tries to roll the ball through the tunnel of legs to the last player in line.

Ruled for 1,800 years by conquerors, Belgium had been invaded by Rome, the Franks, Burgundy, Spain, Austria, and France. It was made part of the Netherlands after 1815 but became independent in 1830.

Directions: On the signal "Go!" the front player of each team bends forward and rolls the ball through the tunnel of legs to the last player in line. Players forming the tunnel are not allowed to touch the ball with their hands while it passes through the tunnel. When the last player receives the ball, she/he carries it to the front of the line and rolls the ball through the line to the new last player. This continues until the original first player returns to the front of the line with the ball.

If the ball rolls out of the tunnel between two players, it is brought back to the front and rolled again without players changing positions.

Adaptation: For younger players just learning the activity, the player in line where the ball stops inside or where the ball leaves the tunnel may retrieve the ball and pass the ball from her/his spot in the tunnel.

5-3. Bear Race

Country: Northwest Coast Native Americans, United States (North America)

Type of Game: Race—Animal

Formation: Players stand on their hands and feet behind the starting line.

Equipment: Start and finish lines

Objective: The player tries to imitate the running motions of a bear while traveling as quickly as possible to the finish line.

In this activity, the players imitate the running movements of the bear. It is more important to move correctly than to just be first.

Directions: Beginning behind the starting line, the players run "like a bear" as quickly as possible to a finish line about 60 feet away. Winners are not chosen from the ones who just finished first; rather, they are the ones who finish first *and* perform the actions correctly.

The player must move the right hand and left leg forward at the same time, followed by the left hand and right leg coming forward together. Keeping off the knees is very important to the technique of this activity.

Also See: *Crab Race* (5-4)

Frog Race (5-8)

5-4. Crab Race

Country: Northwest Coast Native Americans, United States (North America)

Type of Game: Race—Animal

Formation: Players stand facing sideways to the starting line.

Equipment: Start and finish lines

Objective: The player tries to move sideways on hands and knees to the finish line.

Northwest Coast Indians would imitate crabs' sideways movements in this relay.

Directions: On the signal "Go!" the players drop down to their hands and knees and crawl sideways to the finish line. The first to finish wins.

Adaptation: Older players go to the turning line and then back to the starting line. When at the turning line, the players may be required to continue to face the same direction so as to move with the other side leading.

Also See: *Bear Race* (5-3)

                 Frog Race (5-8)

5-5. Bunny Hop

Country: Great Britain (Europe)

Type of Game: Race—Animal

Formation: Players squat behind the starting line with their hands placed on the ground in front of the feet.

Equipment: Start and finish lines

Objective: The player tries to be the first to do the Bunny Hop correctly to the finish line.

The United Kingdom of Great Britain and Northern Ireland comprises England, Wales, Scotland, and Northern Ireland. Its capital is London, England. The Normans were the last to successfully invade Britain in 1066 A.D.

Directions: The players squat with their hands on the ground in front of their feet so the hands and feet are touching. On the signal "Go!" the players move their hands forward away from the feet and place them on the ground before their feet are brought to the hands. This movement is repeated to the finish line. It is important for the players to know that the hands move separately from the feet: first the hands move forward, then the feet follow. At no time do the hands or the feet move at the same time.

Also See: *Frog Race* (5-8)

   Kangaroo Jump Race (5-6)

5-6. Kangaroo Jump Race

Country: Australia

Type of Game: Race—Animal

Formation: Players stand behind a starting line.

Equipment: Start, turn, and finish lines

Objective: The player tries to hop like a kangaroo to the turning point and back.

Australia is the home of the kangaroo. The kangaroo is a plant-eating marsupial with weak forelimbs, very strong hind limbs, and a stout tail. The kangaroo family ranges from the size of a rat up to nine feet long from head to tail!

Directions: The players stand with their elbows kept close to the body. The hands are held at shoulder height and flexed forward with their fingers pointing down. The legs are kept together at all times and kept bent. Taking big jumps, the players make quick jumps to the turning point and back.

Variation: If performed as a relay race, team members stand in a single file and take turns to jump to the turning line and back.

Also See: *Bunny Hop* (5-5)

         Frog Race (5-8)

5-7. Lame Chicken

Country: China (Far East, Asia)

Type of Game: Relay Race—Animal

Formation: Teams line up single file behind a starting line. Ten sticks per team are laid out a foot apart and parallel to each other like the rungs of a ladder. The first stick is five yards from the starting line.

Equipment: Start line; 10 sticks per team

Objective: The player tries to hop over the sticks and back.

The country was officially named the People's Republic of China in 1949. The name China *is probably derived from the Qin (Ch'in) dynasty (221–206 B.C.) which first unified the nation. The Chinese people themselves refer to their country as Zhonggua (Chung-kuo, or the Middle Country), due to the early Chinese concept that China was the middle of the world.*

Directions: On the signal "Go!" the first runner hops to her/his team's line of sticks and hops over each stick individually to the last stick. Picking up the last stick, the runner hops over each stick on the way back and places the stick being carried one foot from the first stick closer towards the starting line. Hopping back to her/his team, the second runner is hand-tagged to start her/his turn. This sequence continues until all runners have completed one turn.

The winning team is the team whose runners have completed the sequence once, twice, three times—whatever number has been decided.

Variation: The runner carries the stick back to the starting line instead of placing the stick closer to the starting line. The winning team is the team that has cleared all its sticks from the field.

5-8. Frog Race

Country: Northwest Coast Native Americans, United States (North America)

Type of Game: Race—Animal

Formation: Players squat behind the starting line with arms wrapped around their legs just above the ankles.

Equipment: Start and finish lines

Objective: The player tries to hop like a frog to the finish line.

Living near many rivers and lakes, Native Americans have observed the movements of the animals that live in the water. Here the jumping motion of the frog is used for a race.

Directions: Players stand behind the starting line. On the signal "Go!" players hop to the finish line about 40 feet apart. Any players who lose their balance and fall over must get back onto their feet without letting go of their fingers from in front of their ankles.

Adaptation: Older students race to a turning point and return. On the way back, the players may bump into other runners to knock them over. *These bumps are to be just hard enough to unbalance the other player without hurting her/him.*

Also See: *Bear Race* (5-3)

                  Crab Race (5-4)

5-9. Leapfrog

Country: Europe

Type of Game: Relay Race—Animal

Formation: Teams stand in single file with the first player standing at the starting line. Three or more players are in each line.

Equipment: Start and finish lines

Objective: Each team tries to leapfrog correctly to the finish line.

Leapfrog *was widely played throughout Europe during the Middle Ages. It was so popular that Shakespeare's* Henry V *has mention of it, and people playing* Leapfrog *is found in paintings by Pieter Brueghel.*

Directions: On the signal "Go!" the first player from each team stands at the starting line and performs a standing long jump. Then bending forward, this player grabs her/his ankles to form a position referred to as the "back" position: the head tilts down and the chin touches the chest, out of the way of the next jumper. The second player runs up to the first and places her/his hands on the first player's back. Straddling her/his legs, the second player vaults over the first player. Landing on both feet, the second player then forms a second "back." The leaping frogs must land on both feet without falling over and not take an unnecessary step on landing. (Players who fall down, take extra steps, or knock down a "back" must go to the back of the line to wait for her/his next turn.)

The third jumper runs up to the "backs" and leaps over each in succession without hesitating or knocking them down. The two "backs" must be close enough so the third player need not walk or run to get to the next "back," but also far enough forward from the first to allow the third player room to safely land between the two.

With the last jumper gone, the first "back" stands up and becomes the next jumper. She/he must successfully leap over the line of "backs" before the next "back" can go. If unsuccessful, she/he must repeat process until successful.

Variations: If the "backs" are not sturdy, are easily knocked over, fail to provide a sturdy base, or are too high for other players to vault over successfully, try one of the following changes.

- The "back" slightly bends the knees and bends forward at the waist to place her/his elbows on the knees with arms bent and hands clasped in front of the knees. This forearm/hand position forms the top point of a triangle with an invisible base line between the knees.

- If a standing base is too high for younger players, the "backs" can get on their hands and knees on the floor. The "back" sits back on her/his heels with hands on the floor and arms straight. The head should be dropped down so the chin touches the player's chest, out of the way of the vaulting player.

- If younger players still have a difficult time leaping over the "back," the "back" gets in the position described in the second adaptation and brings her/his elbows to the floor, lowering her/his back even further.

5-10. Hand-Tag Relay Race

Country: Australia

Type of Game: Relay Race

Formation: Teams stand in single file behind a starting line.

Equipment: Start and turn lines

Objective: The team tries to be the first to complete the running course.

Being an island, Australia is surrounded by water. These waters include the Timor Sea and Arafura Sea to the north; the Coral Sea, Pacific Ocean, and Tasman Sea to the east; the Southern Ocean to the south; and the Indian Ocean to the west.

Directions: This is a simple relay where the first runner from each team runs to a turning point away from the starting line, returns, and hand-tags the hand of the next runner, which allows the second runner to begin her/his turn. The first team that has all runners complete the course correctly wins.

Also See: *Tag Relay with Bouncing Ball (5-11)*

5-11. Tag Relay with Bouncing Ball

Country: Australia

Type of Game: Relay Race

Formation: Teams stand single file behind a starting line.

Equipment: 1 bouncing ball for each team; start and turn lines

Objective: The team tries to be the first to have all players run to a turning line and back while bouncing a ball as they run.

Use balls appropriate to the age and development of the players. These balls can range from tennis balls to basketballs.

Directions: The first runner of each team is given a bouncing ball. On the signal "Go!" these runners run to a turning point and back while bouncing the ball as they go. The ball is handed (not thrown) to the next runner so the next runner can have her/his turn to run.

The first team whose runners complete the course wins.

Variation: The player carries the ball to a certain point, usually the turning point, where she/he bounces the ball a predetermined number before returning to the next runner.

Also See: *Hand-Tag Relay Race (5-10)*

5-12. Lamjei (The Race)

Country: India (Asia)

Type of Game: Race

Formation: Two racers start behind a starting line. The finish line is 100–400 yards away.

Equipment: Start and finish lines

Objective: The runner tries to be the fastest.

Lamjei *is a popular annual race in Manipur, India.*

Directions: On the signal "Go!" two runners race to the finish line. After all sets of runners have raced, the winners race against each other, continuing to compete until only one runner remains undefeated.

Losing runners might compete against other losing runners.

5-13. Menomini Foot Race

Country: Menomini Native Americans, United States (North America)

Type of Game: Race

Formation: Runners begin 50–75 feet behind the starting line. Paired runners hold a stick between them.

Equipment: 15- to 18-inch long sticks; start and finish lines

Objective: The paired runners try to run across the starting line at the same time, and then race separately to the finish line to see who is faster.

Once past the starting line, the Menomini runners were allowed to interfere with the progress of the other runner. They could trip, hold, hit, kick, push, shove, or shoulder each other in an effort to slow her/him down. This is not recommended for today's races!

Directions: Beginning 50–75 feet behind the starting line (and the actual start of the race), the runners approach the starting line next to each other in an effort to cross the line at the same time. To help them do this, the runners hold a stick between them. This way a runner can tell when she/he or the other runner is ahead or behind.

Once both runners pass the starting line together, the stick is dropped and the real race begins. The length of the race depends on the age and ability of the runners. The first runner across the finish line wins.

5-14. Chung Tou Teh Tou (Plant Beans, Reap Beans)

Country: Hong Kong (Far East, Asia)

Type of Game: Relay Race

Formation: Teams stand single file behind the starting line. The first runner for each team has five checkers. Five circles are marked on the floor at the turning point.

Equipment: 5 checkers per team; 5 circles per team marked on the floor; start and turn lines

Objective: Each runner tries to place or pick up a checker.

Great Britain leased the islands of Hong Kong for 99 years from China. In 1997 Hong Kong returned to Chinese rule, but under agreement with Britain, Hong Kong will be able to keep its capitalistic system for another 50 years.

Directions: Taking only one checker at a time, the first runner for each team runs down to the circles on the floor and places the checker in one circle. Returning to the starting line, the first runner picks up a second checker and returns to the circles and places it in a different circle. Making five runs, the first runner "plants the beans."

When finished planting the five beans, the first runner tags the hand of the second runner. The second runner runs down and grabs one checker and brings it back, "reaping" the bean. The second runner repeats this four more times until all the beans are harvested before tagging the hand of the third runner who plants the beans.

Each runner continues the pattern of either "planting" or "reaping" the beans until all runners have had a turn. Each relay team is to have the same number of runners, even if some teams need to have a player have more than one turn.

Variations:

- Have one bean for each runner in line. Each runner runs one time to place her/his bean in a circle on the floor. The second time a runner runs down, she/he reaps a bean before coming back with it. This pattern continues until all runners have planted and reaped a bean for a predetermined number of times.

- The first runner places all five beans in separate circles before returning. The second runner runs down and picks up the five beans before returning. This sequence repeats itself until all runners have either planted or reaped the beans, or done both.

Also See: *Harvest Race (5-15)*

5-15. Harvest Race

Country: China (Far East, Asia)

Type of Game: Relay Race

Formation: Teams stand single file behind a starting line.

Equipment: 1 small garden shovel; 3 plastic flowers; 1 watering can; bucket of dirt; 1 spray can; 1 basket for each team; start and turn (garden) lines

Objective: The team tries to be the first team to return with the flowers.

This activity demonstrates that many jobs need to be done for a flower to grow. Each runner has a different job to perform, so cooperation of all is necessary in order for the flowers to grow.

Directions: Each runner on the team has a different function to perform. All equipment is left at the garden (turn line). Before the race, each job to be performed is assigned and its importance and sequence explained.

On the signal "Go!" the first runner on each team runs to the garden and digs three holes in the bucket of dirt with the shovel. Dropping the shovel, the runner runs back to her/his line to tag the second runner. The second runner runs to the garden, plants the plastic flowers in the holes, covers the "roots" with dirt (so they stay up), and runs back to tag the third runner. Runner three "waters" the flowers. Runner four "sprays" for bugs. Runner five "picks" the flowers, puts them in a basket, and brings them back to the line.

For more or fewer runners, jobs will be increased or decreased for each runner. All jobs must be performed in their proper sequence.

Also See: *Chung Tou Teh Tou (Plant Beans, Reap Beans) (5-14)*

5-16. Fielding Race

Country: Australia

Type of Game: Relay Race

Formation: Teams stand single file behind a starting line.

Equipment: Start and turn lines; ball

Objective: Each runner tries to roll a ball to the turning line, run down, and retrieve it for the next runner.

The runners learn how hard to roll or throw the ball so it will pass the turning point but not go far beyond. Following the ball after it is thrown is good practice in fielding a ball for other games.

Directions: Standing behind the starting line, each runner in turn rolls or throws the ball towards the turning line. As soon as the ball leaves the player's hand, she/he runs to the turn line to retrieve the ball and carry it back to the next runner.

If the ball does not cross the turn line, the runner is to pick up the ball, return to the starting line, and roll or throw it again. (Players who cannot throw the ball past the turning line on one throw may pick up the ball between the starting and turning lines and throw it a second time to the turning line.)

The first team to complete the course wins.

5-17. Indian Foot Race

Country: Plains Native Americans, United States (North America)

Type of Game: Race

Formation: Field marked with two starting lines far apart and opposite from each other. A center line is marked halfway between for the finish line. One runner stands at each starting line facing the center finish line.

Equipment: Start lines and center finish line

Objective: Each runner (coming from opposite directions) tries to cross the center line before the other runner.

This race was originally used to show courage along with speed. The temptation to dodge or swerve or reduce speed near the finish line to avoid a collision would be great.

Directions: Runners face each other at the start of the race. On the signal "Go!" both runners race to the center finish line trying to cross the center line first. Runners need to be careful to run past the other runner, *not directly towards* the other runner.

Safety: A perpendicular line may be drawn between the two starting lines to help the runners avoid a collision. Each runner needs to stay to the right side of the line (much like the center line marked on a roadway to keep traffic on the proper side of the road).

5-18. Tipi Race

Country: Plains Native Americans, United States (North America)

Type of Game: Race/Relay Race

Formation: Circle of 44-foot diameter is drawn on the ground. One runner stands at each marker outside the circle. (See Illustration 1.)

Equipment: Markers (cones); 2 markers (cones) are placed inside the circle 4 feet apart; 44-foot circle

Objective: Each team's runners try to run around their marker inside the circle and back to her/his place outside the circle.

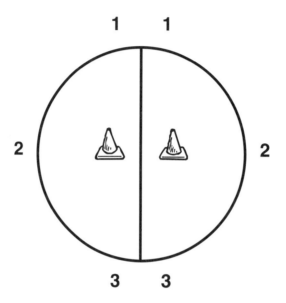

Illustration 1: *Tipi Race*

Native American Indians considered the circle the perfect form. They believed the circle added wings to their feet in racing, allowing them to run faster.

Directions: There are several ways to perform the Tipi Race. If there is only one runner at each marker around the circle, the runner at number 1 for each team runs around her/his center marker and back following the "Go!" signal from the leader. As soon as the first runner returns to her/his marker, the runner at number 2 can run. This continues until all runners have run. The first team to have all runners complete the course wins.

Variations:

- In races involving more than one runner at each marker, one of three ways can be performed. Played as described, the first runner at each marker runs before the second runner begins. When the first runner at the last marker finishes her/his run, the second runner at the first marker begins. This continues until the last runner at the last marker has finished.

- A second way to perform the Tipi Race with multiple runners at each marker is to have all runners at the first marker to run in turn before the first runner at the second marker begins. This pattern continues until the last runner at the last marker has completed the course.

- A third way for multiple runners at each marker is to have all first runners at each marker run at the same time. This takes care and talking to ensure that an understanding of safety and fair play is followed to prevent accidents. During the progress of the relay, faster runners will separate from the slower runners and the runners will spread out, reducing the number of runners at the center marker where all make their turns before heading back to her/his line.

5-19. Juego De Panuelo
(Handkerchief Game)

Country: Bolivia (South America)

Type of Game: Race

Formation: Players form four single files to create a plus design. The first runner of each line is in the center. One player (IT) stands outside the formation holding a handkerchief. (See Illustration 1.)

Equipment: Handkerchief

Objective: The chosen line tries to run around the other lines and return to its original order.

Bolivia, at an altitude of 12,000 feet, is a great central plateau in South America. Lake Titacaca on the Peruvian border is the world's highest lake (at 12,506 feet) on which steamboats are used.

Directions: IT travels around the formation carrying the handkerchief and drops the handkerchief when behind one of the lines. All the runners in that line run clockwise around the other lines and back to their places in the original order. As these runners are racing around the circle, IT takes the vacated space of one of the runners. The runner whose place is taken by IT becomes the new IT.

Variation: IT drops the handkerchief and runs around the formation, racing to get back to the line and in place of one of the other runners.

Illustration 1: *Juego De Panuelo*

5-20. Bokwele

Country: Africa

Type of Game: Relay Race

Formation: Hula hoops are placed in a circle 8–10 feet apart. Players stand behind a hoop containing 3–4 items inside.

Equipment: 1 hula hoop for each team; 3–4 objects (blocks, balls, etc.) in each hoop

Objective: Each team tries to get the most items in its hoop.

The Sahara Desert in northern Africa is 3,500,000 square miles in size, the largest desert in the world. It is larger than the continental United States!

Directions: Each team has a hula hoop with 3–4 items inside. On the signal "Go!" the runners run to other team's hoops taking only one object and returning it to their own hoop. Runners take turns running one at a time in a relay. (In games of five or more teams, players may not take items from hoops next to her/his own hoop.) This continues for a predetermined amount of time. At the end of the game, the team with the highest number of objects in its hoop is the winner.

Safety: Runners may not guard or prevent others from taking from their hoop.

Also See: *Herqr Relay Race (5-22)*

        Ver Ver Aras Lama (5-21)

5-21. Ver Ver Aras Lama

Country: New Guinea (Oceania)

Type of Game: Relay Race

Formation: Center circle is drawn with 5–7 balls inside. Smaller circles (hula hoops) are in front of each team. Runners (in 4 teams) stand behind one of the smaller circles around the center circle.

Equipment: Large center circle; 5–7 balls; 4 hula hoops

Objective: Each team tries to collect the most balls in its hula hoop.

New Guinea is an island found in the Pacific Ocean north of Australia. The eastern half of the island is the country of Papua New Guinea; the western half is part of Indonesia. The island of New Guinea is slightly larger than the state of West Virginia.

Directions: One large circle is drawn in the center of the playing area with 5–7 balls inside. Four hula hoops are spaced evenly around the center circle.

At the signal "Go!" the first runner runs from each team to the center, takes one ball and brings it back to her/his team's hoop. Placing it inside (not throwing), the runner goes to the end of the line, and the second runner goes to the center for another ball. When no more balls are in the center circle, the runners may take balls from the other teams' hoops. This is to be done without interference from the other players. The game ends when one team has captured at least three balls in its hoop at one time.

Also See: *Bokwele (5-20)*

Herqr Relay Race (5-22)

5-22. Herqr Relay Race
(Arrow Relay Race)

Country: Scandinavia (Europe)

Type of Game: Relay Race

Formation: Each team forms a single file behind a starting line. A hula hoop for each team is placed equal distance from the starting line. An equal number of sticks is placed in each hula hoop.

Equipment: Start line; 1 hula hoop for each team; sticks

Objective: Each team tries to have the fewest number of sticks in its circle at the end of the race.

Scandinavia is a region in northern Europe including Norway, Sweden, and Denmark (and sometimes Iceland). A Nordic custom was to shoot an arrow (herqr) to announce the coming of an enemy and to prepare for war.

Directions: On the signal "Go!" the first runner from each team runs to her/his circle of sticks, takes one out, and places it in another team's circle. After doing so, this first runner returns to her/his own circle of sticks, takes another, and brings this second stick back to the next runner on her/his team. Once the second runner has received the stick from the first runner, she/he runs and places it in another team's circle, grabs one from her/his own circle, and returns to her/his own line to hand it off to the third runner.

This process continues until the timekeeper calls time is up. The team with the fewest arrows in its circle is the winner.

Also See: *Bokwele* (5-20)

   Ver Ver Aras Lama (5-21)

5-23. Dzien Dobry (Good Morning)

Country: Poland (Europe)

Type of Game: Race

Formation: All but one player (IT) sit in a single circle. IT stands outside the circle.

Equipment: None

Objective: The player tries to be the first to return to the vacant spot in the circle.

Dzien dobry, *pronounced "jane dough-bri," means "Good Morning."*
Jak sie masz, *pronounced "yok heh mush," means "How are you?"*

Directions: Walking around the outside of the circle of players, IT taps a player on the shoulder, says "Dzien dobry," and continues to walk around the circle. The tapped circle player gets up quickly and begins to walk around the circle in the opposite direction. When the two players meet, they stop, face each other, and say three times "Jak sie masz," bowing as they do so. Both walkers continue to walk around the circle to the vacated spot of the tapped player. The first player back sits in that spot and the remaining player is IT for the next turn.

It should be stressed that *dzien dobry* and *jak sie masz* should be said loud enough for all players to hear.

Variation: IT and the tapped player can walk around the inside of the circle (if made large enough). To ensure that no player cuts corners to beat the other, the two walkers must give each player of the circle a "high five" as they travel around.

Circle players need to keep their feet and legs pulled in so as to not trip either walker.

Also See: *Handshake Race (5-24)*
                  Run for Your Supper (5-25)

5-24. Handshake Race

Country: Sweden (Europe)

Type of Game: Race

Formation: All but one player (IT) sit in a single circle. IT stands outside the circle.

Equipment: None

Objective: The player tries to be the first to return to the vacated spot in the circle.

Goddag *(gŏd/dăg) is Swedish for "good day."*

Directions: IT runs around the outside of the circle, taps a player on the shoulder, and continues around. The tapped player runs around the circle in the opposite direction. When the two runners meet, they stop, shake hands with each other, and say "Goddag" before continuing on their way around the circle to the vacant spot. The first player back sits in that spot and the remaining player is IT for the next turn.

Also See: *Dzien Dobry (5-23)*

Run for Your Supper (5-25)

5-25. Run for Your Supper

Country: United States (North America)

Type of Game: Race

Formation: All but one player (IT) stand in a single circle. IT stands outside the circle.

Equipment: None

Objective: The player tries to race around the circle and be the first to tag IT's hand.

The total landmass for the United States is 3,540,000 square miles including Alaska and Hawaii. The total landmass for the Sahara Desert is 3,500,000 square miles.

Directions: IT walks around the outside of the circle. At any point, IT stops and places her/his hands together and reaches between two players of the circle. These two players run around the circle in opposite directions (running away from IT). The first racer back to tag IT's hand becomes the new IT.

Circle players who have run sit down until all circle players have had a turn to race. Circle players, when stranded by themselves, may need to be moved from time to time to match up with other runners who have not yet run.

Also See: *Dzien Dobry* (5-23)

Handshake Race (5-24)

5-26. Circular Race in Zigzag

Country: Bolivia (South America)

Type of Game: Race/Relay Race

Formation: Players sit in a single circle with space between them so runners may pass through.

Equipment: None

Objective: The player tries to run around the circle, weaving in and out between the circle players.

Bolivia is named after Simon Bolivar, an independence fighter who helped free Bolivia from Spanish rule in 1825.

Directions: The circle is divided in half. Players on each half are numbered off so both teams have identical numbers. When the leader calls a number, the player from each team having that number called runs around the circle to her/his right, weaving in and out between the players of the circle until the players reach their home spot. The first player to return wins.

Variation: A player from each team stands in the center of the circle holding a basketball. The leader calls a player's number and the center player quickly passes the basketball to that player. As soon as the ball is caught, that player begins running, weaving in and out around the circle while dribbling the basketball.

Once the runner returns to her/his place in the circle, the ball is passed back to her/his team's center (or may dribble the ball to the center her-/himself). The runner then becomes the next center player to pass the ball to the next runner.

5-27. Spinning the Plate

Country: Australia

Type of Game: Race

Formation: All players but one (IT) sit in a single circle. Each circle player chooses a name of a town. IT stands in the center of the circle with a plastic plate.

Equipment: 1 plastic plate

Objective: The player tries to get up and catch the spinning plate before it stops or falls.

Once ruled by Great Britain, Australia gained its independence in 1901 although the head of state is still Queen Elizabeth II of England.

Directions: IT spins the plate on its side in the center of the circle and calls out the name of a town. The player called must jump up and catch the plate before it falls over. If successful, she/he is the next IT. If not, the player is eliminated and sits outside the circle.

Players (including IT) are eliminated if she/he:

- Misses or knocks over the plate.
- Calls a town already eliminated.
- Calls a town name a player does not have.

The last player left wins.

Variation: A player who successfully catches a plate gets to spin it. While the plate is spinning, the player must correctly spell a word called out by the leader before the plate stops spinning.

Also See: *Kaipsak* (5-28)

Memutar Pinggan (5-29)

Spinning Tops (5-30)

5-28. Kaipsak (Spinning Tops)

Country: Inuit Native Americans, United States (North America)

Type of Game: Race

Formation: Players sit in a single circle. A top (or plastic plate) is in the center of the circle.

Equipment: 1 top or plastic plate

Objective: The player tries to spin the top or plate and run around the circle before the top or plate stops spinning.

Inuit children would spin a top, run around the outside of the icehouse, and try to get back before the top stopped spinning. A block of ice would be used during winter months, whereby other players would sit on top of the ice as it was spun around.

Directions: One player from the circle is chosen to be first to spin a top or plate in the center of the circle. Once the plate or top is spinning, the player runs around the outside of the circle and tries to return to her/his spot before the top or plate stops. If the first player is successful, she/he chooses the next spinner. If unsuccessful, the next player in the circle goes.

Variation: Have the circle players spread out so the plate spinner can weave in and out of the circle as she/he runs around before ending at her/his home spot.

Also See: *Memutar Pinggan* (5-29)

Spinning the Plate (5-27)

Spinning Tops (5-30)

5-29. Memutar Pinggan
(Plate Spinning)

Country: Malaysia (Asia)

Type of Game: Race

Formation: Players sit or stand in a single circle. A plastic plate or Frisbee™ is in the center of the circle.

Equipment: 1 plastic plate or Frisbee™

Objective: The player tries to reach a spinning plate or Frisbee™ before it stops.

At 127,316 square miles, Malaysia is slightly larger than New Mexico. Malaysia is on the southern tip of the Malay Peninsula and the eastern shore of the island of Borneo.

Directions: One player is chosen to be first to spin the plate or Frisbee™ in the center of the circle. Once the plate or Frisbee™ is spinning, the spinner calls out the name of a circle player. The called player must try to catch the plate or Frisbee™ before it stops spinning and falls off its spinning edge. If successful, the circle player becomes the new spinner. If not successful, the first player spins again and calls a new circle player.

Players who are unsuccessful in catching the plate or Frisbee™ before it falls score a point. The player with the most points at the end of the game must perform a stunt or some sort of trick.

Variations:

• The called player tries to catch the spinning plate with only one hand.

• The called player tries to respin the plate as the plate continues to spin.

Also See: *Kaipsak (5-28)*

          Spinning the Plate (5-27)

          Spinning Tops (5-30)

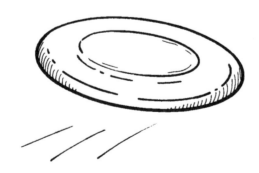

5-30. Spinning Tops

Country: United States (North America)

Type of Game: Race

Formation: Players sit in a single circle.

Equipment: 1 top

Objective: The player tries to run around the circle and catch the top before it stops.

Rhode Island is the smallest state with only 1,212 square miles within its borders. Alaska is the largest in area with 591,000 square miles.

Directions: A player enters the circle and spins the top in the center. While the top is spinning, the player exits the circle, runs around the outside of the circle, and reenters the circle through her/his vacant spot to try to catch the top before it stops or falls.

Also See: *Kaipsak (5-28)*

   Memutar Pinggan (5-29)

   Spinning the Plate (5-27)

5-31. Kiwa Trail (Twisted Trail)

Country: Northwest Coast/Woodlands Native Americans, United States (North America)

Type of Game: Race

Formation: Start and finish lines are drawn 40 feet apart. Each team of runners has a marker (cone) placed 10 feet from the starting line, and a second marker placed 10 feet from the finish line. Four more markers are placed evenly between the first and last markers. Runners stand in single file behind the starting line in line with their markers. (See Illustration 1.)

Equipment: Start and finish lines; 6 markers for each team

Objective: The team tries to run the course as described and finish first.

Native American Indians would use trees as markers to run around. Many times the trees used would not be lined up straight, so the runners needed to watch their pathway so as not to run head first at full speed into a tree.

Directions: Younger runners should travel in only one direction, whereas older runners can run to the far line and return to the starting line. On the signal "Go!" the first runners on each team run to the first marker and circle it once before going to the second marker. Runners run around each marker once before proceeding to the next and then the finish line. The first team to finish wins.

Start Line   **Finish Line**

Illustration 1: *Kiwa Trail*

Variations:

- Runners run both directions and hand-tag the next runner to go.

- All runners run at the same time staying in line. Without passing other runners on one's own team, the team runs through the course to the finish line.

- Divide the teams evenly: half at the start line and the other half at the finish line. On "Go!" the first runner from the start line runs through the course and tags the first runner on her/his team at the finish line. This runner runs the course and hand-tags the next runner on her/his team at the start line. This continues until all runners have run.

- Use ten markers instead of six.

- Have all runners run twice around each marker before going to the next marker.

Also See: *Obstacle Run* (5-32)

5-32. Obstacle Run

Country: Northwest Coast/Woodlands Native Americans, United States (North America)

Type of Game: Race—Obstacle Course

Formation: Different obstacles are chosen to hinder the progress of the runners.

Equipment: Various manufactured or natural obstacles

Objective: The player tries to run through the course and finish ahead of the other runners.

Covering long distances to test the skill of the runner, natural obstacles were used to impede the runner's progress. Such obstacles were rivers, hills, ravines, large hollow logs, and underbrush.

Directions: To challenge the modern runner, large sheets fastened to the ground at each corner may represent a river to cross. Large sacks with bottoms cut out and one side fastened to the ground can be the log to crawl through. Wide planks fixed at an incline can represent hills to climb.

Each runner must complete the course as laid out, trying to beat the other runners.

Also See: *Kiwa Trail* (5-31)

5-33. Cross-Country Relay

Country: Northwest Coast/Plains/Woodlands Native Americans, United States (North America)

Type of Game: Relay Race—Obstacle Course

Formation: Relay teams stand behind the starting line.

Equipment: Ropes; lime; poles; cones; extra players not on any team; start line

Objective: The runner tries to run through the cross-country course as quickly as possible and return to the starting line for the next runner to go.

Native American Indians traveled by foot until the horse was brought to the U.S. from Europe. The cross-country relay was a challenge where runners would run through different obstacles to reach their destination.

Directions: Set up identical course challenges in front of each relay team. (See Illustration 1.) On the signal "Go!" the first runner from each team runs to the rocks (cones) and circles each rock before running to and leaping over a 4-foot stream (marked off with ropes). After leaping over the stream, the runner weaves through a set of four or five trees (cones). The trees are set in a scattered line and spread far enough apart so the runner can pass through. The runner passes each tree in turn to the outside of the trees. The runner proceeds to a 7-foot wide river (marked off with lime) and leaps over it without touching between the banks into the water. After the river is crossed, the runner must climb over one or two mountains (leapfrog over nonplayers' backs) and into another set of trees (cones). The runner must again weave through these trees to the last tree.

Once past the last tree, the runner runs straight back to the starting line to tag the next runner.

Runners who fail to perform an obstacle challenge correctly must do that obstacle a second time before continuing to the next.

Illustration 1: *Cross-Country Relay*

Variation: Once past the last tree at the end of the course, the runner reruns the course back to the starting line to tag the next runner.

5-34. Ball Relay

Country: Northwest Coast/Plains/Woodlands Native Americans, United States (North America)

Type of Game: Relay Race—Manipulative

Formation: Teams stand single file behind a starting line. Players for each team stand 15–20 feet apart. A finish line is drawn 10 feet in front of the first runner.

Equipment: 1 soccer ball for each team; start and finish lines

Objective: The player tries to foot-dribble the ball to the next player in line without the ball going beyond the next player.

Native Americans made a lightweight ball from an animal's bladder that was stuffed with dried grass. A mesh net was woven closely around the bladder to protect the ball from rough ground and rough play.

Directions: The last player in each line has the ball. On the signal "Go!" the ball is foot-dribbled up to the next player in line. The next player cannot go until being hit with the ball in the legs. If the ball is kicked to the next player but misses her/his legs, the dribbler must retrieve the ball and bring it back to the player and try again.

When the ball gets to the front player on the team, that player dribbles the ball to a finish line and places her/his foot on top of the ball on or past the line to be finished.

Variation: A line is drawn 10 feet behind the last player in line. The race is performed as above, but continues with the front player dribbling the ball back after reaching the finish line and passing the ball back down the line in reverse order. This race is finished when the last person in line (first to dribble) has the ball and has dribbled it to and stopped it on or past the finish line behind her/his starting place. (See Illustration 1.)

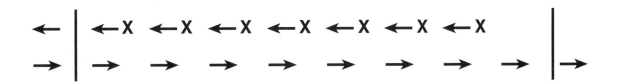

Illustration 1: *Ball Relay*

Also See: *Stick Relay* (5-35)
    Double Relay (5-36)
    Lance Head (5-37)

5-35. Stick Relay

Country: Northwest Coast/Plains/Woodlands Native Americans, United States (North America)

Type of Game: Relay Race—Manipulative

Formation: Players for each team stand 15–20 feet apart, with the front player standing 15–20 feet from a turning line.

Equipment: 1 stick and 1 small ball for each team; start and finish lines (Beginning players can use hockey sticks; advanced players can use a stick with a knob at the end for added difficulty.)

Objective: The player tries to relay the ball and stick to the front player who then dribbles the ball with the stick to the finish line.

Native American Indians would use a stick to control a ball while moving.

Directions: The last player in each relay line begins with the stick and ball. On the signal "Go!" this player uses the stick to dribble the ball to the next person on the team. The ball must hit the next player in the team before the stick is passed to that player. The ball and stick are passed from player to player until they reach the front player, who dribbles the ball to the finish line. The first team to finish wins.

Adaptation: A second line is drawn for advanced players 15–20 feet behind the last player. Once the front player dribbles the ball with the stick to the finish line in front of the relay line, the ball is dribbled back with the stick from player to player until returned to the player who started the ball. When this player receives the ball and stick, she/he dribbles the ball to the finish line behind the relay line. (See Illustration 1.)

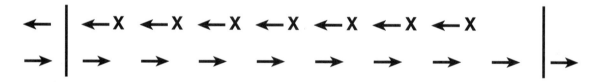

Illustration 1: *Stick Relay*

Also See: *Ball Relay* (5-34)

Double Relay (5-36)

Lance Head (5-37)

5-36. Double Relay

Country: Northwest Coast/Plains/Woodlands Native Americans, United States (North America)

Type of Game: Relay Race—Manipulative

Formation: Each team is in single file, with players spread 10–15 feet apart. A turning line is marked 10–15 feet in front of the front player and one marked 10–15 feet behind the last player. A stick is placed behind each front turning line.

Equipment: 1 stick and 1 ball for each team; turn lines (Use hockey sticks; see *Stick Relay* activity.)

Objective: The player tries to dribble the ball with the feet and with the stick.

A combination of Ball Relay *and* Stick Relay, *this activity is used to develop foot–hand coordination.*

Directions: The last player in line has the ball and foot-dribbles to the next player. The ball is passed so it hits the legs of the next runner to signal the change of possession. (If passed but misses the next player, the dribbler must retrieve the ball and quickly make a better pass.)

Once the front player has possession of the ball, she/he foot-dribbles the ball to the front turning line and picks up the stick. The stick is used to help dribble the ball back down the relay line, handing it off to the next player in line. When the last player (who started the relay) has the stick and ball, she/he dribbles the ball with the stick to the finish line. (See Illustration 1.)

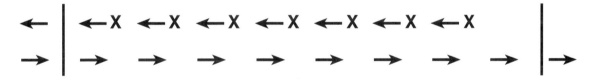

Illustration 1: *Double Relay*

Also See:　　*Ball Relay* (5-34)

　　　　　　　Stick Relay (5-35)

　　　　　　　Lance Head (5-37)

5-37. Lance Head

Country: Plains Native Americans, United States (North America)

Type of Game: Relay Race

Formation: Relay teams spread out with runners 15–20 yards apart. The back runners are apart from the other lines. The front runners converge towards the leader to form a lance head formation. (See Illustration 1.)

Equipment: 1 feather per team

Objective: The team tries to pass the feather from runner to runner to the leader.

The formation resembles a lance or arrowhead. The leader is the point of the lance. The relay lines extend away from the leader to form the wide end of a lance or arrowhead.

Illustration 1: *Lance Head*

Directions: Runners are in line from the leader to the last runner. Each line fans out from each other so that the ends are an equal distance from each other. Runners in the lines stand 15–20 yards from each other. Runners at the end of each line (the farthest away from the leader) stand and hold feathers. On the signal "Go!" these runners go to the next person in line and pass the feathers on. This continues until each runner in line has carried the feather closer to the leader. The feather that reaches the leader first wins.

Also See: *Ball Relay* (5-34)
        Stick Relay (5-35)
        Double Relay (5-36)

5-38. Corkscrew

Country: Great Britain (Europe)

Type of Game: Relay Race

Formation: Teams of 6–10 runners each are lined up in single file spaced 5–7 feet apart. A marker (cone) is placed 15–20 feet in front of each front player.

Equipment: 1 marker (cone) for each team; start line

Objective: The team tries to be the first to complete the race.

Once the largest empire in the world, the British colonies were so vast that it was said the "Sun never set on the British Empire."

Directions: The runner farthest from the turn marker is the first runner. On the leader's signal "Go!" the first runner runs in a straight line past the runners standing in front of her/him. As the runner passes the runner directly in front, that runner follows her/him running towards the turning point. As runner number 2 passes runner 3, runner 3 leaves the line and follows runner 2. This continues until all runners are following the first runner, all staying in the correct order. (See Illustration 1.)

The lead runner runs around the turn marker and heads back to the starting line. Once runners return to where they started, they stand still in line. The first team to get all runners back and in the correct place in line wins.

Variations:

- As the runners return, the lead runner stops where the front player stood at the front of the line. The second runner lines up behind her/him and so on. Thus, positions in line end up reversed from that at the beginning of the relay.

- As the runners at the end of the line run up past the runners in front, they weave through the line until they get past the first player. When returning, the front runner takes the first spot in line and the rest file in line behind, weaving through the line as enough runners return. (See Illustration 2.)

Illustration 1: *Corkscrew*

Illustration 2: *Corkscrew*

5-39. Ball Toss Race

Country: Plains/Southwest Native Americans, United States (North America)

Type of Game: Race

Formation: Players stand at the starting line. The course may be straight, an oval pathway, or cross-country.

Equipment: Skin-covered balls measuring 2-1/2 inches in diameter; 3-pronged tossing sticks 26-1/2 inches long; start and finish lines

Objective: The player tries to use the stick to propel the ball forward to a finish line.

Traditionally played by Native American Indian women, the distance for this race varied from 500 yards up to several miles.

Directions: Players use the throwing stick to throw the ball forward towards the finish line. Care must be taken to make sure the ball and the stick do not hit anyone. The first player to cross the line without touching the ball with a foot or hand is declared the winner.

Also See: *Stick vs. Foot* (5-43)

Toss a Ring Race (5-44)

5-40. Indian Kickball

Country: Hopi Native Americans/Tarahumara Indians, United States/Mexico (North America)

Type of Game: Race

Formation: Each team has 3 runners. Racers stand behind a starting line with a ball near their feet. The finish line is marked so the course covers a distance equal to the runners' abilities.

Equipment: Start and finish lines; 1 ball for each team (the ball should be a kind that cannot be kicked long distances). (For beginning/less experienced players, use a regulation softball; for more experienced players, use a regulation baseball or something smaller.)

Objective: Each team member tries to help keep the ball moving forward toward the finish line while kicking the ball only once before another team member kicks it forward.

The Hopi Indians would use a round stone while the Tarahumara Indians used a ball carved from the root of a tree. For over a thousand years both Indian groups would participate in this activity in celebrations and rituals. Sometimes the run would be between different villages and would be 20–30 miles long!

Directions: Each team stands behind the starting line with a ball near the feet of the first kicker. On the signal "Go!" the ball is kicked forward in such a way that one of the other two players on the team can run to it and kick it before it stops rolling. Without any set order of kicking the ball, the players take turns kicking the ball through the course to the finish line. The running course can range from a flat course without any obstacles in the way to a cross-country course where players have to run up and down hills, around trees, and other obstacles found in the way. Each kicker kicks the ball only one time before another player must kick it.

Also See: *Kickball Races (5-41)*

Kick Stick Races (5-42)

5-41. Kickball Races

Country: Southwest Native Americans, United States (North America)

Type of Game: Race

Formation: Players stand behind a starting line.

Equipment: 1 ball for each racer; start and finish lines

Objective: The player tries to kick the ball along a course to the finish line.

Hopi Indians used kickballs 4-1/2 inches in diameter, Mojave Indians used kickballs 2-1/4 inches in diameter, and Yuma Indians used kickballs 3-1/4 inches in diameter. The kickballs were made of various materials including tree roots, bush, fiber, woven weeds, bone, wood, and stone. The item would be wrapped and held together using natural adhesive gums and hides. Hairs from fast horses and cottontail rabbits—and even toe hairs from the fastest kickball racers—were placed inside the ball to help "keep the ball fast." Some races would be from 20–40 miles long!

Directions: Starting behind a starting line, racers begin kicking a ball through a course to a finish line. The course for beginners should be flat and free of obstacles. As players' skills improve, obstacles may be placed for the runners to pass around (cones) or through (boxes opened at both ends); players can also run up and down hills. Teams of up to four runners for each ball may be used to work together to pass the ball forward to a teammate who is closer to the finish line.

Also See: *Indian Kickball* (5-40)

Kick Stick Races (5-42)

5-42. Kick Stick Races

Country: Zuni/Southwest Native Americans, United States (North America)

Type of Game: Race

Formation: Players standing behind a starting line.

Equipment: Sticks 5 inches long, 3/4 to 1-1/2 inches thick; start and finish lines

Objective: The player tries to kick the stick through a running course to the end.

Each racer would identify her/his stick with special painted designs or burnings, which were believed to help the runner along.

Directions: As in *Kickball Races,* the runners kick the stick through a running course as quickly as possible to the finish. No hands must touch the stick at any time. Native Americans would choose a course traveling through woods and along stream beds. For beginning players, select an open course such as a playground free from objects in which the stick could get trapped. As students' ability improves, create an obstacle course using cones to direct the path to run.

Safety: Be sure no one is hit with a kicked stick.

Also See: *Indian Kickball* (5-40)

     Kickball Races (5-41)

5-43. Stick vs. Foot

Country: Apache/Southwest Native Americans, United States (North America)

Type of Game: Race

Formation: Players stand behind the starting line.

Equipment: 2 small balls attached with string for each girl; 4-foot long throwing stick for each girl; 1 kickball for each boy; start and finish lines

Objective: The girls try to use the stick to throw the balls forward, while the boys try to kick the balls forward through the course.

Apache women would throw the double ball with a throwing stick while men of the tribe would kick a ball as they raced together. These races would range from 1 to 5 miles in length.

Directions: While running along the course (playground or obstacle course), the girls use the stick to throw the balls forward. They place the end of the stick behind the string holding the balls together. The end of the stick flies forward, throwing the balls ahead. Boys kick a ball over the same course. Beginning at the start line, the competitors race to see who is the first to complete the course.

Safety: Be sure no one is hit with a kicked ball or thrown double ball.

Also See: *Ball Toss Race* (5-39)

  Toss a Ring Race (5-44)

5-44. Toss a Ring Race

Country: Southwest Native Americans/Northern Mexican Indians, United States/Mexico (North America)

Type of Game: Race

Formation: Players stand behind a starting line.

Equipment: Rings 3–5 inches in diameter; sticks about 29 inches long; start and finish lines

Objective: Player tries to throw or flick the ring using the stick along a course to the finish line.

Native Indian women of the Southwest United States and Mexico were the ones to perform this race, which could range in distance from 500 yards to a mile or more! Hands were never allowed to touch the woven ring during the race.

Directions: From the starting line, racers use a stick to flick, throw, and move a ring through a course to the finish line. The ring is not allowed to be carried at any time. The first racer to finish wins. The course for beginning players is flat without any obstacles to hinder their progress. When players' skills improve, obstacles like cones and boxes are placed on the course. Natural obstacles like trees and bushes may be used as well.

Also See: *Ball Toss Race* (5-39)
    Stick vs. Foot (5-43)

5-45. Three-Legged Race

Country: (Europe)

Type of Game: Race

Formation: Partners stand side by side and place their near legs into a sack, which becomes a third leg.

Equipment: 1 sack big enough for each pair of runners to put one leg each into and strong enough to not come apart or rip; start and finish lines; (optional) obstacles

Objective: The partners try to work together to race to the finish line.

This is a favorite activity for all ages at field days, picnics, and family get-togethers.

Directions: Using sacks as a means to connect two runners, the runners must work in unison to run through a course. The course may be a straight run or an obstacle course to challenge the runners' abilities to move together.

In the event of a large number of participants, each set of partners may be timed as to how long they took to complete the run. The lowest time wins.

5-46. Blindfolded Horse Relay

Country: Nigeria (Africa)

Type of Game: Relay Race—Communication

Formation: Teams start behind a starting line. Identical courses are set for each team.

Equipment: 1 blindfold for each team; 2–3 cones for each running course; start and turn lines; cones

Objective: The Rider tries to direct the horse through the course.

The Horse needs to rely on the Rider to guide her/him through the course safely.

Directions: Teams are set up into partners. One partner is the Horse, the other is the Rider. The Horse is blindfolded so she/he cannot see. (Decide ahead of time if the Riders are to ride piggyback on the Horse or walk behind. All relay pairs need to do the same. Walking Riders place their hands on the shoulders of their Horse.)

On the signal "Go!" the first set of Horse and Rider starts through the running course of cones. The Rider uses nonverbal clues to direct the Horse through the course. Once at the turning point (a line beyond the last cone or the last cone itself), the Horse and Rider go straight back to the start/finish line.

Variation: This activity can be performed as a race for each Horse and Rider or a relay race for each team.

Also See: *War Canoes* (5-48)

5-47. Asol-Tale Aap
(Canoe Race on Sand)

Country: India (Asia)

Type of Game: Race

Formation: Players sit on one scooter and prop one leg on a second scooter behind the starting line.

Equipment: 2 scooters per player; start and finish lines

Objective: The player tries to use both hands and one foot to maneuver to the finish line.

Traditionally performed in sand, the players sit on a canoe made from the stem of a coconut tree. Using a paddle and one foot, players race their way to a finish line.

Directions: On the signal "Go!" racers use one foot and both hands to propel their "canoes" towards the finish line. The first player to cross the finish line wins. Racers need to be careful not to interfere with other racers; this would result in disqualification from the race.

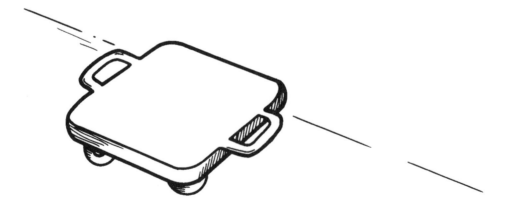

5-48. War Canoes

Country: Nigeria (Africa)

Type of Game: Race—Communication

Formation: Two teams of 4–8 players each stand behind a starting line, straddling a long pole. Only one player per team is allowed to face forward. A finish line is marked 15–20 feet away. Objects are placed in the "river" to represent natural river obstacles—rocks, trees, and—in these parts of Africa—crocodiles!

Equipment: Start and finish lines; long poles; various objects (cones, boxes, etc.) to represent river hazards; rope or markers to show the river banks

Objective: The lone player facing forward tries to guide the canoe safely through the river to the finish line.

Nigerian children pretend the teams are rowing war canoes down river, avoiding rocks, crocodiles, and the riverbank.

Directions: On the signal "Go!" the two teams are guided down river by their one guide player facing forward. The other players must not look behind them to see the locations of the river hazards.

Teams that hit an obstacle are eliminated from the race (or pay a time-taking penalty before continuing). The winning canoe is the team that reaches the finish line first without hitting obstacles.

POSSIBLE PENALTIES:

- Add three seconds to a team's time for each obstacle touched.

- Have different time values for each river obstacle: 3 seconds for each rock touched, 4 seconds for touching a riverbank, 5 seconds for touching a crocodile.

- Have the canoe turn around one complete time before continuing.

   The number of teams playing can determine how the races are run:

- For a short amount of time for a large number of teams, have winning teams race for the overall winner.

- For a low number of teams and more time, have each team race each other. The team with the most wins is the winning team.

   The number of players per team can control the number of teams. Teams should have between 4 and 8 players each.

Safety: Make sure the pole length allows for safe movement for the size of the players.

Also See: *Blindfolded Horse Race (5-46)*

5-49. Australian Bottle Game

Country: Australia

Type of Game: Relay Race

Formation: Teams stand single file behind a starting line. (Distance between starting line and water buckets is 20–30 feet.)

Equipment: 1 plastic bottle, 1 bucket of water, and 1 cup for each team; start line

Objective: Each team tries to fill its bottle with water as quickly as possible.

Half of the world's diamonds are mined in Australia.

Directions: On the signal "Go!" the first runner of each team runs to the bucket of water carrying the team's bottle. The runner scoops up one cup of water and pours it into the bottle before carrying it back to her/his line. The first runner hands the bottle to the second runner to take her/his turn. The relay continues until a "Stop!" signal is given or all runners have gone a predetermined number of turns. The team with the most water in its bottle wins.

5-50. Nut Relay

Country: Europe

Type of Game: Relay Race

Formation: Each team forms a single file behind a starting line.

Equipment: Spoons; nuts; start and turn lines

Objective: The player tries to carry the nut in the bowl of the spoon without dropping it.

Try this with two spoons and two nuts—one in each hand.

Directions: The first runner on each team has a spoon and a nut. The nut is placed in the bowl of the spoon and the spoon is held only by the tip of the handle. On the signal "Go!" the first runner of each team carries the nut on the spoon while walking as quickly as possible around a turning point and back to her/his next player in line.

At no time during the race is the runner to touch the nut with any part of her/his body to prevent it from falling. In the event the nut does fall from the spoon, the nut is scooped up with the opposite hand and held in that hand to the starting line where it is replaced in the spoon for the next runner or the race is finished.

5-51. Bottle Relay

Country: Uganda (Africa)

Type of Game: Relay Race

Formation: Teams stand single file behind the starting line. The turning line is 15–20 feet away.

Equipment: Plastic cup for each team; start and turn lines

Objective: The player tries to run to the turning point and back while balancing the cup on the head—no hands allowed.

Uganda was once under British rule (1894–1962). Traditional tribal kingdoms were abolished in 1967, strengthening the central government.

Directions: The first runner for each team balances the cup on top of her/his head. On the signal "Go!" the racers go to the turning line and back without using their hands to keep the cup from falling. When each runner returns to her/his team, the cup is handed to the next runner for her/his turn.

If the cup falls off and lands on the floor, it is replaced on the head and the runner continues. But if the cup is caught before hitting the floor, or a hand touches it while on the head, the runner must return to the previous line crossed and replace the cup on the head before continuing the race.

The first team to finish wins.

5-52. Feather Racing

Country: United States (North America)

Type of Game: Race/Relay Race

Formation: Players stand behind a starting line with a paper plate in hand and feathers on the ground.

Equipment: Paper plates; feathers; start and finish lines

Objective: The player tries to carry the feathers on the plate through the course to the finish line.

This race is believed to have begun in the midwestern United States where feathers were plentiful on farms.

Directions: Either as individuals or the first runner of a relay team, the first racers stand behind the starting line. On the signal "Go!" the racers pick up a feather, place it on the plate, and carry it through the course to the finish line. At no time may a player touch the feather to keep it on the plate.

In the event the feather does come off the plate while enroute to the finish line, the player may pick up the feather, carry it back to the starting line, and begin again.

5-53. Plate, Potato, Broom Relay

Country: Germany (Europe)

Type of Game: Relay Race

Formation: Players stand single file behind a starting line. A turning line is marked 20–25 feet from the starting line. The plate, potato, and whisk broom are with the first runner.

Equipment: Start and turn lines; 1 plastic plate, 1 potato, and 1 small whisk broom per team

Objective: Each runner tries to carry the plate, potato, and whisk broom to the turning line and back without dropping any item.

Following World War II, Berlin—the capital of Germany—was divided by the Berlin Wall into East and West Berlin. East Berlin became a Soviet sector; West Berlin was influenced by western governments.

Directions: On the signal "Go!" the first runner from each team places the potato between her/his knees, balances the plate on her/his head, and places the string of the whisk broom over one finger. The player must shuffle to the turning point without dropping the potato or plate and while twirling the whisk broom around her/his finger. If any object is dropped, it is replaced and the runner continues. The first team to have all its members complete the course wins.

Adaptation: Younger runners may have the turning line closer to the starting line.

Variation: The plate, potato, and whisk broom start at the turning line. On the signal "Go!" the first runner runs to them, puts them in place, and brings them back to the second runner. This runner takes them back to the turning line, leaves them there, and runs back to hand-tag the third runner. This continues until all runners have had a turn.

5-54. Balon en el Aire
(Ball in the Air)

Country: Argentina (South America)

Type of Game: Relay Race

Formation: Divide into two teams. Team A stands in single file with the first runner behind a starting line. Team B forms a single circle facing the left. Four cones are set up to form a square outside the circle that Team B forms. The ball is placed in the center of the circle.

Equipment: Ball (basketball, volleyball, soccer, or playground); 4 cones; start line

Objective: The passing team tries to make as many passes as possible while the running team runs around the circle of players.

The whole western border of Argentina is found in the Andes Mountains. The highest peak outside Central Asia is found within these mountains—Aconcagua at 22,834 feet in elevation. Other noteworthy peaks are Ojos del Salado at 22,615 feet; Cerro Tupungato at 22,310 feet; and Mercedario at 22,211 feet.

Directions: One player for Team B is designated as its first player. A ball is placed in the center of the circle. On the signal "Go!" the first runner for Team A runs around the four cones surrounding Team B. When returning to the line, the lead runner tags the hand of the second runner for that runner to begin. As Team A is running around the cone, Team B is passing the ball around the circle. On the same signal "Go!" the first player for Team B runs into the circle to get the ball and returns to her/his place in the circle. Once back in place, the ball is passed with two hands overhead to the next player in the circle. Make sure the passes are performed with two hands and all players handle the ball. Team B leader counts the number of passes made.

As the last runner for Team A returns to the start/finish line, Team A yells "parar!" (stop!). The number of passes made is recorded and the two teams exchange places. The activity is repeated so Team A has a score for the number of passes made. When all runners for Team B have run, the two scores are compared and the higher number of passes wins.

Make sure both teams have the same number of runners. If one team has an extra runner, the other team has its first runner run twice (first and last) to make the number of runners equal.

Variations for Passing Team:

- Players face left around the circle and pass the ball between the legs to the next player.
- Players face left around the circle and pass the ball sideways with two hands. Players need to twist to reach around to pass.
- Players face center and pass the ball sideways.
- Players face out and pass the ball sideways.

- Circle players count off. Odd-number players face center; even-number players face out. They pass the ball sideways so the ball is weaving in and out around the circle.

- Facing left, the first player passes the ball with two hands overhead. The second player passes the ball with two hands between the legs. They keep alternating around the circle.

- Facing left, the first player passes the ball sideways to the left (outside the circle). The second player passes sideways to the right (inside the circle). They alternate in and out of the circle so the ball is weaving in and out as it travels.

- Combine any of the above. Each time the ball comes back to the lead player of the passing team, a new form of passing is performed.

- Perform the above passes while facing to the right.

Make sure both teams perform the same type of pass in the same sequence. Count only the passes correctly made. Stress that incorrect passes cost points due to lost time and effort.

Also See: *Tadpole Relay (5-56)*

Thread the Needle (5-55)

5-55. Thread the Needle

Country: Great Britain (Europe)

Type of Game: Relay Race

Formation: Divide into two teams. Team One stands single file behind a starting line. Team Two forms two single files standing side by side, 8–10 feet apart facing towards the other line with players staggered.

Equipment: Start and finish lines for Team One; ball

Objective: Team One tries to run around Team Two in relay-race fashion (one runner at a time) while Team Two tries to pass the ball back and forth from one end to the other.

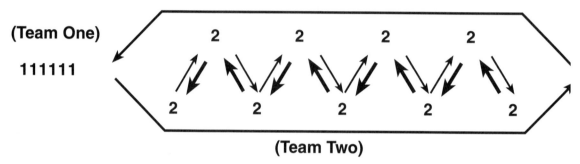

Illustration 1: *Thread the Needle* (Team One begins at the end of Team Two.)

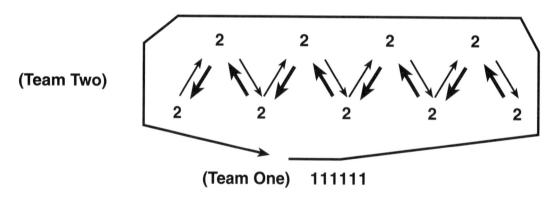

Illustration 2: *Thread the Needle* (Team One begins at the side of Team Two.)

Directions: On the signal "Go!" the first runner for Team One runs around Team Two and tags the hand of the second runner to run. Beginning at the left end of one line, Team Two passes the ball back and forth between the lines to the right end until all have touched the ball. Once the last player has received the ball at the right end, the path of the ball is reversed, being passed between the lines to where the ball began.

Team Two keeps passing the ball up and down the line until all the runners from Team One have completed the relay run around Team Two. Team Two counts the number of passes made during this time.

The two teams change places and Team One passes the ball as Team Two relay-races around. Team One tries to perform more passes as Team Two tries to run faster than Team One around the line.

If one team has more runners than the other team, the running team with fewer runners will need to have some runners run a second time.

Variation: Have the passing team perform different passes from one line to the other. For example, the first line may make a basketball chest pass and the second line may make a bounce pass in return.

When Team One runners pass the farthest end of Team Two, individual runners may pass the ball and the next team member use the same passing style as Team Two. When the next runner receives the passed ball, she/he begins her/his turn around Team Two.

Also See: *Balon en el Aire* (5-54)

Tadpole Relay (5-56)

5-56. Tadpole Relay

Country: United States (North America)

Type of Game: Relay Race

Formation: Divide into two teams. Team One stands single file behind a starting line. Team Two forms a single circle with one player standing in the center with a ball.

Equipment: Start and finish lines; ball

Objective: The running team tries to perform a relay race around the circle made by Team Two, while Team Two tries to pass the ball from the center player to each circle player in turn.

The center player inside the circle needs to be a good passer and catcher. Quickness is necessary for Team Two to get as many passes as possible while Team One is running.

Directions: On the signal "Go!" the first runner for Team One runs around the circle formed by Team Two. Meanwhile Team Two passes the ball from the center player to a circle player and back to the center player, going around the circle and counting the number of passes caught by the center player.

When the last runner completes the run and hand-tags the first runner (who does not run a second time), "Stop!" is called out by the running team and the ball is stopped. The two teams change places to allow Team Two a chance to run the relay around Team One, who will be passing the ball for points. The team finishing with the higher number of passes is the winner.

Variations:

- Use different types of passes.
- Use different types of passable equipment (fleece balls, beanbags, footballs, etc.).
- Count only the number of catches made by the center player, or by all players.
- After the ball has been passed to all circle players, the center player passes the ball to the first player passed to and the two players exchange places.
- Have the runners dribble a basketball while running, handing the ball off to the next runner or passing the ball (the same type of pass as the circle players) when reaching a passing line marked on the ground.

Also See: *Balon en el Aire* (5-54)

Thread the Needle (5-55)

Section 6
Sports

Many of the sporting activities you see in this section are different from what many students play today. If you look at them closely, however, you will be able to see fundamental activities of modern sports. Use these old games as lead-up activities when developing the skills and basics of such games as baseball and soccer.

In this section you will find 44 games from 20 different countries and 6 continents/regions.

Asia

Khong Kangjei (Wrestling Hockey) (6-42)—India
Tskhenburti (Polo) (6-44)—Republic of Georgia

Australia

Bowls (6-7)—Australia
Continuous Cricket (6-18)—Australia
Crazy Golf (6-13)—Australia

Caribbean Islands

Bamboula (Center Pole) (6-43)—Caribbean Islands
Tossing the Ball (6-29)—Caribbean Islands

Central America (North America)

Chapete (6-30)—Central America (North America)
Pin (6-5)—Guatemala (North America)

Europe

Battledore and Shuttlecock (6-26)—Ancient Greece
Bocci (Lawn Bowls) (6-6)—Italy
Broom Croquet (6-39)—Germany
Continuous Rounders (6-21)—Great Britain
Danish Rounders (6-19)—Great Britain
Gaelic Football (6-38)—Ireland
Les Boules (6-9)—France
Quoits (6-12)—Great Britain
Saskatch Soccer (6-37)—Great Britain
Schlagball (6-16)—Germany
Skittles (6-2)—Germany/Netherlands
Stool Ball (6-17)—Great Britain

Far East (Asia)

Handball (6-23)—Korea
Jae Gi (6-31)—Korea
Kick Swing (6-32)—Vietnam

North America

Bas-Quoits (6-11)—Native Americans
Battledore and Shuttlecock (6-27)—Native Americans
Bowling (6-3)—Colonial America
Bowling the Maika Stone (6-8)—(Hawaii) United States
Football (6-34)—Colonial America
Goal Kickers (6-33)—United States
Home Plate Baseball (6-20)—United States
Hurling (6-36)—Colonial America
Shinny (6-41)—Canada
Shuttlecock (6-24)—Colonial America
Sidewalk Golf (6-14)—United States
Skittles (6-1)—United States
Snow Football (6-35)—(Alaska) United States
Stickball (6-22)—United States
Stool Ball (6-15)—Colonial America 296

South America

Bola (Ball) (6-4)—Peru
Chueca (Twisted) (6-40)—Chile
Le Harradura (Horseshoe Quoits) (6-10)—(Inca Indians/Spanish Conquistadors) Peru
Le Pelota (6-28)—Argentina
Peteca (6-25)—Brazil

6-1. Skittles

Country: Colonial America (North America)

Type of Game: Sports—Bowling

Formation: Nine skittles (bowling pins) are set up in a diamond shape with one in the center at the end of a lane. Players stand behind a rolling line and roll a wooden ball trying to knock down the skittles.

Equipment: Ball; 9 skittle pins; bowling lane with rolling line

Objective: The player tries to roll the ball to knock down the skittles.

Skittles *was known as* Nine-Pin Bowling, *a bowling activity brought to the colonies in America by the Dutch and English—and later outlawed! A tenth pin was later added and today's game of* Bowling *was born.*

Directions: *West County Skittles* is a game of skittles played today. Eight skittles are set up in a diamond shape with the ninth skittle set in the center. (See Illustration 1.) A rolling line is 24 feet from the head skittle. Each player has three attempts to knock down the skittles with the maximum score of 27 points for one turn.

If all skittles are knocked down on the first roll, the player receives 27 points ($3 \times 9 = 27$). If all skittles are knocked down in two rolls, the player receives 18 points ($2 \times 9 = 18$). If all skittles are knocked down in three rolls, 9 points are scored or the total of skittles knocked down after all three rolls. The skittles are set back up for the next roller.

Illustration 1: *Skittles*

6-2. Skittles

Country: Germany/Netherlands (Europe)

Type of Game: Sports—Bowling

Formation: Nine pins are set in a diamond formation. Players stand behind a rolling line 25–30 feet away.

Equipment: 9 pins; ball; bowling lane with rolling line

Objective: The player tries to roll the ball and knock down as many pins as possible on each turn.

Artifacts found in Egyptian tombs dating around 5000 B.C. have led historians to believe that the game of Skittles *was played with stone balls.*

Directions: The pins are set up in a traditional diamond shape with eight pins forming four sides and the ninth pin in the center. Different shapes may also be used for setting up the pins—circles, lines, triangles, etc.

Standing behind the rolling line, the player rolls the ball to knock down as many pins as possible. Each pin knocked down is worth one point. The player retrieves the ball and sets up the pins for the next roller.

6-3. Bowling

Country: Colonial America (North America)

Type of Game: Sports—Bowling

Formation: Players stand behind a rolling line. The first bowler rolls the Jack ball before rolling the larger team ball.

Equipment: Small Jack ball; 2 sets of 4 team balls marked to identify the two teams; bowling lane with a rolling line

Objective: The player tries to roll a team ball closer to the Jack than the other team.

King Henry VII of England outlawed this game to the lower classes, who were to practice their archery skills so they could defend their land.

Directions: The first player from Team One rolls the Jack ball. The player then rolls a larger team ball as near the Jack ball as possible. Team Two players take turns trying to roll a ball closer to the Jack ball than Team One's. Once Team Two has a ball closer, Team One players take turns trying to roll a ball closer than Team Two's. The object is to have one of a team's ball closer to the Jack ball after all balls have been rolled. This scores one point for the closer team. The team that scores 21 points first wins.

Variation: Two players can play, each player taking a color of ball to roll.

6-4. Bola (Ball)

Country: Peru (South America)

Type of Game: Sports—Bowling

Formation: Three pins are set in a triangle. The bowler stands with the ball behind a bowling line 25–30 feet away.

Equipment: 3 pins; 1 large ball to roll; bowling line; grassy area

Objective: The player tries to roll the ball and knock down the pins.

The Inca Empire flourished in the Andean highlands of Peru until it came under Spanish domination for nearly 300 years. Today the Incas (known as Amerindians) remain the largest ethnic group in Peru, comprising 45 percent of the population.

Directions: Standing behind the bowling line, the bowler rolls the ball to try to knock down the three pins. Each pin is worth a certain number when knocked down: the front head pin is worth 12 points, the back two are worth 6 points each. The bowlers get one roll each turn to knock down the pins. The first bowler to reach 100 points wins.

6-5. Pin

Country: Guatemala (Central America, North America)

Type of Game: Sports—Bowling

Formation: The player stands behind a rolling line 12–15 feet from a single target pin.

Equipment: Rolling line; 2 balls; 1 pin (milk carton or cone)

Objective: The player tries to bump the first ball to touch the pin without knocking it over.

The Mayan way of life brightens the country's villages. Native clothes are vivid in colors and are still woven in precolonial designs.

Directions: The bowler rolls the first ball toward the pin to have it stop before knocking it down. The bowler then attempts to bump the first ball closer toward the pin by rolling the second ball into it. The first player retrieves the second ball and gives it to the second bowler. The second bowler rolls the ball to try to bump the first ball to the pin. This continues until the first ball touches the pin without knocking it down.

Variations:

- If played by teams, each team tries to see how few rolls it takes to get the first ball to touch the pin without knocking it down.

- Setting the first ball on a given spot, individual bowlers or teams may try to see how many rolls it takes to get the first ball to touch the pin without knocking it down.

6-6. Bocci (Lawn Bowls)

Country: Italy (Europe)

Type of Game: Sports—Bowling

Formation: Players stand at one end of the playing area. Teams or partners stand together, but apart from opponents.

Equipment: Small white cue ball; 1 rolling ball for each player on each team (teams have different identifiable balls); rolling line; grassy playing area

Objective: Each team tries to roll the ball closer to the cue ball than the other team.

United under one flag since the 1870s, the loyalty of Italians is first to the family and the community, then the central government.

Directions: Team captains decide which team is to go first. The team bowling first is Team One. Team One chooses which player is to bowl first. The captain rolls the cue ball to the other end of the playing area for the target. The first bowler rolls her/his ball to have it stop as close to the cue ball as possible.

The captain of Team Two chooses a player (or her-/himself) to roll first for her/his team. If her/his ball fails to stop closer to the cue ball, a second player from Team Two is chosen to roll to try to get closer. Once Team Two has a ball stop closer to the cue ball than Team One, Team Two stops bowling.

The captain of Team One chooses a player to bowl to see if she/he can get closer to the cue ball than Team Two's closest ball. This changing continues every time the other team places a ball closer than the opponents.

When all players from both teams have bowled, the team gets one point for each ball closer to the cue ball than the other team's best ball. Thus, if each team has three players, the winning team can score 3 points if all three of that team's balls are closer than the opponent's best ball.

Only one team can score in each frame, and that team bowls first the next frame, first rolling out the cue ball. The first team to reach 21 points wins.

Adaptation: Advanced players on each team can try to bump their own team's ball closer to the cue ball—or even try to bump an opponent's ball away from the cue ball!

6-7. Bowls

Country: Australia

Type of Game: Sports—Bowling

Formation: Bowlers stand behind a rolling line holding the ball they will roll. A white Jack ball is rolled or placed some distance from the rolling line.

Equipment: White Jack ball; 1 ball for each bowler; bowling line; grassy playing area

Objective: The player tries to roll the ball closest to the Jack ball.

Australia is the world's smallest continent, but the sixth largest country. Located completely in the Southern Hemisphere, Australia is the flattest and driest continent.

Directions: Each bowler in turn rolls her/his ball towards the Jack ball. The ball closest to the Jack earns one point for its bowler. A ball hitting the Jack is worth 3 points. All balls are rolled before any are picked up. If a ball hits another player's ball and moves it to a better position, the owner of the moved ball earns the possible points earned.

After all the balls are bowled, the points are awarded to the closest ball and the next round begins in which the second bowler becomes the first and the first bowler becomes the last. The first player to reach 21 points wins.

6-8. Bowling the Maika Stone

Country: Hawaii, United States (North America)

Type of Game: Sports—Bowling

Formation: Two sticks are driven vertically in the ground 6–12 inches apart. The bowler stands behind a rolling line 20–25 feet away.

Equipment: 2 sticks for the goal; 1 Maika stone (round and flat); rolling line; playing area

Objective: The bowler tries to roll the stone on end so it rolls between the goal sticks.

A good player could roll a Maika stone through a goal from 100 yards away! Originally made from lava, the Maika stone was heavy and more difficult to bowl accurately than the stones used today.

Directions: Standing behind the line, the bowler attempts to roll her/his Maika stone so it passes through the goal (3 points) or stops closest to the goal (1 point if no other stone passes through the goal). The first player to reach 11 or 21 points wins.

Variations:

- This can be played in teams with members bowling in turn and accumulating points for the team.
- Vary the distance of the bowling line to the goal based on the skill and ability of the players.

6-9. Les Boules

Country: France (Europe)

Type of Game: Sports—Bowling

Formation: For two players—both stand at one end of the bowling area behind the line. For four players—two players (opponents) stand at each end of the bowling area behind the line.

Equipment: Jack ball; 3 balls per team (marked to distinguish between teams); grassy playing area 30 feet long

Objective: Each player (or team) tries to roll the balls closer to the Jack ball than the other player (or team).

Paris, France is the home of the 984-foot high Eiffel Tower. It was built for the International Exposition of 1889.

Directions for 2 Players: The first bowler stands behind a bowling line and rolls the Jack ball to the other end of the bowling area, 30 feet away. The first player then rolls one bowling ball at a time, trying to have the balls stop as close to the Jack as possible.

The second player now rolls her/his three bowling balls in an attempt to get closer to the Jack ball. The second player may try to knock the first player's balls away from the Jack ball in order to get closer.

The closest ball after all balls have been rolled scores 1 point. The first player to reach 11 points wins.

Directions for 4 Players: *Les Boules* is played as for two players. One player from each set of partners bowls from opposite ends of the bowling area.

BOWLING FIRST:

- The position of the first bowler alternates each time the Jack ball is rolled.

- The player/team scoring the last point becomes the first bowler the next time the Jack ball is rolled.

6-10. Le Harradura
(Horseshoe Quoits)

Country: Inca Indians/Spanish Conquistadors, Peru (South America)

Type of Game: Sports—Horseshoes

Formation: Two stakes are driven into the ground 40 feet apart. Players stand behind one stake while tossing a heavy ring or horseshoe at the other stake.

Equipment: 2 stakes; horseshoes or heavy rings for each player; playing area

Objective: The player tries to toss a heavy ring or horseshoe so it lands encircling the far stake.

Le Harradura (Horseshoe Quoits) *was played by the Inca Indians and Spaniards before spreading into the United States and Australia.*

Directions: The players, in turn, stand behind the near stake and toss a heavy ring/horseshoe towards the far stake. If the ring/horseshoe lands so the stake is inside, the player scores 3 points. If it lands touching the stake with the stake outside, 2 points are scored. If no ring/horseshoe is around or touching the stake, 1 point is awarded to the closest ring/horseshoe to the stake. The first player/team to reach 21 points wins.

Adaptation: Younger/weaker players may have a closer tossing line.

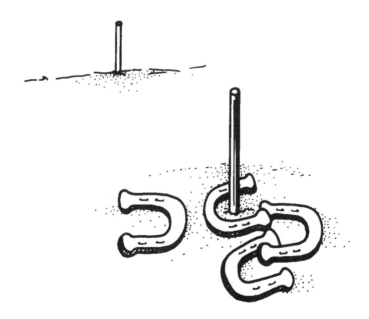

6-11. Bas-Quoits

Country: Native Americans, United States (North America)

Type of Game: Sports—Horseshoes

Formation: Two stakes are driven in the ground 20 feet apart with 12 inches of the stakes above the ground. Players stand behind one stake.

Equipment: 2 stakes; 4 rope rings (quoits) 4–5 inches in diameter (half of each ring is white, the other half is green); playing area

Objective: The player tries to toss the quoit to land with the stake inside.

Bas-Quoits *is based on the game of* Horseshoes, *and was well organized in the fifteenth century.*

Directions: The player stands behind one stake and tosses all four quoits, one at a time, at the far stake. The second player retrieves the quoits and takes her/his turn. When both players have tossed to one stake, both stand at the far stake and toss back to the first stake. Points can be scored for both players on each turn.

Points are awarded for each player's best toss as follows:

- Ringer (stake inside the quoit)—3 points
- Leaner (quoit leaning against the stake) with green side up—2 points
- Leaner with white side up—1 point
- All other tosses—0 points.

The first player to reach 11 points wins.

6-12. Quoits

Country: Great Britain (Europe)

Type of Game: Sports—Horseshoes

Formation: Stakes are driven into the ground 11 yards apart in the center of a 3' x 3' clay pit. A stake must be 6 inches above the surface of the ground. Players stand behind the stake at one end.

Equipment: 2 stakes; 2 quoits (5-1/2-inch rings weighing nearly 1 pound each) for each player; playing area

Objective: The player tries to toss the quoit so that it lands as close to the far stake as possible, if not around it.

Quoits were designated as illegal in 1388 by the Sporting Regulations act of that year.

Directions: The players stand behind one stake and take turns tossing her/his quoits at the other stake. Alternating turns, the players each toss two quoits. When all four quoits are tossed, players go to the far end to toss them back to the first stake.

The first player to toss is determined by a single toss by each player. The player with the closest toss to the far stake goes first. During a match, the player who scored the last point goes first.

When a quoit lands surrounding the stake (ringer), the player is awarded 2 points. If more than one quoit lands scoring a ringer, only the top quoit scores. If no ringers are tossed, the closest quoit scores one point. The first player to reach 21 points wins.

6-13. Crazy Golf

Country: Australia

Type of Game: Sports—Golf

Formation: The players begin behind a starting line and follow a cross-country course to a target.

Equipment: Tennis balls; stick; targets; challenges; playing area

Objective: The player tries to hit the ball with the stick through a challenging course to a target.

This is a different kind of golf game that is performed as a race among players.

Directions: On the signal "Go!" all players begin to hit their ball toward the target, moving along the agreed-upon route. Touching the ball with the foot or hand causes that player to start over at the beginning of the "hole" (challenge).

The first player whose ball touches the target wins the game.

Also See: *Sidewalk Golf* (6-14)

6-14. Sidewalk Golf

Country: United States (North America)

Type of Game: Sports—Golf

Formation: Players stand at a designated starting place and decide on the first target.

Equipment: Bottle caps; stone; obstacles found on a golf course; playing area

Objective: The player tries to "golf" from one challenging hole to the next.

Using their imagination, the players develop a golf course including sand traps, water hazards, and miniature trees.

Directions: Players stand at the first tee and in turn toss their stone towards the first hole. Stones landing in a hazard either completely or partially must be placed outside and a penalty stroke added.

After all players have completed the first hole, the second player designs the next hole and direction for all to follow. When the course is finished, the player with the lowest overall score wins.

Also See: *Crazy Golf* (6-13)

6-15. Stool Ball

Country: Colonial America (North America)

Type of Game: Sports—Baseball/Cricket

Formation: A milking stool or upside-down basket is placed 20–25 feet from a throwing line. One player stands near the stool as its defender. Other players stand at the throwing line or scattered in the playing area.

Equipment: Stool or basket; soft ball; throwing line; playing area

Objective: The defender tries to protect the stool from being hit with the pitched ball. The thrower tries to hit the stool with the ball. The fielders try to catch the batted ball on the fly.

An ancestor to the game of Cricket *in the sixteenth century,* Stool Ball *was as popular with the women then as* Cricket *is now with men.*

Directions: The thrower stands 20–25 feet from the stool and pitches the soft ball in an attempt to hit the stool. A lone defender stands near the stool to try to bat the ball away using only her/his hand.

The throwing player becomes the new defender when the defender misses the ball and/or the ball hits the stool. A fielding player who catches a batted ball on the fly becomes the new defender.

Also See: *Stool Ball* (6-17)

6-16. Schlagball

Country: Germany (Europe)

Type of Game: Sports—Baseball

Formation: One team lines up to bat. The second team spreads out in the playing area as in baseball. Home base and the single goal base are 30–40 feet apart.

Equipment: Home base; goal base; soft playground ball; playing area

Objective: The batter tries to hit the ball and run to the goal base before the fielding team hits the runner with the ball.

This game has no pitcher to throw the ball to the batter, and only one base to which the batter runs.

Directions: The batter stands at home base with the ball. Tossing the ball up to her-/himself, the batter strikes the ball with an open hand and runs to the goal base.
The fielding team retrieves the ball and throws the ball at the runner, trying to hit the runner with the ball (below shoulder level) before she/he reaches the goal base. If the ball hits the runner, the runner is out. If the runner reaches the goal base without being hit, the runner scores a point. Teams switch positions after each out.

Adaptations:

- Use a batting tee for younger players.
- Have the goal base closer for younger players.

Variation: Throw the ball to a fielding player standing at the goal base. If the ball gets there first and is caught, the runner is out. Don't throw at the runner.

6-17. Stool Ball

Country: Great Britain (Europe)

Type of Game: Sports—Baseball/Cricket

Formation: One team bats. The other team spreads out in the field.

Equipment: Milking stool or milk crate; bat; soft ball; playing area

Objective: The batter tries to protect the stool by batting the ball away.

This game was first played by milkmaids using their milking stools, which were called "crickets."

Directions: The batter stands close to the milking stool and tries to protect the stool by hitting the ball with the bat (or her/his hand). Taking turns pitching the ball, the fielders stand 20–25 feet from the batter when throwing the ball. The batter is out if a pitched ball hits the stool, or if a fielding player catches the ball on the fly. When all batters have batted, teams change places. The team with the higher score after everyone has batted wins.

Variation:

- If played as individuals, one batter is up and the other players are in the field. A batter stays to bat until the ball hits the stool on a pitch, or a fielding player catches the ball on the fly. When a pitched ball hits the stool, the pitcher becomes the new batter. When a fielder catches the ball on the fly, that player becomes the new batter.

- Place a second stool for a base the batter runs to after hitting the ball. The batter scores a run by running between the two bases, but is out if tagged by a fielder holding the ball if the batter is not touching one of the bases.

Also See: *Stool Ball* (6-15)

6-18. Continuous Cricket

Country: Australia

Type of Game: Sports—Baseball

Formation: The batting team stands outside the play area. The batter stands in front of the wicket. The fielding team spreads out in the playing area. One fielder stands 12–15 yards from the batting area at the "bowler's crease" (pitcher's mound).

Equipment: Wicket (1-1/2 feet high x 2-1/2 feet wide) made of wood or wire; bat; tennis ball; base; playing area

Objective: The batters try to hit the ball (protecting the wicket) and run to the base and back before the pitcher gets the ball and pitches. The pitcher tries to throw the ball to knock over the wicket whether the batter is ready or not.

The origin of the game of Cricket *dates back to medieval England of the 1100s and 1200s. Rules for today's game of* Cricket *were adopted in 1744 by the London Cricket Club's revision of the 1727 Articles of Agreement.*

Directions: The pitcher stands at the bowler's crease and tosses the ball underhand at the wicket. The ball may bounce, but doesn't have to. The batter tries to hit the ball into the fielding area. If the ball is hit, the batter drops the bat, runs to the base and back, and prepares to hit the ball again. If the batter returns before the pitcher gets the ball and makes another pitch, the batter scores one run for her/his team.

The fielders must quickly retrieve the ball and get it back to the pitcher to pitch again at the wicket before the batter returns from the base. If the ball is missed by the batter and also misses the wicket, the catcher throws the ball back to the pitcher for another pitch.

The batter remains at bat until a pitch knocks down the wicket, the ball goes through the wicket, or a batted fly ball is caught. As soon as the batter is out, the next batter quickly comes to bat before the pitcher pitches the ball at the wicket again.

When all players on the batting team are out, the teams change places. After both teams have batted, the team with more runs wins.

6-19. Danish Rounders

Country: Great Britain (Europe)

Type of Game: Sports—Baseball

Formation: The pitcher's mound (4-foot circle) is 10–15 yards from home plate (hula-hoop). Three (3-foot square) bases are placed like a baseball diamond with home plate. There are 15 yards between bases. (See Illustration 1.)

Equipment: Tennis ball; hula hoop; 3 bases; playing area

Objective: Players try to advance from base to base before the pitcher "downs" the ball.

Hula-Hoop/Home Plate   **Third Base**

Pitcher's Mound

First Base   **Second Base**

Illustration 1: *Danish Rounders*

Directions: The pitcher stands on the pitching mound and tosses the ball higher than the batter's head so it bounces inside the hula-hoop home plate. (The batter stands next to the hula hoop or home plate.) The batter must hit the ball with an open hand before the ball hits inside the hula hoop. The batter gets only one pitch to try to hit. Once the batter hits the ball (or if the ball is missed or the pitch is poor), the batter runs to first base.

The fielders retrieve the ball and quickly return it to the pitcher who touches it to the ground somewhere inside the pitching mound and calls "Down!" Any base runner not standing on a base is out at that point. If the ball is batted in the air and caught by a fielder before hitting the ground, the batter and any base runner between bases are out. Three outs end the batting team's turn at bat, and teams change positions.

Runners on base are not forced to run to the next base on a batted ball. Multiple runners can remain on any base and may run when they feel it is safe for them to get to the next base. Runners should also know that they cannot score until they reach home base.

A batting team is not out until it has three outs or no more batters. In the event that all batting players but one are on base, that batter bats until three outs are made or a base runner comes home. Base runners bat a second time according to the order they reach home (or are put out). This way batters do not necessarily bat after the same teammate the second time.

The team with the higher score after an equal number of turns batting wins.

Also See: *Home Plate Baseball (6-20)*

6-20. Home Plate Baseball

Country: United States (North America)

Type of Game: Sports—Baseball

Formation: Four bases are placed 15–20 feet apart to form a square (baseball diamond). Batting team stands in line near the home plate. Fielding team spreads out in the playing area. The pitcher stands at the pitcher's mound 15 feet in front of home plate. The catcher stands behind the batter, out of the way.

Equipment: 4 bases; tennis ball; pitcher's mound (circle); playing area

Objective: The batter tries to hit the ball with her/his open hand and get to a base before the pitcher receives the ball and touches the ball to the home plate.

Playing Home Plate Baseball *is similar to* Danish Rounders *with the exception of the pitcher touching the ball to home plate to get a batter/runner out.*

Directions: One batter stands at home plate as the pitcher softly tosses the ball underhand for the batter to hit. The pitcher tosses the ball until the batter successfully hits the ball. Once the ball is hit, the fielders retrieve the ball and throw it to the pitcher at home plate. The pitcher touches the ball to home plate calling "Down!" If done before the batter reaches first base, the batter is out; otherwise, the batter is safe. If a batter touches first base and is on her/his way to second when "Down!" is called, the batter returns to first base. Base runners between bases when "Down!" is called return to the last base touched.

The fielding team rotates before the ball is pitched to the next batter. The pitcher becomes the new catcher, the catcher goes to the field, and a new fielder becomes the new pitcher. Pitching order for the fielding team should be set up before beginning play to save time and make sure all fielding players are allowed a turn to pitch.

Teams change positions when the batting team has three outs. After both teams have had a predetermined number of times at bat, the game is over and the team with the higher score wins.

Also See: *Continuous Rounders* (6-21)

Danish Rounders (6-19)

6-21. Continuous Rounders

Country: Great Britain (Europe)

Type of Game: Sports—Baseball

Formation: The batting team is lined up at the batting area. The fielding team spreads out in the play area. Four bases form a square (baseball diamond). Bowler's area (pitcher's mound) is 10–15 yards in front of the batting area.

Equipment: Ball; four bases; pitcher's mound; playing area

Objective: The base players try to pass the batted ball to all four bases before the batter can run and touch all the bases.

This game allows the players to practice throwing, tossing, catching, retrieving, batting, and running bases.

Directions: The bowler (pitcher) tosses the ball underhand so it passes the batter between her/his knees and shoulders. The ball may or may not bounce. The batter hits the ball with her/his open palm into the playing area and runs to touch all four bases.

The fielding players quickly retrieve the ball and throw the ball to the nearest base. From this base, the ball is thrown to the other three bases and then back to the first base where it began. If the batter touches all four bases before the ball returns to the base where it began, the batter scores a run for her/his team. If the ball returns to where the ball started before the batter has touched all four bases, the batter is out. If the ball is batted in the air and a fielder catches it, the batter is out.

Teams switch places when the batting team players have all batted one time.

Also See: *Danish Rounders* (6-19)

Home Plate Baseball (6-20)

6-22. Stickball

Country: United States (North America)

Type of Game: Sports—Baseball

Formation: Set up two teams, as in baseball.

Equipment: Tennis ball; broom handle for bat; home plate; three bases; playing area

Objective: The batting team tries to score runs. The fielding team tries to get the runners out.

This form of baseball is played on the narrow streets of cities where there are no fields to play ball.

Directions: This game is played the same as baseball with the following exceptions:

- *Playing field:* Usually played on the narrow streets of local neighborhoods. The bases are not so wide due to the narrow streets.

- *Hitting:* Hitting the ball into unfriendly territories is not a homerun but an out. The batter needs to retrieve the ball.

- *Pitching:* The ball is thrown so it bounces once before it reaches the batter. There is a new pitcher for each batter.

- *Equipment:* No gloves are used by the fielders. The bat is a broom handle. The ball is a tennis ball or other same-sized rubber ball. Bases are landmarks, whatever is handy (fire hydrants, marks on the curb, cars, etc.).

- *Balls and strikes:* There are no walks in *Stickball*. The batter either hits the ball or strikes out.

- *Ghost runners:* Ghost runners are used for small teams. If all runners are on a base, a ghost runner takes the place of the runner closest to home base. That player comes up to bat. The ghost runner advances the same number of bases as the runner behind her/him. As base runners advance, ghost runners can score.

6-23. Handball

Country: Korea (Far East, Asia)

Type of Game: Sports—Tennis

Formation: Rectangular playing area (28' x 16') has a midcourt line. One team is on each half of the playing area.

Equipment: Rectangular playing area; small rubber ball

Objective: Each team tries to throw the ball from one team to the other.

Handball *is played with the idea of tennis, but the players/teams catch and throw the ball in place of hitting the ball with a racket.*

Directions: Players begin in two equal teams. A player on Team One throws the ball to Team Two at shoulder height so it can be caught. If the ball is caught before it bounces, it is thrown back. If the ball hits a player and bounces before being caught, the player is eliminated. The game continues until one team or the other is completely eliminated from the game. The ball must be thrown in a way that it can be caught or the thrower is eliminated.

Variation: When a player is eliminated, she/he goes to the other team.

6-24. Shuttlecock

Country: Colonial America (North America)

Type of Game: Sports—Badminton

Formation: Teams stand on opposite sides of a dividing line.

Equipment: Racket for each player; shuttlecock made by stuffing a rag into a ball and leaving a tail of cloth to flutter (or commercially produced shuttlecock); dividing line

Objective: Each team tries to hit the shuttlecock to the other team to get them to miss the shuttlecock.

Through the years, Battledore *and* Shuttlecock *have become competitive. In the 1850s the name* Badminton *came about from the Duke of Beaufort's residence—Badminton House—in Gloucestershire, England (now Avon).* Badminton *became a full medal sport at the 1992 Olympic games in Barcelona, Spain.*

Directions: Played with or without a dividing line, players hit the shuttlecock back and forth trying to get the opposing players to miss it. When one team cannot return the shuttlecock before it hits the ground, the other team scores a point.

Variation: This may also be played with only two players.

Also See: *Battledore and Shuttlecock* (6-26)

                  Battledore and Shuttlecock (6-27)

                  Le Pelota (6-28)

6-25. Peteca

Country: Brazil (South America)

Type of Game: Sports—Badminton

Formation: Players stand in a circle with one player holding the shuttlecock.

Equipment: Shuttlecock; playing area

Objective: The player tries to strike the shuttlecock with the hand to keep it in the air.

Brazilian children would make the peteca from a cone-shaped leather bag about the size of a tennis ball and fill it with sand. Long feathers would be inserted where the bag is tied.

Directions: The player holding the shuttlecock strikes it with one hand to another player in the circle. Taking turns striking the shuttlecock, the players count the number of times it is hit in the air before it hits the floor. Players may also call out letters of the alphabet as they strike the shuttlecock.

Variations:

- Players hit the shuttlecock around the circle clockwise, then counterclockwise.

- Have several circles perform the activity at the same time. The circle able to keep its shuttlecock up the longest (greatest number of hits) wins.

- Call the player's name to make the next hit. As a player hits the shuttlecock, she/he calls the name of another circle player to make the next hit. Players may not call out the name of the player who hit it to them.

- Players are scattered from a starting line to a finish line. The player at the starting line strikes the shuttlecock forwards to the next player down the line. The shuttlecock is passed from player to player until it crosses the finish line. If it is missed, falls to the ground, or is caught, play starts again at that point (or at the beginning, depending on the ability of the players).

Also See: *Shuttlecock (6-24)*

Battledore and Shuttlecock (6-26)

Battledore and Shuttlecock (6-27)

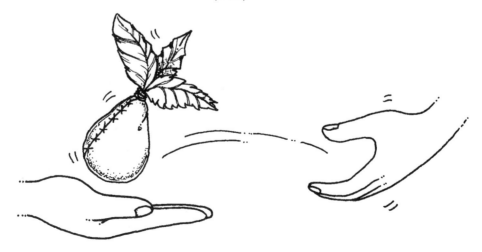

6-26. Battledore and Shuttlecock

Country: Ancient Greece (Europe)

Type of Game: Sports—Badminton

Formation: Two players face each other holding rackets.

Equipment: Rackets; shuttlecock; playing area

Objective: The players try to hit the shuttlecock back and forth as many times as possible without it hitting the ground.

Believed to have developed in Ancient Greece about 2,000 years ago, Battledore and Shuttlecock *spread to China, Japan, India, and Siam (now Thailand). Early shuttlecocks were made by sticking feathers into cork. It was a popular game in England with the peasant children in the sixteenth century and with the European classes in the seventeenth century. In 1830 the record number of hits without a miss was apparently 2,117 by the Somerset family in England.*

Directions: Partners stand 4–6 feet apart. They use their rackets to hit the shuttlecock back and forth as many times as possible, trying to keep it from hitting the ground.

Also See: *Shuttlecock (6-24)*

Peteca (6-25)

Battledore and Shuttlecock (6-27)

6-27. Battledore and Shuttlecock

Country: Native Americans, United States (North America)

Type of Game: Sports—Badminton

Formation: Players stand 4 feet apart in a circle. Each player holds a wooden paddle, one holds the shuttlecock.

Equipment: Wooden paddles; shuttlecock; playing circle

Objective: The players try to keep the shuttlecock in the air.

Native American Indians made the shuttlecock by attaching feathers to a small bag of seeds with a string of hide or gut.

Directions: The first player strikes the shuttlecock with an underhanded motion of the paddle. The shuttlecock is passed to the next player in the circle to the right or left (decide earlier). The shuttlecock must stay in the circle. Players may move into the circle to strike the shuttlecock, but never backwards out of the circle.

   If the shuttlecock is hit out of the circle, the player responsible leaves the circle.

Variation: As players leave the circle, they form a second circle. As players are eliminated from the first circle and added to the second, no player is eliminated from the second circle. Only when one player is left in the first circle do players begin being eliminated from the second; they return to the first circle and begin the process again.

Also See: *Shuttlecock (6-24)*

              Peteca (6-25)

              Battledore and Shuttlecock (6-26)

6-28. Le Pelota

Country: Argentina (South America)

Type of Game: Sports—Volleyball

Formation: A net separates the teams.

Equipment: Net; ball; playing area

Objective: Each team tries to hit the ball over the net to the other team.

Argentina was first settled in the 1500s by Spanish adventurers looking for precious metals. They soon realized that Argentina's true value was in agriculture and grazing.

Directions: The game begins with one team throwing the ball over the net to the other team. Once over the net, no one is allowed to hit the ball with the feet or fists. Any other part of the body can be used. Once the ball falls to the floor, the other team earns one point. Teams take turns serving the ball regardless of which team allowed the ball to fall to the floor. Players on each team take turns serving the ball.

Variation: Vary the height of the net. Play with the net high (as in volleyball or badminton) or low (as in tennis).

6-29. Tossing the Ball

Country: Caribbean Islands

Type of Game: Sports—Soccer (Juggling)

Formation: Players are scattered but standing close.

Equipment: Lightweight small ball; playing area

Objective: The player uses her/his feet to try to keep the ball in the air.

The Caribbean is a series of island countries stretching from Venezuela in South America to the southern tip of Florida in North America.

Directions: To begin, the ball is tossed in the air. That is the last time the ball is touched with the hands. Players use their feet (soles and heels) to keep the ball in the air by carefully kicking it up so other players can do the same.

Count the number of kicks on the ball before the ball falls to the floor or is touched by a player's hands. Try to beat that number.

Also See: *Chapete* (6-30)

   Jae Gi (6-31)

   Kick Swing (6-32)

6-30. Chapete

Country: (Central America) (North America)

Type of Game: Sports—Soccer (Juggling)

Formation: Players stand in small groups.

Equipment: 1 small ball or beanbag for each group

Objective: The players try to keep the ball in the air by using any part of the body below the waist.

Marketed in the United States under the name of Hacky Sack, *this activity has been played in Mexico and Central America for centuries.*

Directions: This is a game of kicking a small ball/beanbag into the air under control so another player can kick it into the air again.

Only parts of the body below the waist (knees, ankles, foot) are allowed to touch the ball. Count the number of kicks made on the ball before it hits the ground and then try to beat that score.

Adaptation: This can be played by individual players, too. Each player tries to keep the ball/beanbag under control for as long as possible.

Also See: *Tossing the Ball* (6-29)

Jae Gi (6-31)

Kick Swing (6-32)

6-31. Jae Gi

Country: Korea (Far East, Asia)

Type of Game: Sports—Soccer (Juggling)

Formation: Each player stands in a personal space to play by her-/himself.

Equipment: 1 soft spongy ball or beanbag for each player

Objective: The player tries to keep the *jae gi* in the air using only the feet.

To make a jae gi*: Place a large washer on a 10" x 10" piece of paper at the center of the near side. (See Illustration 1.) Roll the washer in the paper so the paper is around the washer, keeping the washer in the center. Cut the paper from the center hole. Slide both ends of the paper through the hole and cut this excess paper in vertical strips so it fans out for the tail.*

Directions: Using the inside part of the foot, players keep their *jae gi* in the air by kicking it repeatedly. The player keeping her/his *jae gi* in the air for the most number of kicks is the winner.

Also See: *Tossing the Ball* (6-29)

   Chapete (6-30)

   Kick Swing (6-32)

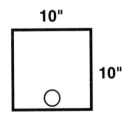

Illustration 1: *Jae Gi*

6-32. Kick Swing

Country: Vietnam (Far East, Asia)

Type of Game: Sports—Soccer (Juggling)

Formation: Two teams stand 4–10 feet apart.

Equipment: 1 soft spongy ball or beanbag; playing area

Objective: The teams kick the ball/bag back and forth using only the bottoms of the feet.

Wrap a coin in tissue paper to make a shape of a bag. Wrap string around to hold it together. The top of the bag is flared out to form a tail.

Directions: The game begins by one team kicking the ball/bag to the other team using the bottom of the foot. Kicking the ball/bag back and forth, the teams keep it in the air for as many kicks as possible. When the ball/bag falls to the ground or is touched by a player's hand, a point is scored against that team.

Also See: *Tossing the Ball* (6-29)

Chapete (6-30)

Jae Gi (6-31)

6-33. Goal Kickers

Country: United States (North America)

Type of Game: Sports—Soccer

Formation: Divide into two teams. One team stands on each side of a center line in a 20' x 40' playing area.

Equipment: 1 soccer ball; playing field; center line; goal lines

Objective: Each team tries to kick the ball past the goal line protected by the other team.

Directions: Standing in the center of the playing area, one player from each team begins the game with a basketball-type jump ball. Once the tip-off is done, the ball is not to be touched by the hands again. Players stay on their own side of the playing area and use only their feet to kick the ball back and forth, trying to kick the ball through the other team and past the back boundary line for a score.

   When the ball goes out of bounds and after each score, the two teams face off for another tip-off. The first team to reach 21 points wins.

Also See: *Football* (6-34)

Snow Football (6-35)

Saskatch Soccer (6-37)

6-34. Football

Country: Colonial America (North America)

Type of Game: Sports—Soccer

Formation: Divide into two teams. A goal is set up on each end line by sticking two sticks in the ground 2–3 feet apart.

Equipment: 1 soccer ball; 4 sticks for goals; playing field

Objective: Each team tries to kick the ball through the other team's goal.

Football *in Colonial America meant that only the feet were used to propel the ball.*

Directions: Without using the hands on the ball, players kick the ball to try to get the ball past the other team and through its goal.

Also See: *Goal Kickers (6-33)*

Snow Football (6-35)

Saskatch Soccer (6-37)

6-35. Snow Football

Country: Alaska, United States (North America)

Type of Game: Sports—Soccer

Formation: Two teams stand on opposite ends of a playing field. Goals (sticks) on each end line are 4–6 feet apart. The ball is placed in the center of the field.

Equipment: 1 soccer ball; 4 sticks; playing area

Objective: Each team tries to kick the ball through the other team's goal.

Although called Football, *this game resembles European Football, which is known in the United States as* Soccer. *The Eskimo children play* Snow Football *on hard-packed snow during the winter months using a leather pouch stuffed with moss or animal hair.*

Directions: Teams begin by standing on opposite goal lines. The ball is placed in the center of the playing field. On the signal "Go!" both teams rush out for the ball. There are no official positions in *Snow Football,* so any player from either team may go after the ball, but some may stay back to protect the goal.

The team that kicks the ball through the goal of their opponent scores 1 point. The ball begins in the center of the field and teams return to their goal line after each score to begin play again.

Adaptation: Two large boxes can be used as goals.

Also See: *Goal Kickers (6-33)*

Football (6-34)

Saskatch Soccer (6-37)

6-36. Hurling

Country: Colonial America (North America)

Type of Game: Sports—Football

Formation: Two teams begin at opposite goal lines 70 yards away. Each player wears two football flags, one on each hip.

Equipment: Playground ball the size of a softball; football flags (or handkerchiefs); waist belts; goal lines; playing field

Objective: Each team tries to get the ball past the other team's goal line by running past it.

In colonial days, players were able to stop a player with the ball by "laying hold of him." Some contests were between towns and parishes and would travel cross-country through all kinds of terrain.

Directions: Beginning at the goal lines, the team with the ball (offense) begins running it towards the other team's goal. The team without the ball (defense) runs up to try to stop the advancement of the ball. Only one defensive player at a time may confront the player with the ball. To stop the player with the ball, the defensive player can pull one of the two flags from her/his waist belt. At that point, the offensive player must stop moving forward and drop the ball for the defense to get it (becoming the offense). If the offensive player can pass the ball before a flag is pulled, the ball remains in possession of her/his team. All passes to teammates must travel backward away from the goal line, never forward.

An offensive player may dodge, sidestep, or spin away from a defender, but another defender may be waiting and ready. The ball must be carried across the goal line for a score.

Once a score is made, the team scored upon begins the next round. The first team to reach a predetermined score wins.

Also See: *Gaelic Football (6-38)*

6-37. Saskatch Soccer

Country: Great Britain (Europe)

Type of Game: Sports—Soccer

Formation: Divide into teams of six players each. Each team has four field players who link hands together and two goalie players who link together. Each team has one goal; goals are separated throughout the play area. The number of teams can be unlimited, as long as each has its own goal.

Equipment: 1 soccer ball per team; 1 goal per team; playing field

Objective: Each team's field players try to touch the ball before shooting at any opponent's goal.

This game is also played in Spain and France.

Directions: Each team's four field players must remain connected while dribbling the soccer ball towards a goal. Before shooting at a goal, the four players must each touch the ball at least once. If a player of another team touches the ball, all four field players must touch the ball again before shooting at the goal.

When a team does score, two members of the shooting team that just scored replace the goalies, and the goalies become part of the field players.

Also See:　　*Goal Kickers* (6-33)

　　　　　　　Football (6-34)

　　　　　　　Snow Football (6-35)

6-38. Gaelic Football

Country: Ireland (Europe)

Type of Game: Sports—Soccer/Rugby

Formation: Divide into two teams on a large rectangular field with soccer goals. Each team has 15 players.

Equipment: 1 soccer ball; goals; playing field

Objective: Each team tries to get the ball into the soccer goal or above the top of the goal of the other team's.

This type of football is a mix of soccer and rugby.

Directions: Starting with the ball at its goal line, one team moves the ball towards the other team's goal by kicking, fisting, throwing, and dribbling the ball forward to teammates or themselves. A player is not allowed to carry the ball more than four consecutive steps before giving it up to a teammate.

Once near the other team's goal, the offensive players try to kick, fist, throw, or bounce the ball into the other team's soccer net (3 points) or above the goal's crossbar (1 point). If successful, the other team starts the ball when both teams are at their respective goal lines. If unsuccessful, the other team begins the ball at its goal line, with the offensive team close at hand to try to take the ball away.

Safety: Body contact between teams other than incidental bumping is not allowed. Players playing rough are suspended from the game.

6-39. Broom Croquet

Country: Germany (Europe)

Type of Game: Sports—Hockey

Formation: Two teams stand on opposite sidelines. Teams are counted off from left to right so number 1's begin on the left end of the line near the opponent's goal. Goals are set on opposite ends of the playing area. A rag ball is placed in the center of the play area with push brooms placed halfway between the goals and the ball. The handles of the push brooms are pointed toward the team that guards that goal. (See Illustration 1.)

Equipment: 1 rag ball; 1 push broom for each team; 1 goal for each team (chair with open legs for ball to pass through); sidelines; playing area

Objective: The player uses the push broom to try to push the ball through the opponent's goal (chair legs).

Otto von Bismarck, Chancellor of Prussia, united the independent German states into the German Empire in 1871.

Directions: The leader calls out a player's number. That player from each team runs out and grabs her/his team's broom and tries to push the rag ball through the legs of the opponent's chair for a goal. The ball may go through the legs of the chair in any direction from any side. The first player to do so scores 1 point for her/his team.

Following each score, the equipment is replaced for the leader to call the next number. Play continues until all players have been called.

The team with the higher score following the last player's turn wins.

Variation: Use different types of brooms or sticks to move the ball.

Also See:　　*Chueca (Twisted) (6-40)*

　　　　　　Shinny (6-41)

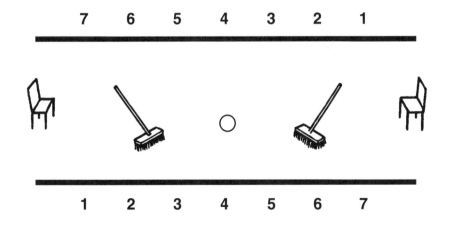

Illustration 1: *Broom Croquet*

6-40. Chueca (Twisted)

Country: Chile (South America)

Type of Game: Sports—Hockey

Formation: Divide into two teams. A field is marked off with two sidelines, end lines used as goals, and a 3-foot wide circle in the center of the field. A tennis ball is placed in the center of the circle. Teams are lined up on opposite sidelines and counted off from left to right. (See Illustration 1.) Each player has a hockey stick.

Equipment: 1 tennis ball; 1 hockey stick for each player; colored shirts or armbands for each team's identification (or hockey sticks colored or marked for identification of each team); playing field with center hole, sidelines, and end lines for goals

Objective: Each team tries to score by putting the ball across the goal line of the other team.

Larger than the state of Texas at 92,257 square miles, Chile's width ranges from 100 to 250 miles. Chile's length of 2,700 miles north to south makes it a long thin band of land on the western side of South America from the Andes Mountains to the Pacific Ocean.

Directions: Teams stand on opposite sidelines. The leader calls a number and the player from each team with that number runs out to the center circle and tries to get the ball out of the circle and towards the other team's goal line. Once the ball is out of the circle, the teams still standing on the sidelines are allowed to come onto the field and play.

Using only the hockey stick, both teams try to gain control of the ball and work it towards the other team's goal line while trying to prevent the other team from doing the same. When a team scores, the ball is replaced in the center circle on the field. Teams return to their sidelines in proper order and a new number is called.

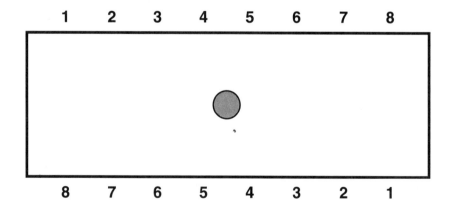

Illustration 1: *Chueca (Twisted)*

Adaptation: For advanced players, a 4–5-foot wide circle is placed at the center of each goal line. Goals are scored when the ball goes into one of these circles. Care should be taken on the shot on goal because only one shot is allowed. If the ball goes in, 1 point is scored. If the ball misses the circle, the ball is replaced at the center of the field and a new number is called.

Also See: *Broom Croquet* (6-39)

Shinny (6-41)

6-41. Shinny

Country: Canada (North America)

Type of Game: Sports—Hockey

Formation: A rectangular playing field is marked off with goals in the center of opposite end lines and a line through the center of the field. Two teams of 7 to 10 players each start on their half of the playing field. Each player has a hockey stick.

Equipment: Playing field; center line; goals; 1 hockey puck or spongy ball; 1 hockey stick for each player

Objective: The player uses the hockey stick to try to gain control of the puck and put the puck into the other team's goal.

Many Native American Indians play variations of Shinny *and there are many levels of rules for playing. The game presented here is a simple form of hockey played throughout Canada.*

Directions: A referee drops the puck in the center of the playing area between one player from each team. These players try to gain control of the puck and pass it to teammates who move into the opponent's half of the playing area towards the goal.

Each team passes the puck from teammate to teammate or tries to intercept it from the other team by using only the hockey stick. When one team hits the puck through the other team's goal, 1 point is scored and play begins again in the center of the field. Games are played in two 10–15-minute periods.

Rules:

1. The hockey stick blade is kept below knee level.

2. Players cannot use their feet on the puck to move it or stop it.

3. Infractions of rules 1 or 2 result in a free shot for the opponents at the point of infraction. Defensive players stand behind the puck if closer than 15 feet to the goal. Only the goalie may be in front of the goal.

4. When the puck goes out of bounds, the other team hits it back in play. Defensive players must be 5 yards away until the puck is hit.

Safety: Be sure the children are closely supervised while playing this game.

Also See: *Broom Croquet* (6-39)

              Chueca (Twisted) (6-40)

6-42. Khong Kangjei
(Wrestling Hockey)

Country: India (Asia)

Type of Game: Sports—Hockey

Formation: Divide into two teams of 7 players each. Players each have a hockey stick and are scattered on own side of playing area.

Equipment: 1 tennis ball; 1 hockey stick for each player; goal lines; playing field

Objective: Each team tries to hit the ball past the other team's goal line (end lines).

With origins traced to prehistoric times, Khong Kangjei *has developed into a team activity having specific positions as in hockey, field hockey, and soccer.*

Directions: The game begins with the ball being tossed at the center line. These players use their stick to gain control of the ball. Any player at any time may kick the ball, carry it, or use the stick to control the ball; but in order to score, the player must hit the ball past the goal line (end line) with the hockey stick.

When a player carries the ball, opponents originally were allowed to tackle and wrestle with that player in an attempt to free the ball. Today, however, the opponents tag a player holding the ball, who must release it to the ground and continue play.

The game continues until one team hits the ball past the other team's goal line. After each score, players get back in position and the ball begins again in the center.

Safety: This game must be played under close supervision.

6-43. Bamboula (Center Pole)

Country: Caribbean Islands

Type of Game: Striking with Paddles

Formation: Teams stand spread out on their own half of the marked playing area. A pole (*bamboula*) marks the center of the field when play begins. A board is put at each end of the playing area as a team's goal. Each player has two rackets.

Equipment: Playing field; pole (*bamboula*); boards at each goal line (for goals); 2 rackets (badminton rackets or ping-pong paddles with extended handles attached) for each player; 1 ball

Objective: Each team tries to gain control of the ball with the rackets and pass it to the goal for a score.

Cuba is the largest island of the Caribbean and the most northern, about 90 miles from the southern tip of Florida in the United States.

Directions: The ball is tossed at the *bamboula* and the players carefully try to gain control of the ball using the rackets. Using only the rackets to move the ball, players may strike the ball to teammates or scoop the ball from the ground.

When close enough, players try to hit their team's goal (board) with the ball for 1 point. The first team to reach a predeterminded score wins.

6-44. Tskhenburti (Polo)

Country: Republic of Georgia (Asia)

Type of Game: Sports—Polo

Formation: Divide into two teams. Within each team, teammates have partners: one partner is the Horse that stands in front of the Rider. A jump rope is put around the Horse's chest and under the arms to make reins. The Rider stands behind the Horse and holds a croquet mallet. Each team begins on its own half of the playing field. Goals are marked off on opposite end lines using poles stuck into the ground 2 yards apart.

Equipment: Jump ropes; croquet mallets (or other form of equipment with a striking surface); low-bouncing ball; goals; playing field

Objective: The Rider tries to strike the ball to control, pass, or hit towards the other team's goal to score, while the defending riders try to defend their goal and try to intercept the ball to score for their own team.

Annexed by Russia in 1801, Republic of Georgia became an independent state when the Soviet Union disbanded in 1991.

Directions: The ball starts in the center of the playing area. One set of Horse and Rider from each team meet at the ball and try to gain control of the ball on the signal to start play. Only the Riders are allowed to strike the ball and only with the croquet mallet. Any infraction of this results in control going to the other team at that spot. By passing the ball or dribbling to oneself, the ball is worked towards the other team's goal in an attempt to score. When the ball is hit between one team's goal post, a point is scored. Play is restarted at the center of the field.

The first team to reach a predetermined score wins.

Safety: For safety and ease of play, instead of using a croquet mallet, the Riders may use their feet to kick the ball. The Horses are not allowed to touch the ball; but if the ball is kicked into the feet of the Horse, no penalty is called unless the Horse kicks the ball away.

Section 7
Toss-Throw-Catch

Tossing or throwing to a partner or a target is the main objective of this unit. Catching activities are also involved but not in all the activities. Many types of targets are used in these activities, from tossing to oneself, to holes, cans, pails, and rocks, to partners. Propelling an object to a target using an underhand or overhand motion is the key to this unit.

In this section you'll find 50 activities from 28 countries and 7 continents/regions around the world.

Africa

Goose Feather Throwing Game (7-28)—Africa
Haba Gaba (7-27)—Sierra Leone
Mulambilwa (7-42)—Nigeria
Pebble Toss (7-18)—Guinea
Spearing the Disk (7-44)—Ethiopia

Asia

Hole Ball (7-23)—Russia
Sticks (7-41)—Pakistan

Australia

Donkey (7-7)—Australia
Down Ball (7-12)—Australia
Sevens (7-13)—Australia

Caribbean Islands

Catch the Bag of Sand (7-8)—Caribbean Islands
Sticks and Stones (7-40)—Caribbean Islands

Central America (North America)

Off the Wall (7-15)—Guatemala

Europe

Ball in the Decker (Pillar the Hat) (7-24)—
  Ireland
Call Ball (7-10)—Austria
Hit the Stones (7-36)—Portugal
Hook the Driftwood Stick (7-31)—Greece
Hoopla Stalls (7-32)—Great Britain
London (7-16)—Great Britain

Mat Ball (7-49)—Great Britain
Monday, Tuesday (7-11)—Great Britain
Name the Animal (7-9)*—Switzerland
Pass and Catch (7-3)*—Great Britain
Pass Ball (7-47)—Great Britain
Pitch Ball (7-26)*—Ireland
Queenie (7-5)—Great Britain
Quilles (7-17)—France
Seven-Up (7-14)—Great Britain
Skyros (7-50)—Greece
Swedish Meatball (7-4)*—Sweden

Far East (Asia)

Ang-Konnh (7-34)—Cambodia
Chuck Stones (7-35)—China
Nekki (7-39)—Japan

Middle East (Asia)

Button Toss (7-22)*—Lebanon
Kukla (7-38)—Turkey
Magura (Pecan Hole) (7-19)*—Iraq
Tiger's Ball (7-46)*—Israel

North America

Catch the Ball (7-2)*—Canada
Hit the Tree (7-29)—Native Americans
Keep Away (7-48)—United States
Monkey in the Middle (7-45)—United States
Pine Cone Toss (7-30)—Native Americans
Pitch and Hustle (7-20)*—Colonial America

North America *(continued)*

Oceania

*Games that may be played in the classroom.

7-1. Throwing Sevens

Country: Colonial America (North America)

Type of Game: Toss and Catch

Formation: Players stand in personal space with a ball or beanbag.

Equipment: 1 ball or beanbag for each player; list of stunts/challenges

Objective: Each player tries to toss and catch while performing the stunts/challenges.

The balls in colonial times did not bounce.

Directions: The first player chooses a stunt from the list of stunts/challenges. After performing the first stunt seven times without a miss, the player chooses a second stunt to perform. This continues until she/he misses; then the second player performs the stunts performed by the first player. When the second player surpasses the stunts of the first player, she/he chooses the next stunt from this list to be performed.

This process continues until one player has completed seven stunts/challenges.

LIST OF ONE-OR TWO-HANDED STUNTS/CHALLENGES:

- Toss—clap—catch.

- Toss—clap behind the back—catch.

- Toss—clap once—touch right shoulder with left hand, right hand to left shoulder—catch.

- Toss—twirl around once—catch.

- Toss—bend forward and clap behind both legs—catch.

- Toss—clap behind right leg—catch.

- Toss—clap behind left leg—catch.

- Toss—clap behind right leg—clap behind left leg—catch.

- Toss—clap under lifted right leg—clap under lifted left leg—catch.

- Toss—touch toes—catch.

- Toss—lift left leg and touch heel in front and behind—catch.

- Toss—lift right leg and touch heel in front and behind—catch.

- Toss—lift right leg and touch heel—lift left leg and touch heel—catch.

- Toss and catch seven times while hopping on right or left foot—catch.

- Toss—jump on both feet seven times—catch.

- Toss and catch seven times while standing on right or left foot—catch.

LIST OF ONE-HANDED STUNTS/CHALLENGES:

- Toss left—catch right.
- Toss right—catch left.
- Toss right—catch left—hand off to right—toss right.
- Toss left—catch right—hand off to left—toss left.
- Toss from behind the back—catch with opposite hand.
- Toss from behind the back—catch with same hand.
- Toss right under right leg—catch with left hand.
- Toss left under left leg—catch with right hand.
- Toss left under left leg—catch with right hand reaching under right leg.
- Toss right under right leg—catch with left hand reaching under left leg.
- Toss left under right leg—catch left.
- Toss right under left leg—catch right.

    Encourage players to make up more stunts/challenges of their own, keeping in mind that the balls in colonial times did not bounce.

Variation: Each stunt/challenge may be performed three times instead of seven.

Also See: *Sevens* (7-13)

                 Seven-Up (7-14)

                 Off the Wall (7-15)

7-2. Catch the Ball

Country: Canada (North America)

Type of Game: Toss with Partner

Formation: Players form a single circle. One player has a ball.

Equipment: 1 ball

Objective: The players try to toss the ball to other players in the circle as many times as possible and as quickly as possible without dropping it.

Canada has the longest total coastline in the world at 152,100 miles.

Directions: On the signal "Go!" players begin to toss the ball to different players around the circle. Toss the ball as quickly as possible. Care needs to be taken not to make a bad toss. A player making a toss that another player is not capable of catching is eliminated. A player missing a toss eliminates the catcher.

The last player left is the winner.

Variations:

- Use different size/shaped tossing equipment.
- Play in different body positions—sitting, kneeling, and so on.
- Use more than one ball at a time.

Also See: *Pass and Catch* (7-3)

Catch the Bag of Sand (7-8)

Name the Animal (7-9)

7-3. Pass and Catch

Country: Great Britain (Europe)

Type of Game: Toss with Partner

Formation: Teams stand single file with each first person standing 10 feet in front, facing her/his line.

Equipment: 1 ball for each team

Objective: The lead player tries to toss the ball to all players in her/his line so they can catch the ball and toss it back.

This was played during the time of Queen Elizabeth I (1558–1603), daughter of Henry VIII and Anne Boleyn.

Directions: The front player of each line stands 10 feet in front of the line, facing the team and holding a ball. On the signal "Go!" the ball is tossed to the next player in line who catches the ball, tosses it back, and goes to the end of the line. If the catcher in line misses the ball, she/he retrieves it and tosses it to the front player who throws it to that player again. Good tosses are the key.

When all players in the line have successfully caught and tossed the ball, the line is finished.

Variations:

- When the first player is back to the front of the line, the tosser goes to the end of the line. The first player in line goes 10 feet in front to become the new tosser to everyone in line. This rotation continues until all players in the line have been the tosser.

- This activity can be performed as a relay race with more than one line.

Also See: *Catch the Ball* (7-2)

Name the Animal (7-9)

7-4. Swedish Meatball

Country: Sweden (Europe)

Type of Game: Toss with Partner

Formation: Players are scattered throughout a small playing area. One player has the ball.

Equipment: 1 ball; playing area

Objective: The players try to pass the ball from player to player so everyone has a chance to toss and catch it.

Use a variety of balls (basketballs, footballs, volleyballs, fleece balls, tennis balls, etc.) and a variety of passes (bounce, chest, one-handed, overhead, etc.) for a well-rounded experience.

Directions: On the signal "Go!" the ball is passed from player to player until all players have tossed the ball. Before tossing to a player, the tosser needs to call the name of the player to whom she/he is tossing. It is the responsibility of the tosser to make the best possible toss.

Variations:

- After a player passes the ball, she/he sits down to show that she/he has had a turn.

- Divide into teams to race against each other.

- Players stay in a scattered formation. The lead passer must toss and catch with each player. Each player should sit down after her/his turn.

7-5. Queenie

Country: Great Britain (Europe)

Type of Game: Toss with Partner

Formation: Players stand side by side in a line. One player ("Queenie") stands 10 feet in front, facing away.

Equipment: 1 ball

Objective: Queenie tries to toss the ball backward over her/his head so that players can catch it.

The United Kingdom has had six women rulers: Mary I (from 1553–1558), Elizabeth I (from 1558–1603), Mary II along with William III (from 1689–1694), Anne (from 1702–1714), Victoria (from 1837–1901), and Elizabeth II (from 1952 to present day).

Directions: When the players in line are ready, Queenie tosses the ball backward over her/his head. The players in line try to catch it before it falls to the ground. If caught, that player is the new Queenie. If it falls to the ground, one player picks up the ball and hides it behind her/his back. Before Queenie turns around, all the line players put their hands behind their backs pretending to have the ball. When all are ready, Queenie turns around and tries to guess who has the ball. If Queenie correctly guesses who has the ball, Queenie has another turn. If incorrect, the player with the ball becomes the new Queenie.

7-6. Folding Arms

Country: New Zealand (Oceania)

Type of Game: Toss with Group

Formation: Players stand side by side facing one direction with arms crossed in front. One player stands in front with the ball.

Equipment: 1 ball

Objective: The player in line tries to catch the ball if tossed, but keeps the arms folded if not tossed.

New Zealand is found in the Southwest Pacific with Australia, Fiji, and Tonga as neighbors. New Zealand is 103,736 square miles in size, about the size of the state of Colorado.

Directions: The player in front of the line tosses the ball to any player in line. The player in line has to unfold her/his arms in time to be able to catch the ball. If too slow, the ball can be missed and the player leaves the line with a miss.

The front player may pretend to toss the ball to a player. If the player unfolds her/his arms and the ball is not tossed, that player is eliminated from the line. Players who catch the ball when tossed to them remain in line to try the next time it is their turn. Players who reach for the ball when not tossed to them can be eliminated when it becomes a problem for the intended player to catch the ball. The tossing player must toss the ball in such a way (speed and accuracy) to allow the line player a chance to catch the ball.

The remaining player in line is the winner and becomes the new tosser for the next game.

7-7. Donkey

Country: Australia

Type of Game: Toss with Partner

Formation: Parallel lines are marked 70 feet apart (or whatever is appropriate for the ability of the players). Opponents stand behind opposite lines.

Equipment: Parallel lines 70 feet apart; 1 tennis ball

Objective: The players try to throw the ball over the other line in an area where it has a chance to be caught.

Australia's coastline is 16,000 miles long—compared with Canada's 152,100 miles!

Directions: Standing behind one line, the ball is thrown so it will pass over the other line in reach of a player at that line. If the ball is caught, that player throws it back. If the ball does not pass the second line, the thrower takes the first letter to the word DONKEY. If the throw is poor and cannot be caught, a letter goes to the thrower. If the throw is long enough and can be caught, but the catcher misses it, the catcher receives a letter in DONKEY.

The first player to spell DONKEY loses.

Variations:

- This game can be played by partners or in teams.
- This game can be played in a circle. Players who do not catch the ball or who make a bad toss earn a letter.

7-8. Catch the Bag of Sand

Country: Caribbean Islands

Type of Game: Toss with Partner

Formation: Players form a circle.

Equipment: 1 large leaf flexible enough to be filled with sand and wrapped with twine to form a ball; playing area; (optional) bases

Objective: The players try to toss and catch the leaf of sand from player to player without breaking.

Large palm leaves are used in the Caribbean and tropical islands.

Directions: Standing in a circle, the players toss the leaf of sand to each other. The player who catches the leaf when it breaks attempts to run to the nearest tree (or base) and touch it before she/he is tagged by another player.

Variation: Use a water balloon instead of a sand-filled leaf.

Also See: *Catch the Ball (7-2)*

7-9. Name the Animal

Country: Switzerland (Europe)

Type of Game: Toss to Group

Formation: Players stand in line side by side and face a leader.

Equipment: 1 ball

Objective: The leader tosses the ball to each player in line and gives a clue for the line players to try to answer.

Switzerland's national languages are German, French, Italian, and Romaresh. German is the predominant language, spoken by 65% of the inhabitants.

Directions: The leader tosses the ball to her-/himself and calls out: "Name the animal. The first letter is O." This is a signal for the line players to get ready. The leader tosses the ball to the first player in line, who answers: "Is it an owl?" If owl is correct, the player becomes the new leader. If owl is not correct, the line player tosses the ball back to the leader, who then tosses the ball to the next player in line. When the ball has been tossed to all players in the line and no one has named the right animal, the leader begins at the first player again and says, "Name the animal. The first two letters are OT." The procedure is repeated until the correct animal has been named; in this example, OTTER.

This can continue using different categories, such as: foods, countries, states, or anything else with which all players would be familiar.

Also See: *Catch the Ball* (7-2)

Pass and Catch (7-3)

7-10. Call Ball

Country: Austria (Europe)

Type of Game: Throw at Wall

Formation: All players stand facing a wall that is 10-15 feet away. One player has the ball and may choose to stand 15-20 feet away from the wall.

Equipment: 1 ball; wall

Objective: The players try to catch the ball after it is thrown against the wall.

All children in Austria go to school between the ages of 6 and 14. After completing four years of elementary school, they choose the type of secondary school to go to. They may choose a nonacademic career and attend a trade school, art school, or technical school. Colleges in Austria are called gymnasiums. *The oldest gymnasium is the University of Vienna, founded in 1365.*

Directions: The player with the ball throws it against the wall and calls out a name of another player. As the ball bounces off the wall, the named player must make the catch.

If a named player misses the ball, all other players run away. The named player retrieves the ball as quickly as possible and yells "Stop!" All runners stop where they are. The ball is thrown in an attempt to hit a player below the waist. The player thrown at may move one foot or leg to dodge the ball, but can't move both feet or jump.

When the throw hits a player's legs, the thrower becomes the next player to throw the ball against the wall. If the throw is unsuccessful, the thrower leans forward with feet away from the wall and hands against the wall. Beginning with the player farthest away from the thrower leaning against the wall, each player has a turn to toss the ball in an effort to come near one of the thrower's hands (within 12-18 inches). The first to do this is the next thrower. If none of the players are successful, the thrower has another turn.

Variations:

- Don't throw the ball at the thrower if the player misses the ball.

- If throwing at the player, have players throw with her/his opposite hand.

- If the throw misses the target player, the target player is the next thrower.

Also See: *Monday, Tuesday (7-11)*

7-11. Monday, Tuesday

Country: Great Britain (Europe)

Type of Game: Throw at Wall

Formation: Seven players stand at a throwing line facing a wall 15 feet away. Players are assigned a day of the week.

Equipment: Throwing line; 1 ball; wall

Objective: The named player tries to catch the ball after it bounces against the wall.

In 1215 an aristocratic rebellion against the royal absolutism of King John led to the royal acceptance of The Magna Carta that helped lay the foundations of parliamentary government. Around 1688 the English Bill of Rights established the supremacy of parliament and made the government a model of constitutional monarchy.

Directions: The player assigned "Sunday" is the first thrower. Sunday throws the ball and calls another day of the week, perhaps "Wednesday." Wednesday rushes in and tries to catch the ball before it bounces on the floor. If successful, Wednesday is the next thrower. If Wednesday misses the ball, Sunday has to get the ball as all other players scatter. Sunday throws the ball at the other players, trying to hit one below waist level. If Sunday hits a player, Sunday is the next thrower. If Sunday misses, Monday is the next thrower.

Variations:

* For 12 players, use the months of the year.
* For 9 players, use the names of the planets.

Adaptations:

* Younger players may let the ball bounce once before a player has to catch it.
* If you don't want players to throw a hard ball at the player against the wall, do this: Place a Nerf™ ball at either end of the throwing line. Before a player can throw a ball at a player, the ball used against the wall is retrieved and placed near one of the Nerf™ balls. The Nerf™ ball taken is then thrown at players running away.

Also See: *Call Ball (7-10)*

7-12. Down Ball

Country: Australia

Type of Game: Throw at Wall

Formation: Two players stand facing a wall with a 15-foot surface width marked. The court length (end line) is 15–20 feet from the wall.

Equipment: 1 tennis or rubber ball; wall; chalk

Objective: The player tries to hit the ball off the wall so the other player cannot return it.

Although no longer a colony of Great Britain, Australia still recognizes the British royal family as its own. Queen Elizabeth II is Australia's head of state.

Directions: Standing behind the end line across from the wall, one player begins play by throwing the ball so it bounces off the floor before it bounces off the wall. The second player must rush to the ball before it hits the floor and hit the ball so it hits the floor before hitting the wall again. Alternating between players, this pattern continues until one player misses the ball, makes a mistake in hitting the ball, or the ball goes out of bounds either on the wall or on the floor.

The player earning a point on an opponent's mistake is the next server.

Adaptation: Younger players may be allowed to catch and quickly throw the ball instead of hitting it following the service.

7-13. Sevens

Country: Australia

Type of Game: Throw at Wall

Formation: Partners stand near a wall.

Equipment: 1 tennis ball for each set of partners; wall

Objective: The player tries to perform a desired stunt for a predetermined number of times, first with both hands together, then right hand only, then left hand only.

The Great Barrier Reef lies off the northeast coast of Australia and is 1,245 miles long, making it the longest coral reef in the world. In some places the reef is 400 feet thick.

Directions: The first player begins the following stunts/challenges:

1. For seven times, the player bounces the ball against the wall and catches it.

2. For six times, the player throws the ball against the wall and claps her/his hands once before catching it.

3. For five times, the player throws the ball against the wall and touches both hands to her/his head, then shoulders, before catching it.

4. For four times, the player throws the ball under one leg against the wall and catches it.

5. For three times, the player throws the ball against the wall, claps her/his hands in front, claps hands behind the back, claps hands in front again, and catches the ball.

6. For two times, the player throws the ball against the wall, squats to touch the floor with both hands, and catches it.

7. For one time, the player throws the ball against the wall, spins around one complete time, and catches the ball.

A player's turn is over if the ball hits the ground before being caught, the player fails to complete a stunt, or the player performs a trick the wrong number of times. The next player then begins her/his turn. On a player's second turn, she/he begins at the level she/he previously stopped.

Once a player performs all seven levels, the activity is repeated two more times: once using only the right hand, and then the left hand. The first player to complete all three rounds is the winner.

Adaptation: Younger players may allow the ball to bounce off the floor once before catching.

Variation: Do the above stunts without a wall by tossing the ball into the air.

Also See: *Throwing Sevens* (7-1)

Seven-Up (7-14)

Off the Wall (7-15)

7-14. Seven-Up

Country: Great Britain (Europe)

Type of Game: Throw against Wall

Formation: Players stand behind a tossing/catching line five feet from the wall.

Equipment: Wall; 1 ball; throwing/catching line

Objective: The players try to perform a series of stunts/challenges before the ball hits the floor.

The most famous British universities are Oxford and Cambridge, each dating back to the thirteenth century. There are about seventy other universities in England.

Directions: Standing behind the throwing/catching line, each player in turn throws the ball against the wall and performs a required stunt before catching the ball. If a player drops the ball or fails to perform the stunt correctly (including the correct number of times), the next player starts. The second (and subsequent) turn for a player begins at the level causing the loss of turn, whereby the player performs the total number of stunts/challenges required for that level.

There are seven levels to complete in this activity. Each level must be completed before going on to the next. The stunt/challenge is repeated the number of times equaling the level of the stunt/challenge:

Throw the ball against the wall and...

1. ...catch it.
2. ...spin around once and catch it.
3. ...clap once and catch it.
4. ...clap hands in front of the body, in back of the body, and catch.
5. ...slap both hands on thighs, slap hands on opposite shoulders, and catch it.
6. ...lift one leg, clap hands under the leg, lift the other leg, and clap under this leg. Do this three times (3 x 2 = 6).
7. ...throw the ball under one leg and catch.

When a player misses the ball or fails to complete a level, her/his turn is over and the next player begins her/his turn. A player begins her/his second turn at the level missed and performs the required activity before advancing to the next level.

Variations:

- Catch the ball by reaching one or both hands under one leg.
- Catch behind the back.
- Catch below knee level.
- Catch while jumping—just be in the air at the time of the catch to count.

Also See: *Throwing Sevens (7-1)*

Sevens (7-13)

Off the Wall (7-15)

7-15. Off the Wall

Country: Guatemala (Central America, North America)

Type of Game: Toss against Wall

Formation: Players stand 6–8 feet from a wall. Each player has her/his own rubber/tennis ball.

Equipment: 1 rubber/tennis ball for each player; wall

Objective: The player tries to perform each stunt/challenge three times while reciting the descriptive line each time.

The major products of Guatemala are furniture, rubber, sugar, chemicals, and textiles.

Directions: In rhythm with each other, each player recites the descriptive lines as she/he tosses the ball against the wall and performs the described stunt/challenge *three times*. Players who miss are eliminated at that point.

The challenges are:

- We bounce our ball…
    (We bounce our ball…)
    (We bounce our ball…)

- Against the wall…
    (Against the wall…)
    (Against the wall…)

- Without moving…

- Without laughing…

- Without talking…

- On one foot…

- With one hand… (use same hand)

- In front… (throw, clap, catch)

- Behind… (throw, clap behind back, catch)

- Little horse… (clap under lifted leg)

- Right now… (keep arm in front for catch)

- Half turn… (turn half turn to right, turn back to left)

- Full turn… (turn all the way around)

    After the first round, any players who are left should repeat each stunt/challenge *two times*. Perform only one stunt/challenge in the third round.

    When players are learning the stunts/challenges, do not eliminate any players. After a miss, players get back into rhythm with the others and continue to the finish.

Also See: *Throwing Sevens* (7-1)

            Sevens (7-13)

            Seven-Up (7-14)

7-16. London

Country: Great Britain (Europe)

Type of Game: Toss at Target

Formation: The *London* diagram (see Illustration 1) is drawn on pavement with chalk. The outer dimensions are three feet wide and five feet long. The players stand at the tossing line.

Equipment: *London* diagram; stone to slide; chalk; tossing line

Objective: The player tries to be the first to draw three men in one section of the *London* diagram.

This is a larger version of a game played on a tabletop board.

Directions: Standing behind a tossing line at the bottom of the *London* diagram, players in turn slide or toss a stone to land completely between two of the lines. The player draws a circle for a man's head in that section and writes her/his initials inside the circle. As play continues, different players may have circles and initials in the same areas. (Stones landing on a line between sections do not count for drawing men or adding to them on that turn.)

In following turns, when a player's stone lands in sections where she/he has a circle drawn, that player adds a body and legs to the stickman. When the stone lands in the top space labeled "London," the player places a part of a stickman in all sections of the diagram.

A single line connects the player's three stickmen: arms are added when a player has three stickmen drawn in one section, each having a head, body and two legs.

The first player to have three stickmen in one section is the winner.

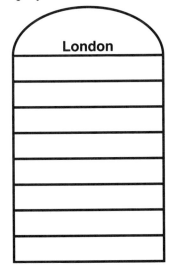

Tossing Line

Illustration 1: *London*

7-17. Quilles

Country: France (Europe)

Type of Game: Toss at Target

Formation: A rope or cord is attached above the area where 9 bowling pins are set up in a diamond formation. Players stand 5–6 feet away from the pins and hold the ball attached to the other end of the rope.

Equipment: Rope; overhead support; ball; 9 bowling pins

Objective: The player tries to release the ball so it will swing and knock down the bowling pins.

Although not a true tossing game, releasing the ball so it will swing to hit a target requires good eye–hand coordination to line up the swing of the ball.

Directions: Holding the ball away from the pins, the player lines up the ball so that when it is released, it will swing down and hit the target pins. The player has two tries to knock down as many pins as she/he can. The number of pins knocked down is the score for that turn. The first player to reach a total score of 100 wins.

Variation: The player swings the ball around/past the pins so that when it swings back towards the bowler, it knocks down the pins from behind.

7-18. Pebble Toss

Country: Guinea (Africa)

Type of Game: Toss at Target

Formation: Players stand on a tossing line that is 10 feet from a hole in the ground (or a can or pail target).

Equipment: Small nuts or pebbles; small hole (or large food can or small pail); tossing line

Objective: The player tries to toss the nut or pebble into the target.

Guinea is found on the Atlantic Coast of west Africa. Its neighbors are Guinea-Bissau, Senegal, Mali, Côte d'Ivoire, and Liberia. Guinea is slightly smaller than the state of Oregon with 94,964 square miles.

Directions: Each player in turn tries to toss a small pebble into the target hole. When a player's pebble successfully lands and stays in the hole, the player sits guard behind the hole without blocking it from the other tosses. As the other players toss their pebble to the hole, the Guard tosses her/his pebble in an effort to knock the other player's pebble while in flight. When a new player's pebble does drop into the hole, she/he becomes the new Guard for the hole.

Variations:

- Vary the size of the hole or the distance to the hole according to the players' ability.
- Have more than one hole (pail).

Also See: *Button Toss* (7-22)

   Hole Ball (7-23)

   Pitch Ball (7-26)

   Haba Gaba (7-27)

7-19. Magura (Pecan Hole)

Country: Iraq (Middle East, Asia)

Type of Game: Toss to Target

Formation: Players stand behind a tossing line 7 feet from a hole or milk carton. The hole is placed in front of a backstop.

Equipment: Hole (4 inches in diameter, 3 inches deep) or milk carton; 10 pecans for each player; tossing line; backstop or wall

Objective: The player tries to toss all pecans at one time for an even number of pecans to land in the hole. The player tries to accumulate as many pecans as possible.

Iraq, then known as Mesopotamia, had an advanced civilization by 4000 B.C. and was the center of ancient Babylonian and Assyrian Empires by 2000 B.C. In 1922 A.D. following the end of World War I, Great Britain was given a mandate over the area of Mesopotamia, which was then renamed Iraq. Iraq gained full independence in 1932.

Directions: One player is chosen to be the "owner" of the hole. The first player tosses all her/his pecans at one time to the hole. The owner counts the number that falls into the hole. If an even number is in the hole, the tosser gets these back; the owner keeps those that did not fall in. If an odd number of pecans fall into the hole, the owner gets these and the tosser gets back the pecans outside the hole. Each tosser has one toss before the next person has a turn.

The owner may sell the hole to a tosser at any time for an agreed number of pecans. The game is over when one tosser is out of pecans. The winner is the player who has the highest number of pecans at the end.

Variation: Players take turns being the owner. When all players have tossed one time, the first player to toss becomes the new owner. The game continues until all players have been an owner.

7-20. Pitch and Hustle

Country: Colonial America (North America)

Type of Game: Toss at Target

Formation: All players stand behind a tossing line facing a designated target 8–10 feet away.

Equipment: Two-sided flat objects (coins) that have distinguishing marks on the "heads" and "tails" sides; tossing line; target (cone, bowling pin, or wall)

Objective: The player tries to toss her/his coin closest to the target.

Colonial children frequently did not have coins with which to play. They used flat stones and marked one side with an "X" for heads and "O" for tails.

Directions: To begin this game, one player at a time tosses her/his coin at the target. The players form a line according to how close their coin landed. The player whose coin landed closest gathers up all the coins and tosses them into the air. All coins landing "heads up" belong to the tosser. The others go to the players in line according to the order of closeness to the target until the coins run out. (If three coins come up heads, the last two players in line would not get a coin back.)

When the coins are all passed out, the remaining players again toss at the target and play continues as before.

Also See: *Pitch-Penny (7-21)*

7-21. Pitch-Penny

Country: Colonial America (North America)

Type of Game: Toss at Target

Formation: Players stand behind a tossing line.

Equipment: Pennies; wall; tossing line

Objective: The player tries to toss a penny against the wall so that it lands closer than the other pennies.

When pennies were available in the U.S., children would get together and pitch pennies to try to add to their pockets. Colonial children used stones.

Directions: Squatting behind a tossing line, the players toss or thumb-flip their pennies so they hit the wall before landing. The penny closest to the wall wins the other pennies. If no penny is closer to the wall than a finger span (fingers spread wide, thumb to pinkie), or no penny bounces off the wall, the pennies are left on the ground. The winner of the next round would then pick up all pennies.

Variation: A flat target, perhaps another coin, is placed a short distance from the wall. The pennies are bounced off the wall and the closest penny to the target wins the pennies and the target.

Also See: *Pitch and Hustle (7-20)*

7-22. Button Toss

Country: Lebanon (Middle East, Asia)

Type of Game: Toss at Target

Formation: Each player has a can. Cans are placed in a straight line close to each other. Players stand on a parallel line 8 feet away.

Equipment: 1 can for each player; 3–4 buttons for each player

Objective: The player tries to toss the buttons into her/his own can.

Lebanon is located at the far eastern end of the Mediterranean Sea. Its neighbors are Syria to the east and Israel to the south. At 4,015 square miles, Lebanon is smaller than the state of Connecticut.

Directions: Each player tosses one button at a time in an effort to have it fall into her/his assigned can. One player may toss as the others watch, or all players may toss one button each at the same time.

Once all buttons are tossed, the player with the most buttons in her/his can is the winner. Sometimes players will have buttons in her/his can that were tossed by other players!

Variations:

- Pebbles may be used in place of buttons.
- Players stand in a circle 16 feet in diameter. The cans are placed in the center close to each other in a group instead of a line.

Also See: *Pebble Toss* (7-18)

Hole Ball (7-23)

Ball in the Decker (7-24)

Pitch Ball (7-26)

Haba Gaba (7-27)

7-23. Hole Ball

Country: Russia (Asia/Europe)

Type of Game: Toss at Target

Formation: A series of holes are dug 2–3 feet apart in a straight line, one hole per person. (See Illustration 1.) A tossing line is marked 10 feet from the nearest hole. Players stand behind the tossing line.

Equipment: Tossing line; hole targets; balls

Objective: The player tries to toss the ball into a hole and score as many points as possible.

---

*In 1987 the Soviet government initiated a program of reforms through openness (*glasnost*) and restructuring (*perestroika*), which was opposed by some Eastern bloc countries and many old-line Communists in the U.S.S.R. In 1991 several Soviet republics declared their independence. The Soviet Union officially broke up December 26, 1991 into 15 independent republics.*

Directions: Each player has a hole to call her/his own. The first player has hole number one, the second has hole number two, and so on.

   The first player tosses her/his ball in an attempt to land in a hole. If it lands in the third hole, the tosser gets three points and player number three is the next tosser. When a toss fails to land in a hole, the player with the lowest score is the next tosser. The winner is the first player to reach a predetermined score, or who has the highest score when time runs out.

Variation: Use cans as targets instead of holes.

Also See: *Pebble Toss* (7-18)

   Button Toss (7-22)

   Pitch Ball (7-26)

   Haba Gaba (7-27)

Tossing Line

Illustration 1: *Hole Ball*

7-24. Ball in the Decker
(Pillar the Hat)

Country: Ireland (Europe)

Type of Game: Roll at Target

Formation: Hats with bills are set upside down so the bill acts as a ramp into the hat. Players stand 10 feet from the hats.

Equipment: 1 hat for each person; ball; pebbles; rolling line

Objective: The player tries to roll the ball into a hat.

Ireland is an island in the Atlantic Ocean off the coast of Great Britain. At 27,137 square miles, Ireland is slightly larger than the state of West Virginia.

Directions: Standing behind the rolling line, the first player rolls the ball in an attempt to get it to roll into one of the hats. When it does go in a hat, the owner of the hat runs to the hat, takes out the ball, and throws it at one of the other players. If a player is hit with the ball, a pebble is placed in that player's hat.

When a player has five pebbles in her/his hat, she/he stands by a wall and tries to catch all the other players' balls thrown to her/him.

Also See: *Button Toss (7-22)*

7-25. Skelly

Country: United States (North America)

Type of Game: Toss at Target

Formation: Players toss a checker into the boxes of the diagram while standing 3 feet away.

Equipment: Diagram drawn as shown 4' x 4'; checker for each player

Objective: The player tries to toss the checker into each box in sequence.

Skelly *was usually played on the sidewalks and streets of New York City.* Skelly *is also known as* Skully. *Each numbered box is called a "skelly."*

Directions: Standing three feet from the diagram (see Illustration 1), the first player tosses her/his checker to try to have it land in box 1. If successful, player number one finger-flicks the checker to box 2. A player's turn ends when she/he is not successful in getting the checker into the appropriate square. Player number one now waits for all the other players to finish their turns before playing again.

When a player's checker stops in an area inside the diagram but outside a numbered box, that player cannot shoot again until the checker is knocked out of bounds or into a numbered box by another player. The first player to reach box 21 wins.

Variation: Play so that when a player's checker lands inside a skelly, the player's turn is over, but may continue to play the next time it is her/his turn.

Adaptation: Beginning players may take 2–3 shots per turn to try to get the checker inside a numbered box.

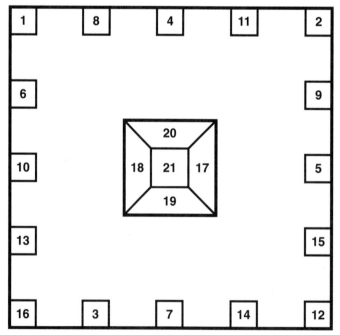

Illustration 1: *Skelly*

7-26. Pitch Ball

Country: Ireland (Europe)

Type of Game: Toss at Target

Formation: A tossing line is drawn 9 feet from containers of different sizes. Each container has a different point value.

Equipment: Ball; 5–7 containers of different sizes; tossing line

Objective: The player tries to toss the ball into the containers while standing behind the line.

Ireland is the second largest island of the British Isles. Ireland has 32 counties, 6 of which are in Northern Ireland which is part of the United Kingdom of Great Britain.

Directions: The first player stands behind the tossing line and tosses the ball at the containers. The player is awarded the number of points assigned to the container in which the ball drops. The winner is the first player to reach a predetermined number of points.

Also See: *Pebble Toss* (7-18)

Magura (7-19)

Button Toss (7-22)

Hole Ball (7-23)

Haba Gaba (7-27)

7-27. Haba Gaba

Country: Sierra Leone (Africa)

Type of Game: Toss at Target (Translation of "Haba Gaba" is "Tossing Target.")

Formation: A target board set at a 45-degree angle is placed 10 feet from a tossing line. Players stand behind the tossing line in order of their turns.

Equipment: Target board with holes measuring 2, 3, and 4 inches in diameter; beanbags; tossing line

Objective: The player tries to toss the beanbags through the holes in the target.

Plywood targets with cut-out holes make good targets. These may be painted with faces or scenes using the holes for eyes or mouths on the faces. Each hole may be given a different point value.

Directions: Standing behind the tossing line, the player tosses the beanbag at the target. If the beanbag goes through a hole in the target, the player is awarded the designated points. Players take turns retrieving the beanbags, keeping score, and tossing.

After all players have had 8–10 turns, the scores are added; this is one inning. At the end of three innings, the player with the highest total of all innings combined is the winner.

Variation: The players toss more than one beanbag during each turn.

Also See: *Pebble Toss* (7-18)

Magura (7-19)

Button Toss (7-22)

Hole Ball (7-23)

Pitch Ball (7-26)

7-28. Goose Feather Throwing Game

Country: (Africa)

Type of Game: Toss at Target

Formation: A pebble marking a throwing line is placed a reasonable distance from a tree (the target). The feathers are placed to form a circle in front of the pebble.

Equipment: 1 feather for each player; pebble; tree

Objective: The player stands behind the pebble and tries to throw the feather at a marker on the tree.

The Nile River is the world's longest river at 4,187 miles in length.

Directions: While standing behind the pebble, the player picks up a feather from the circle and throws it at a marker on the tree. The winner is the feather closest to the tree. Points are awarded for each feather that hits the tree. The player with the highest number of points after a predetermined number of throws is the winner.

Also See: *Hit the Tree (7-29)*

7-29. Hit the Tree

Country: Native Americans, United States (North America)

Type of Game: Toss at Target

Formation: Players stand 5–10 feet from a tree.

Equipment: Tree; tennis ball; throw line

Objective: The player tries to hit the tree with the ball.

Many times Native Americans would go hunting for small animals using only rocks as weapons. Good aim was necessary for survival!

Directions: Standing at the throw line, the players—one at a time—throw a tennis ball to try to hit the tree. One point is scored for each hit.

Variation: Tie two pieces of bright colored yarn or ribbon around the tree 15 inches apart. If the ball hits the tree between these markers, two points are scored. If the tree is hit above or below these marks, one point is scored.

7-30. Pine Cone Toss

Country: Native Americans, United States (North America)

Type of Game: Toss at Target

Formation: Players stand 15–20 feet from a suspended circle.

Equipment: 3 pine cones; circle made of long weeds/grasses wrapped or interwoven; throw line

Objective: The player tries to throw the pine cones through the suspended circle.

Some Native Americans would wash and dry corncobs to throw through the circle.

Directions: Standing at a designated distance from the target, the thrower is awarded one point for each pine cone she/he can throw through the circle.

7-31. Hook the Driftwood Stick

Country: Greece (Europe)

Type of Game: Toss at Target

Formation: Players stand at a tossing line holding a tin can attached to a long string/cord. Sticks are spread in the playing area away from the players.

Equipment: Sticks; tin cans attached to string/cord; playing area

Objective: The player tries to bring the sticks back using the tin can and string.

Greece is not only a peninsula that stretches into the Mediterranean Sea, but also consists of 2,000 islands. With a coastline of 9,385 miles, this game is often played on Greece's many sandy beaches.

Directions: Standing a few yards from the sticks, the player tosses the tin can beyond the sticks. The player uses the string to pull the can back, trying to drag a stick along with it.

Variation: Use plastic fish and shells instead of sticks.

7-32. Hoopla Stalls

Country: Great Britain (Europe)

Type of Game: Toss at Target

Formation: Players stand several feet from targets (prizes). (Prizes should be fastened down to prevent them from being knocked over.)

Equipment: Hoops; prizes; tossing line

Objective: The player tries to toss the hoop over a prize.

English traveling fairs have booths that players try to toss a rubber ring over a prize to win.

Directions: Standing behind a tossing line, the player tries to toss a ring over a prize. The player wins the prize that the ring lands over.

7-33. Throwing Sticks

Country: Sioux Native Americans, United States (North America)

Type of Game: Throw at Target

Formation: Each player stands on a toss line holding a long stick.

Equipment: Long straight sticks (javelin); tossing line; playing area

Objective: The player tries to throw the highest or farthest.

Early hunters needed the ability to throw a spear-like stick long and high when hunting for food. To develop their skills, the Sioux Indians of North America would throw their sticks for distance. Played in the winter snows, the players would throw their sticks as far as they could and allow them to slide on top of the snow for greater distances.

The game was also played by the Tuaregs, nomadic Arabs in North Africa, who would throw their sticks high into the air. To measure how long each stick was in flight, the Tuaregs would jump up and down as many times as they could until the stick landed. The player with the greatest number of jumps was the winner.

Directions: Each player has a turn to throw her/his stick into the playing area. The player who throws the stick farthest (or highest) is the winner.

Variation: Add feathers to the stick to increase accuracy, as the Sioux did.

Safety: Be sure no one is standing in the field when sticks are thrown.

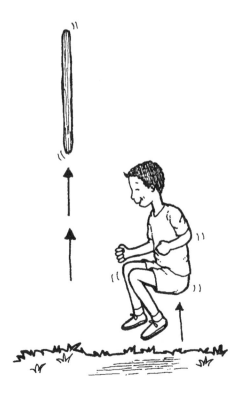

7-34. Ang-Konnh

Country: Cambodia (Far East, Asia)

Type of Game: Toss at Target

Formation: Players stand 6 feet from the target. The target is 5 large stones set in a semicircle.

Equipment: Throwing line; 5 stones per player; 5 larger stones for targets

Objective: The player tries to hit as many stones as possible on each turn.

This game is often played in Cambodia during the celebrations on New Year's Day.

Directions: Standing behind the throwing line, each player in turn tries to hit each target stone with her/his throwing stone. The *first* target stone is hit throwing right-handed. The *second* target stone is hit throwing left-handed. The *third* target stone is hit by throwing the stone under the right leg. The *fourth* stone is thrown under the left leg. The *fifth and final* target stone is hit by a throw made over the left shoulder with the right hand, or over the right shoulder with the left hand.

When a player misses, the next player takes her/his turn. On the *second round*, after all players have missed a target stone, players begin throwing again at the stone and in the manner that they missed the turn before.

7-35. Chuck Stones

Country: China (Far East, Asia)

Type of Game: Throw at Target

Formation: Players stand behind a throwing line. Three (or more) piles of stones are lined up 7–10 feet from the throwing line.

Equipment: 3 or more piles of stones; throwing stone for each player; throwing line

Objective: The player names a pile and tries to hit that pile with the throwing stone.

With borders on the Yellow, East China, and South China Seas, China's total coastline measures about 7,500 miles. China also shares land borders with 14 other countries: North Korea, Russia, Kazakhstan, Kyrgyzstan, Tajikistan, Mongolia, Afghanistan, India, Pakistan, Nepal, Bhutan, Myanmar (formerly Burma), Laos, and Vietnam.

Directions: Standing behind the throwing line, the players must identify which pile of stones she/he will throw to hit. If the player hits the called target and knocks a rock off the pile, she/he gets to keep the stone and has another turn. The player keeps throwing until she/he misses the target. As the piles dwindle, the odd stones remain where they are and continue as the targets.

The winner is the player having the most stones collected at the end.

Also See: *Hit the Stones* (7-36)

7-36. Hit the Stones

Country: Portugal (Europe)

Type of Game: Toss at Target

Formation: Nine large flat rocks are set in three rows of three. One small round stone is set on each flat rock. The player stands 12 feet from the closest set of rocks.

Equipment: 9 flat rocks; 9 round stones; 9 throwing stones; throwing line

Objective: The player tries to knock off as many round stones as possible from the tops of the flat rocks.

Located at the extreme southwest tip of Europe, Portugal's only land border is with Spain. Portugal is 36,390 square miles in size, slightly smaller than the state of Indiana.

Directions: Each player in turn has nine throws to try to knock as many round stones off the flat rocks. One point is scored for each rock knocked off. After all players have thrown, the player with the highest number of rocks knocked off wins.

Also See: *Chuck Stone* (7-35)

Nekki (7-39)

Sticks and Stones (7-40)

Sticks (7-41)

7-37. Salazar's Obelisks

Country: Mexico (North America)

Type of Game: Toss at Target

Formation: Pins are set in two parallel lines with a single pin set in front towards the tossing line. (See Illustration 1.) Players stand behind a tossing line 10 feet away.

Equipment: 9–13 pins; tossing line; beanbag

Objective: The player tries to knock down the pins with the beanbag.

Mexico, known officially as the United Mexican States, has 31 states and a Federal District—the capital city of Mexico City. Spain—where this game is also played—is divided into 17 geographic and historic regions corresponding to the old Christian and Moorish kingdoms of Spain.

Directions: The players stand behind the throwing line and throw the beanbag, knocking down as many pins as possible. The lone front pin is worth double points if knocked down because it can only be knocked down by a beanbag and not by other falling pins.

Variation: Each pin is worth one point when knocked down. When the head pin is knocked down, the player's score is doubled on that throw.

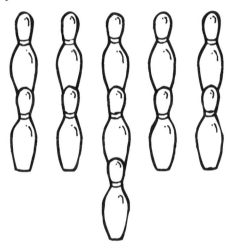

Tossing Line

Illustration 1: *Salazar's Obelisks*

Also See: *Kukla* (7-38)

Nekki (7-39)

Sticks and Stones (7-40)

Sticks (7-41)

7-38. Kukla

Country: Turkey (Middle East, Asia)

Type of Game: Toss at Target

Formation: Players stand behind a throwing line 10–15 feet from a 1-foot diameter circle. A can, pin, or milk carton is placed in the center of the circle. One player is Guard and stands near the circle.

Equipment: 1 beanbag per player; 1 can, pin, or milk carton; circle; throw line

Objective: The player tries to throw the beanbag and knock the can out of the circle.

Children in the Philippine Islands play the same game, named Presohan. *Instead of using beanbags, however, the Philippine children throw cans at the pin.*

Directions: Players stand behind the throwing line and throw the beanbag at the can one at a time. Beanbags are left where they land until the can is knocked down and hopefully out of the circle. When the can is knocked down, players quickly run to grab her/his beanbag and return to the throwing line. As the throwing players retrieve their beanbags, the Guard quickly replaces the can in the circle before trying to tag any player returning to the throwing line. A player tagged becomes the new Guard.

Also See: *Salazar's Obelisks* (7-37)

            Nekki (7-39)

            Sticks and Stones (7-40)

7-39. Nekki

Country: Japan (Far East, Asia)

Type of Game: Toss at Target

Formation: A 12-inch long stick is stuck in the ground so that most of the stick is above ground. Players stand behind a throwing line with a throwing stick.

Equipment: 1 long stick; 1 short stick for each player; throw line

Objective: The player tries to throw her/his stick to knock down the longer stick.

The Nekki *is the pole that supports decorations for Japanese New Year's celebrations.*

Directions: Standing behind a throwing line, one player at a time throws the smaller stick at the upright stick in an attempt to knock it down. The first player to completely knock down the tall stick wins.

Variation: Separate players into teams and see how long it takes each team to knock down the *nekki* stick. All can throw at the same time, or see how many throws a team needs before the *nekki* falls.

Also See: *Sticks and Stones* (7-40)

Sticks (7-41)

7-40. Sticks and Stones

Country: Caribbean Islands

Type of Game: Toss at Target

Formation: Two sticks are stuck in a sandbox to remain vertical. Each player has two stones and stand on a tossing line.

Equipment: 2 sticks; 2 stones for each player; sandbox; tossing line

Objective: The player tries to knock down the sticks with the stones.

Great Britain, France, the Netherlands, and Denmark established colonies on the eastern islands, although Spain controlled the Caribbean Sea.

Directions: Standing a fair distance from the sticks at a tossing line, each player in turn throws her/his stones at the sticks. Each stick a player knocks over is worth one point. Players keep taking turns until one player scores 10 points.

Variation: Use cans instead of sticks.

Also See: *Chuck Stone* (7-35)

   Hit the Stones (7-36)

   Salazar's Obelisks (7-37)

   Kukla (7-38)

   Nekki (7-39)

   Sticks (7-41)

7-41. Sticks

Country: Pakistan (Asia)

Type of Game: Toss at Target

Formation: Six 1-foot long sticks are stuck vertical inside a circle. Players stand behind a throwing line 10–15 feet away.

Equipment: 6 1-foot sticks; circle; throwing line; 2 balls

Objective: The player tries to knock down the sticks with the balls.

On August 14, 1947, Pakistan gained its independence from British rule and was divided into two sections—West Pakistan and East Pakistan. The two areas were nearly 1,000 miles apart on opposite sides of India! On August 15, 1947, India gained its independence from British rule. On March 26, 1971, the western part of Pakistan gained its independence and became the country of Bangladesh.

Directions: Each player in turn has two balls to throw at the sticks. Throwing one ball at a time, five points are awarded for each stick a player knocks out of the circle. Knocked-down sticks are replaced for the next player. The winner is the player with the most points.

Also See: *Chuck Stone (7-35)*

Hit the Stone (7-36)

Salizar's Obelisks (7-37)

Kukla (7-38)

Nekki (7-39)

Sticks and Stones (7-40)

7-42. Mulambilwa

Country: Nigeria (Africa)

Type of Game: Toss at Target—Teams

Formation: Two teams stand on opposite sides of a center line. Sticks are stuck in the dirt vertically. Each player sits or kneels near her/his stick. The goal line is 20 feet behind each team.

Equipment: 1 stick for each player; 1 ball for each player; center line; goal lines

Objective: Each team tries to knock down an opponent's stick with the ball.

In Nigeria, corncobs are stuck vertically in the dirt instead of sticks.

Directions: On the signal "Go!" players roll or throw their balls at the other team's sticks while sitting or kneeling. As balls miss their targets, players get up to retrieve a ball, but they must sit or kneel before throwing/rolling the ball.

When all of one team's sticks are knocked down, all players get up and the team with all sticks down is chased to the goal line behind them. Any players caught "pay a penalty" of some sort of activity to be done or go to the other team.

Safety: Players must move carefully around the sticks when retrieving the balls. Players must also be careful not to hit any other players when throwing the balls.

7-43. Tapu-Ae

Country: New Zealand (Oceania)

Type of Game: Toss at Target—Teams

Formation: Form two teams of 12 players each. Each team has one Guard, two Rovers, three Centers, and six Shooters. (See Illustration 1 for set up.) One Center from each team starts with the ball.

Equipment: 1 pin per team; center line; 2 Rover lines; large shooting circle; smaller circle for Guard and pin; 2 balls

Objective: Each team tries to knock down the other team's pin.

The natives of New Zealand call themselves "Kiwis" due to the large amount of kiwi fruit grown and exported.

Directions: On the signal "Go!" the Centers try to pass the ball to one of their team's Shooters. Only the Shooters can attempt to knock down the other team's pin. The Guards block the pin from the ball. When a Guard intercepts the ball, it is thrown to one of her/his Center players. The Centers throw the ball across the center line to a Rover and then to a Shooter. Rovers attempt to block the ball from being passed to the Centers from the Guard.

Both balls may be in the same circle at one time. At all times players need to stay in their assigned playing areas. When a player has a ball, she/he is not allowed to move with it unless in the throwing motion. Players have only 5–7 seconds before having to get rid of the ball. The ball goes to the other team any time a player breaks a rule.

Each time a pin is knocked down, one point is scored. The team reaching 11 points first wins the game.

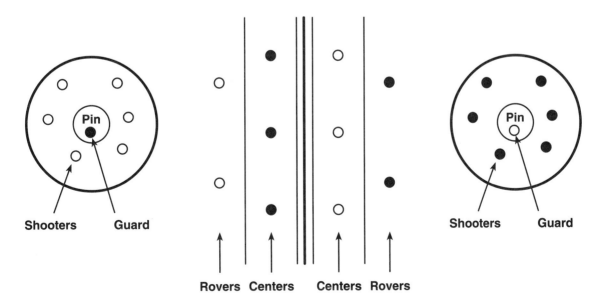

Illustration 1: *Tapu-Ae*

7-44. Spearing the Disk

Country: Ethiopia (Africa)

Type of Game: Throw at Target

Formation: Players stand side by side on a line. One player stands in front and at one end of the line holding a hula hoop.

Equipment: 1 stick or ball for each thrower; 1 hula hoop

Objective: The player tries to throw the ball through the hula hoop.

This game helps Ethiopians to develop hunting skills with a spear.

Directions: The leader with the hula hoop rolls it in front of the line of players. As the hula hoop passes in front, each player throws her/his ball to try to have it go through the hula hoop target as it moves. If the ball passes through, that player remains. If the ball misses the hula hoop, the player is eliminated. The leader continues to roll the hula hoop until only one player remains.

7-45. Monkey in the Middle

Country: United States (North America)

Type of Game: Toss and Catch—Keep Away

Formation: Players are grouped in threes, with one player standing between the other two.

Equipment: Ball

Objective: Two players stand 15–20 feet apart while passing the ball back and forth teasingly, trying to keep it away from the third player standing in the middle.

This keep-away game is a good beginning for partners to try to make good passes to one another, while a third player is in the center trying to take the ball away. Good passes are essential.

Directions: The outside players pass the ball back and forth while the Monkey (player in the middle) tries to intercept the ball. If a passer drops the ball, a scramble for the ball goes on between that player and the Monkey to see who will get the ball first. If the Monkey gets the ball, she/he becomes the new passer. If the passer retrieves the ball first, she/he remains the passer.

Passes between the end players should be so the Monkey has a chance to intercept the ball. For groups that the Monkey cannot get the ball, a limit of passes may be needed to change places before the center player gets frustrated and quits.

Variation: If the pass is not caught by the other end player and is not touched by the center player, then the passer goes to the middle.

7-46. Tiger's Ball

Country: Israel (Middle East, Asia)

Type of Game: Toss and Catch—Keep Away

Formation: Two teams form separate circles. One player from each team is in the center of the other team's circle.

Equipment: 1 ball for each circle

Objective: The circle players try to pass the ball to other circle players, while trying to keep it away from the opponent in the center.

Directions: Circle players pass the ball to one another, trying to keep it away from the opponent in the center. Different types of passes may be used—bounce pass, chest pass—but the ball must always be passed so the center player has a chance to intercept it if moving to the right place at the right time.

When one center player does intercept the ball before the center player in the other circle, one point is scored for her/his team. New center players are chosen from each circle to go to the other team's circle for another round.

When all players from both teams have been in the center of the other circle, the team with the higher amount of interceptions wins.

7-47. Pass Ball

Country: Great Britain (Europe)

Type of Game: Toss and Catch—Keep Away

Formation: Two teams are scattered and mixed up.

Equipment: 1 ball

Objective: Each team tries to make three consecutive passes without an interception by the other team or dropping the ball.

Careful passing to teammates is necessary for success in this game. The passer needs to watch where she/he is passing the ball, making sure her/his teammate is ready and a player from the other team is not ready to intercept the ball when passed.

Directions: Three consecutive successful passes are needed to score a point in *Pass Ball*. Players with the ball are not allowed to move her/his feet. Once a team scores, the ball is started again by the other team. A score of 10 points by one team constitutes a win for that team.

Variations:

- Players might have to perform a certain type of pass. A basketball bounce pass requires the passer to have the ball bounce once on the floor between the passer and the intended catcher.

- Players may play on scooters. Moving only when not having the ball, players try to get into position to receive the ball or intercept the ball if passed to a player from the other team near where she/he is at the time.

7-48. Keep Away

Country: United States (North America)

Type of Game: Toss and Catch—Keep Away

Formation: Two teams stand on opposite parallel lines. The ball is placed in the center of the playing area between the lines.

Equipment: Parallel lines; 1 ball

Objective: The player tries to pass the ball to one's own team, keeping it away from the other team.

Many games and sports that use equipment involve taking possession of that equipment from an opposing team or player. Basketball, football, soccer, hockey, and lacrosse are examples in which specific plans are practiced so one team is able to keep the ball away from the other.

Directions: On the signal "Go!" both teams run to the ball to try to pick it up first. When a team has the ball, it is kept away from the other team by passing it from player to player. A player with the ball is not allowed to walk or run with the ball, but may move one foot leaving the other in one place (basketball pivot).

Successful passes to a teammate count one point each. Players from the other team may not try to hit the ball or take the ball out of an opponent's hands. They may try to intercept a pass when the ball is in the air. If a pass is dropped or falls to the ground, either team may get the ball and begin counting the passes. A missed pass retrieved by the passing team begins at zero again when counting the number of passes.

At the end of the playing time, the team having the higher number of consecutive passes wins.

7-49. Mat Ball

Country: Great Britain (Europe)

Type of Game: Toss and Catch—Keep Away

Formation: Team goals (mats) are placed at opposite ends of the playing area. Players begin standing on their team's mat.

Equipment: 2 mats; 1 ball

Objective: The player tries to gain possession of the ball and pass it to teammates in order to pass the ball to the teammate standing on the other team's mat.

Directions: On the signal "Go!" the player chosen to be on the opponent's goal (mat) runs from her/his own mat to the mat at the opposite end of the playing area. At the same time, the leader of the activity tosses the ball into the air in the center of the playing area. Players from both teams run out to try to be the first to control the ball.

    The team with the ball passes it to other teammates in an effort to get the ball in position to throw it to the teammate standing on the opponent's mat. Players on the other team try to gain possession of the ball so they can try to do the same.

Variation: Instead of tossing the ball in the center of the playing area and having players from both teams run to the ball, begin the activity with a basketball-style jump ball. Players from both teams stand around the center of the area where the leader tosses the ball straight up into the air above the heads and reach of one player from each team. These two players jump up and have to try to tap or hit the ball to a teammate for control. These center players may not catch or grab the ball off the toss of the leader.

Illustration 1: *Mat Ball*

7-50. Skyros

Country: Greece (Europe)

Type of Game: Toss and Catch—Keep Away

Formation: Two parallel lines are 75 feet apart with a third parallel line marking the center. The ball is placed on the center line. Teams stand behind opposite parallel lines. (See Illustration 1.)

Equipment: 3 parallel lines; 1 ball

Objective: The players try to gain possession of the ball and pass to teammates behind the goal line of the other team.

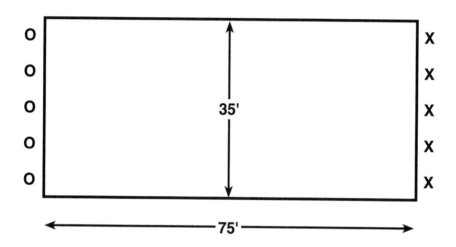

Illustration 1: *Skyros*

Directions: On the signal "Go!" both teams rush out in an effort to gain control of the ball. Once a team has control of the ball, it is passed from teammate to teammate working it towards the other team's goal line. Players without the ball go behind the line in anticipation of receiving the passed ball for a score. The ball must be passed for a score from the playing field to a player behind the goal line. If successful, one point is scored and play begins in the center again. If the ball falls to the floor, the other team gains possession at its goal line.

Safety: Players without the ball may not touch or push an opponent, or try to grab the ball out of an opponent's hands.

Section 8
Tag

Tag is probably the oldest type of game in the world. You can trace it back to prehistoric times by watching the young babies of predators play. If you watch baby lions, tigers, or household cats play, you will see them chasing each other and trying to catch their siblings. Once they are close enough, they will use a front paw to swat the other. They are learning how to hunt through a game of chase and touch—*Tag*.

The following games of *Tag* are arranged so that those played similarly are together in a sequence of easiest to hardest. Games having the same name from the same country are listed on different pages due to a difference in how they are set up. Some may be played arranged in a single circle, others in a double circle, and so on.

In this section you'll find 81 games of *Tag* from 41 countries and 8 continents/regions.

Africa

A Fishing (8-65)—Ghana

Abumbutan (Falling Stick) (8-42)—Nigeria

Beware the Antelope (8-47)—Congo

Boa Constrictor (8-64)—Ghana/Togo

Cat and Lynx (8-24)—Kalahari Desert in Botswana

Catch Your Tail (8-80)—Nigeria

Catching Stars/Gathering Stars (8-53)—(Pygmy Tribes) Gabon

Cho-Cho Chuckie (8-4)—Benin

Four Chiefs (8-68)—Nigeria

Hurley Burley (8-74)—Uganda

Poison (8-13)—Zimbabwe

Asia

Atya–Patya (Lines) (8-49)—India

The Bear (8-63)—Russia

Bell in the Steeple (8-50)—Russia

Eagle and Chickens (8-60)—Asia

Getta–Chutt (The King Ran Away) (8-72)—India

Goellki (8-29)—Russia

Gorelki (8-30)—Russia

Go–Tag (8-18)—India/Pakistan

Kabaddi (8-36)—India

Kho-Kho (8-38)—India

Ribaki (Fishermen) (8-79)—Russia

Saldu (8-69)—India

Australia

A Gecko and a Stag Beetle (8-71)—Australia

Tails (8-78)—Australia

Caribbean Islands

El Gato y El Ratan (The Cat and the Mouse) (8-9)—Puerto Rico

Central America (North America)

El Gavilan, La Coneja, y Los Conejos (The Hawk and the Rabbits) (8-58)—El Salvador

Europe

Capture the Flag (8-77)—England/Scotland

Catch Old Mother Winter and Throw Her in the River (8-70)—former Czechoslovakia

Drei-Mann Hock (Three-Man Deep) (8-16)—Switzerland

King Caesar (8-48)—Italy

Last Couple in the Middle (8-56)—England/Scotland

North Wind and South Wind (8-45)—Sweden

Pebble Tag (8-43)—Greece

Spain (8-22)—Spain

Europe *(continued)*

What's the Time, Mr. Wolf? (8-34)—Great Britain

The Wild Goat Chase (8-7)—Europe

Far East (Asia)

Badger and Sun (8-26)—Ancient Japan

Catching Fish in the Dark (8-40)—China

Chase the Dragon's Tail (8-62)—China

Great Wall of China (8-54)—China

Hawk and Dove (8-19)—China

Leak Kanseng (Hiding the Handkerchief) (8-5)—Cambodia

Loo K' Ba Zee (Tap the Ball) (8-6)—Myanmar (formerly Burma)

Touch-Pole Tag (8-39)—Philippines

Water Sprite (8-33)—China

Middle East (Africa/Asia)

Cat and Mouse (8-10)—Iran (Asia)

Cat and Mouse (8-15)—Iran (Asia)

Don-don Ba Ji (Hyena and Sheep) (8-8)—Sudan

Wolf! Wolf! (8-31)—Egypt (Africa)

North America

Barley Break (8-75)—Colonial America

Baste the Bear (8-44)—Colonial America

Blackberry (8-51)—Canada/United States

Breath-Hold Tag (8-37)—Northwest Coast Native Americans

Cat After Rat (8-2)—Colonial America

Drop the Handkerchief (8-3)—Colonial America

Duck, Duck, Goose (8-1)—Colonial America

Elbow Tag (8-21)—Colonial America

Fish Trap (8-66)—Northwest Coast Native Americans

Fox and Geese (8-32)—Canada

Hook-on Tag (8-61)—Colonial America

January (8-52)—Canada

Lame Fox and Chickens (8-46)—Colonial America

New Orleans (8-67)—United States

Prisoner's Base (8-73)—Colonial America

Puss in the Corner (8-35)—Colonial America

Rabbit (8-20)—Colonial America

Red Lion (8-55)—United States

Spot Tag (8-28)—Mexico

Steal the Bacon (8-23)—United States

Stealing Sticks (8-76)—Choctaw Native Americans

Tierce (8-14)—Colonial America

Touch Iron, Touch Wood, Feet Off Ground (8-27)—Colonial America

Twin Tag (8-57)—Native Americans

Western Round-up (8-81)—United States

Wolf's Tail (8-59)—Colonial America

South America

Cat and Rat (8-12)—Brazil

Squirrel Up a Tree (8-11)—Uruguay

Squirrel Up a Tree (8-17)—Uruguay

Tying the Sun to the Hitching Post (8-25)—Ancient Peru

Worldwide

Blind Man's Bluff (8-41)—Worldwide

One Tagger-One Runner

The following 26 games of *Tag* have at least one Tagger (IT) who is chasing at least one Runner. The formations of the activity area and other players change from single circles to double circles to parallel lines; from partners working together to players scattered throughout the play area to teams—but there is always at least one IT chasing at least one Runner in each game.

8-1. Duck, Duck, Goose

Country: Colonial America (North America)

Type of Game: Tag—One Tagger/One Runner

Formation: Players sit in a single circle with the Fox standing outside.

Equipment: None

Objective: The Fox tries to run around the circle before being tagged by the Goose.

Young children love this activity because it's an early challenge to chasing another student in a game. This game came to the Colonies from Great Britain. Its origin is lost, but the fun of the activity has survived for centuries.

Directions: All students sit in a circle, with arm's length space between neighbors, facing towards the center. One child is chosen to be the Fox. The Fox walks around the outside of the circle, tapping (respectfully) each child on the head or shoulder and saying either "Duck" or "Goose."

When a child is touched and "Duck" is called, that child remains seated. But when a child is touched and "Goose" is called, that child quickly stands up and chases the Fox around the circle in an attempt to tag the Fox before the Fox can run around the circle and sit in the Goose's place in the circle.

If the Goose tags the Fox, the Fox remains seated as part of the circle.

If the Fox is able to run around the circle and sit in the Goose's place, the Fox remains the Fox for the next turn.

Adaptation: If the competition between tagging and not being tagged is too great for some players to accept, change the game so that the Goose becomes the next Fox regardless if the tag is made or not.

Also See: *Cat After Rat* (8-2)

Drop the Handkerchief (8-3)

Cho-Cho Chuckie (8-4)

Leak Kanseng (8-5)

Loo K' Ba Zee (8-6)

8-2. Cat After Rat

Country: Colonial America (North America)

Type of Game: Tag—One Tagger/One Runner

Formation: Players sit in a single circle with the Rat standing outside.

Equipment: None

Objective: The Rat tries to run around the circle before being tagged by the Cat.

This game was brought over from England by the new colonists. It is similar to Duck, Duck, Goose *with the addition of a rhyme to chant.*

Directions: Players sit in a circle facing the center, with the Rat standing outside the circle. The Rat walks around the circle reciting the following rhyme:

> *"I wrote a letter to my love, and on the way I dropped it.*
>
> *A little cat picked it up and put it in his pocket.*
>
> *It isn't you, it isn't you [repeat several times] …It is you!"*

On the call "It is you!" the Rat touches a circle player on the shoulder as a signal to become the Cat who chases the Rat. The two run around the circle with the Cat trying to touch the Rat before she/he can reach the vacated spot on the circle. The Rat may run in and out through the circle (but not across the circle) to avoid being tagged by the Cat.

If the Rat reaches the vacated spot in the circle without being tagged, the Cat is the new Rat for the next game. If a tag is made, the Cat returns to the circle and the Rat remains the Rat for another turn.

Also See: *Duck, Duck, Goose* (8-1)

Drop the Handkerchief (8-3)

Cho-Cho Chuckie (8-4)

Leak Kanseng (8-5)

Loo K' Ba Zee (8-6)

8-3. Drop the Handkerchief

Country: Colonial America (North America)

Type of Game: Tag—One Runner/One Tagger

Formation: Players sit in a single circle with IT standing outside holding a piece of cloth.

Equipment: 1 handkerchief or piece of cloth

Objective: IT tries to run around the circle before being tagged.

Children of wealth used handkerchiefs to play this game similar to Duck, Duck, Goose.

Directions: Players sit in a circle facing the center. IT stands outside with a handkerchief. As IT walks around the circle, all the other children chant or sing:

> *"A tisket, a tasket,*
>
> *A green and yellow basket.*
>
> *I wrote a letter to my love*
>
> *And along the way I lost it."*

Some time during the chant IT drops the handkerchief behind one of the circle players without making it obvious who it is behind.

At the end of the reciting, all the children quickly check behind themselves to see if they had been chosen to chase IT. Whoever finds the handkerchief behind her-/himself, picks it up and chases IT around the circle. IT tries to avoid being tagged before sitting in the vacated seat.

Because IT may not be near the handkerchief when it is found at the end of the chant, the player with the handkerchief needs to quickly decide in which direction to run to try to tag IT before she/he sits in the vacated spot.

If a tag is made, the handkerchief carrier becomes the new IT. If no tag is made, IT has another turn.

Adaptation: If the competitive level of the players is too high for fair play, the handkerchief carrier becomes the new IT for the next game whether IT is tagged or not.

Also See: *Duck, Duck, Goose* (8-1)

               Cat After Rat (8-2)

               Cho-Cho Chuckie (8-4)

               Leak Kanseng (8-5)

               Loo K' Ba Zee (8-6)

8-4. Cho-Cho Chuckie

Country: Benin (Africa)

Type of Game: Tag—One Runner/One Tagger

Formation: Players sit in a single circle with IT standing outside holding a handkerchief or other object.

Equipment: 1 handkerchief or other marker

Objective: IT tries to run around the circle before being tagged.

Benin, Africa at one time was a French colony. The economy is largely agricultural with the labor force engaged in subsistence farming. Found in Western Africa, Benin is on the coast of the Gulf of Guinea and is bordered by Nigeria, Niger, Burkina Faso, and Togo. Only 43,500 square miles in size, Benin is slightly smaller than the state of Pennsylvania.

Directions: Players sit in a circle facing the center. IT stands outside with a handkerchief or other marker (rag, piece of cloth, something that will lie flat and not roll). As IT walks around the circle, she/he calls out "Cho-Cho Chuckie" as if calling chickens. It is during these calls that the marker is dropped behind the back of a circle player.

The circle player must quickly pick up the marker and chase IT around the circle, trying to tag IT before IT can fill the vacated place in the circle.

If safe, IT now must stand on one foot holding the other foot in one hand. The new player with the marker is the new IT and the game continues.

During the game the players who have had their turn to run must remain standing on one foot, but are allowed to switch feet often. If IT catches any player standing on both feet and calls out her/his name, that circle player becomes the new IT.

When all circle players are standing on one foot, IT calls out "It's raining!" and the circle players raise one hand as if holding an umbrella and run away from IT who chases them to tag a new IT for the next game.

Also See: *Duck, Duck, Goose* (8-1)

Cat After Rat (8-2)

Drop the Handkerchief (8-3)

Leak Kanseng (8-5)

Loo K' Ba Zee (8-6)

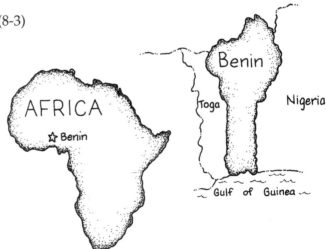

8-5. Leak Kanseng
(Hiding the Handkerchief)

Country: Cambodia (Far East, Asia)

Type of Game: Tag—One Runner/One Tagger

Formation: Players sit in a single circle with IT standing outside.

Equipment: 1 knotted handkerchief

Objective: IT tries to run around the circle before being tagged.

Situated on the coastline of the Gulf of Thailand, Cambodia is a neighbor with Vietnam, Laos, and Thailand. Once part of French-controlled Indochina, Cambodia became independent in 1953. Cambodia is 70,238 square miles in size, roughly the size of the state of Missouri.

Directions: Players sit in a single circle facing the center. IT begins outside the circle carrying a knotted handkerchief. As IT walks around the circle, the handkerchief is dropped behind a circle player and IT begins to run around the circle. If a complete circle is made before the circle player notices the rag is behind her/him, and IT can tag that player on the shoulder, IT remains for another turn.

If the circle player notices the handkerchief is behind her/him, that player picks up the handkerchief and chases IT around the circle trying to tag IT with the cloth. If IT reaches the vacated circle spot before being tagged, IT has another turn. If IT is tagged, the circle player is the new IT for the next game.

Also See: *Duck, Duck, Goose* (8-1)

Cat After Rat (8-2)

Drop the Handkerchief (8-3)

Cho-Cho Chuckie (8-4)

Loo K' Ba Zee (8-6)

8-6. Loo K' Ba Zee (Tap the Ball)

Country: Myanmar (formerly Burma) (Far East, Asia)

Type of Game: Tag—One Runner/Two Taggers

Formation: Players stand in a single circle with IT standing outside holding a small ball or beanbag.

Equipment: 1 small ball or beanbag

Objective: Two players in the circle try to tag the one with the ball.

Burma, called Myanmar since 1989, is part of the Southeast Asia's Indochina peninsula. With a coastline on the Bay of Bengal, Myanmar shares land boundaries with Bangladesh, India, China, Laos, and Thailand. Covering 261,228 square miles in size, Myanmar is almost the size of the state of Texas.

Directions: Players form a circle facing the center with hands placed behind their backs. IT walks around the outside of the circle, pretending to place a ball or beanbag in each player's hands. When the object is finally left in someone's hands, that player tries to leave the circle before her/his neighbors can tag her/him without leaving their places in the circle.

   If tagged, IT remains for another turn. If the circle player escapes before being tagged, she/he is the new IT.

Also See: *Duck, Duck, Goose* (8-1)

                  Cat After Rat (8-2)

                  Drop the Handkerchief (8-3)

                  Cho-Cho Chuckie (8-4)

8-7. The Wild Goat Chase

Country: (Europe)
Type of Game: Tag—Many Runners/One Tagger
Formation: Players stand in a single circle. The Wild Goat stands inside the circle.
Equipment: Playing area
Objective: The Goat tries to chase the players to tag one.

In many European countries, the terrain is such that goats are better suited than grazing cattle. Land is scarce and goats need less than cattle. Europe's landmass is 3,800,00 square miles, the second smallest continent.

Directions: The Goat is in the center of a circle made by the rest of the players. The Goat begins by pretending to be asleep as the circle players recite the following chant. The Goat does what the chant says:

> *"At one o'clock the Goat sleeps.*
>
> *At two o'clock the Goat sleeps.*
>
> *At three o'clock the Goat sleeps.*
>
> *At four o'clock the Goat sleeps.*
>
> *At five o'clock the Goat sleeps.*
>
> *At six o'clock the Goat sleeps.*
>
> *At seven o'clock the Goat wakes up.*
>
> *At eight o'clock the Goat yawns.*
>
> *At nine o'clock the Goat washes.*
>
> *At ten o'clock the Goat dresses.*
>
> *At eleven o'clock the Goat opens the door.*
>
> *At twelve o'clock the Goat runs."*

Once the players say "runs," the Goat begins to run after the circle players to try to catch one. The first player caught by the Goat becomes the new Goat for the next game.

8-8. Don-Don Ba Ji
(Hyena and Sheep)

Country: Sudan (Middle East, Africa)

Type of Game: Tag—One Runner/One Tagger

Formation: Players stand and hold hands to form a single circle. The Hyena stands outside the circle; the Sheep stands inside.

Equipment: None

Objective: The Hyena tries to catch the Sheep.

The Republic of the Sudan is located in northeastern Africa with a coastline on the Red Sea and boundaries with Egypt, Libya, Chad, Central African Republic, Zaire, Uganda, Kenya, and Ethiopia. Sudan is the largest single country in Africa—about 967,495 square miles, one-fourth the size of the United States.

Directions: Players form a circle holding hands with neighbors. One child is chosen to enter the circle as the Sheep. A second player is chosen to stand outside the circle as the Hyena.

Keeping the circle together by holding hands, the circle players move clockwise chanting:

"Don-don ba ji camelot.

Don-don ba ji camelot."

(*Don-don ba ji* means "Hyena" and "Sheep.")

The Hyena tries to enter the circle by going over, under, or (careful not to hurt anyone's arms) through the arms of the circle players to get to the Sheep. The Sheep must stay in the circle. If the Hyena is successful in entering the circle and tagging the Sheep, two new players are chosen to represent the Hyena and Sheep. If the Hyena is not successful, two new players are selected when time is called.

Also See: *El Gato y El Ratan* (8-9)

Cat and Mouse (8-10)

Cat and Rat (8-12)

Squirrel Up a Tree (8-17)

8-9. El Gato y El Ratan
(The Cat and the Mouse)

Country: Puerto Rico (Caribbean Islands)

Type of Game: Tag—One Runner/One Tagger

Formation: Players form a single circle. One player (Mouse) begins inside; a second player (Cat) begins outside.

Equipment: None

Objective: The Cat tries to catch the Mouse.

Puerto Rico was visited by Christopher Columbus on his second voyage in 1493 and claimed for Spain. Following Spain's defeat in the Spanish–American War, Puerto Rico became a territory to the United States. It became the Commonwealth of Puerto Rico in 1952.

Directions: All the players form a circle. Two players are chosen to leave the circle: One becomes the Mouse and stands inside the circle; the other is the Cat who begins outside. The circle players hold hands and try to keep the Cat away from the Mouse.

On the signal "Go!" the Cat runs around the circle, trying to find a way to get into the circle and to the Mouse. The Mouse may come close to the circle to tease the Cat but must be careful not to get too close.

If the Cat gets into the circle, the Mouse (with the help of the Mouse-friendly circle players) leaves the circle with the Cat left inside. If the Cat catches the Mouse, two new players from the circle are chosen to be the Mouse and Cat.

Also See: *Don-don Ba Ji* (8-8)

Cat and Mouse (8-10)

Squirrel Up a Tree (8-11)

Cat and Rat (8-12)

8-10. Cat and Mouse

Country: Iran (Middle East, Asia)

Type of Game: Tag—One Runner/One Tagger

Formation: Players stand in a circle with the Cat inside and the Mouse outside the circle.

Equipment: None

Objective: The Cat tries to catch the Mouse.

Iran is the second largest country in the Middle East and the most populated. Once known as Persia, the name of Iran was requested by the government in 1935. Located on the eastern shores of the Caspian Sea, Iran shares borders with Turkmenistan, Azerbaijan, Armenia, Turkey, Iraq, Afghanistan, and Pakistan. Iran is 632,457 square miles in size, slightly larger than the state of Alaska.

Directions: Players form a circle around the Cat without holding hands. The circle players try to prevent the Cat from leaving the circle.

The Mouse is outside the circle. On the signal "Go!" the Cat tries to escape from the circle and chase the Mouse in an effort to make a tag. If the Cat tags the Mouse, or after a predetermined amount of time, a new Cat and Mouse are chosen for the next game.

Also See: *Don-don Ba Ji (8-8)*

El Gato y El Ratan (8-9)

Squirrel Up a Tree (8-11)

Cat and Rat (8-12)

8-11. Squirrel Up a Tree

Country: Uruguay (South America)

Type of Game: Tag—One Runner/One Tagger

Formation: Players stand in a circle with the Cat inside and the Squirrel outside the circle.

Equipment: None

Objective: The Cat tries to catch the Squirrel.

The second smallest country in South America, Uruguay is found at the southern tip of Brazil on the Atlantic Coast. Argentina is Uruguay's western neighbor. Uruguay is 68,037 square miles in size, roughly the same size as the state of Washington.

Directions: Two players are chosen to leave the circle. One player is the Cat who begins the game inside the circle. The second player is the Squirrel who begins outside the circle. On the signal "Go!" the Cat attempts to escape from the circle to chase the Squirrel. The circle players may not hold hands or use their hands to prevent the Cat from leaving the circle, but do attempt to delay the Cat's escape. Once the Cat escapes the circle, the Cat chases the Squirrel around the circle and tries to tag her/him. Once the Squirrel is caught, or a time limit has expired, a new Cat and Squirrel are chosen for the next game.

Also See: *Don-don Ba Ji* (8-8)

El Gato y El Ratan (8-9)

Cat and Mouse (8-10)

Cat and Rat (8-12)

8-12. Cat and Rat

Country: Brazil (South America)

Type of Game: Tag—One Runner/One Tagger

Formation: Players form a single circle with the Rat inside the circle and the Cat outside.

Equipment: None

Objective: The Cat tries to catch the Rat.

The largest South American country at 3,286,470 square miles, Brazil is the fifth largest country in the world—larger than the continental United States! Brazil was first claimed by Portugal in 1500, even though Spanish explorer Vincente Pizon was the first to touch its northern shores. The name "Brazil" is derived from the Portuguese word for the reddish color of brazilwood that was exported during the sixteenth century. Brazil gained its independence from Portugal in 1822.

Directions: Players form a circle and clasp hands with their neighbors. One player is chosen to start inside the circle as the Rat, and a second player is chosen to begin outside the circle as the Cat.

The Cat taps a circle player on the shoulder. The following conversation happens between the player and the Cat:

PLAYER: *"What do you want?"*

CAT: *"I want to see the Rat."*

PLAYER: *"You cannot see her/him now."*

CAT: *"When may I see her/him?"*

PLAYER: *"At ten o'clock."* [or any other time called out]

The circle players begin to move clockwise in rhythm as they count off the hours by saying, "One o'clock, tick tock, two o'clock, tick tock, three o'clock, tick tock," counting until they reach the announced time. When the number reaches the announced time, the circle stops moving. The Cat comes up again to the same circle player as before and taps her/him on the shoulder.

PLAYER: *"What do you want?"*

CAT: *"I want to see the Rat."*

PLAYER: *"What time is it?"*

CAT: *"Ten o'clock."*

PLAYER: *"All right, come in."*

The circle players allow the Cat to enter the circle without any interference. The Rat escapes being caught by the Cat by leaving the circle. The Cat chases after the Rat, but this time the circle players interfere with the Cat by making it hard (but not impossible) to leave the circle. The Cat must escape the circle in order to chase the Rat. If the Cat catches the Rat, the Rat selects a new Cat and the former Cat becomes the new Rat.

Boundaries for running outside the circle and a time limit may be needed to keep the players close to the circle and keep the turns relatively equal between players.

Also See: *Don-don Ba Ji* (8-8)

El Gato y El Raton (8-9)

Cat and Mouse (8-10)

Squirrel Up a Tree (8-11)

8-13. Poison

Country: Zimbabwe (Africa)

Type of Game: Tag—One Runner/One Tagger

Formation: Players form a single circle with one player standing inside.

Equipment: 1 rag

Objective: The player tries to grab the rag and run outside the circle or to tag the runner who has the rag.

Zimbabwe is landlocked in the southern part of Africa. Formerly known as the British colony of Southern Rhodesia, Zimbabwe declared independence in 1965 as Zimbabwe Rhodesia and then as Zimbabwe in 1980. Zimbabwe shares borders with the countries of Zambia, Mozambique, South Africa, and Botswana. Only 150,872 square miles in size, Zimbabwe is slightly larger than the size of the state of Montana.

Directions: Players are given numbers as they stand in a circle. One player, the leader, begins in the center of the circle next to a rag. The center player calls a player's number who comes into the center of the circle. When both players are at the center of the circle, both try to grab the rag and run outside the circle of players.

The next leader is the player who can both grab the rag and run outside the circle without being tagged, or who tags the other player before she/he can run outside the circle with the rag. A new player's number is called and the game continues until all players have had a turn in the circle.

Also See: *Steal the Bacon* (8-23)

8-14. Tierce

Country: Colonial America (North America)

Type of Game: Tag—One Runner/One Tagger—Exchange

Formation: Players form a double circle with both the Runner and IT beginning outside the circle. The circle players spread out to allow the Runner and IT to pass between the players and through the circle.

Equipment: None

Objective: IT tries to tag the Runner.

Little time was available for play in the Colonies because everyone was expected to help with daily chores around the house. When there was a free moment or two, the children would get together and play simple games.

Directions: All but two players form a double circle. One of the two noncircle players is IT (tagger) and the other is the Runner.

On the signal "Go!" IT begins to chase the Runner in an effort to make a tag. The Runner runs around the circle or between the circle players in an effort to escape the tag by IT. IT follows the Runner or changes course from that of the Runner to try to catch her/him. The Runner may at any time, step in front of the inside circle player to form a group of three-deep. When this happens the outside circle player becomes the new Runner for IT to chase; the inner circle player moves to the outside circle; and the Runner takes the place in the inner circle.

When IT finally does tag a Runner, the Runner becomes IT and IT becomes the new Runner. IT may at any time also step in front of an inside circle player to have the outer circle player of the pair become the new IT to chase the Runner. The game continues until all players have a chance to be the Runner or IT or both.

Also See: *Cat and Mouse* (8-15)

Drei-Mann Hock (8-16)

Squirrel Up a Tree (8-17)

8-15. Cat and Mouse

Country: Iran (Middle East, Asia)

Type of Game: Tag—One Runner/One Tagger—Exchange

Formation: Players stand in a double circle with the Cat and the Mouse both outside the circle. Circle players are spread out to allow both runners to pass between and through the circle.

Equipment: None

Objective: The Cat tries to catch the Mouse.

Iran is the world's major exporter of oil with an output of over 3.5 million barrels per day! Iran controls navigation of the Persian Gulf, the Strait of Hormuz, and the Gulf of Oman.

Directions: In this version of *Cat and Mouse*, the circle players form two circles, one inside the other with the inside players standing in front of an outside circle player.

Circle players are spread out enough to allow the Cat and the Mouse to pass through the circle without running into players. As the Cat is chasing the Mouse, the Mouse can use the circle players as obstacles to block the Cat from making a tag. But when the Mouse is tired and needs a break, feels threatened of being tagged, or has been running for an adequate period of time, she/he may step in front of one of the inside circle players. The outside partner becomes the new Mouse for the Cat to chase. If the Cat cannot make a tag and has been running for a lengthy period of time, she/he may step in front of an inside circle player whose partner becomes the new Cat.

When there is a tag, the Cat is now the Mouse and the Mouse is the new Cat.

Also See: *Tierce* (8-14)

Drei-Mann Hock (8-16)

Squirrel Up a Tree (8-17)

8-16. Drei-Mann Hock
(Three-Man Deep)

Country: Switzerland (Europe)

Type of Game: Tag—One Runner/One Tagger—Exchange

Formation: Players stand in a double circle with IT and the Runner starting outside. Circle players are spread out to allow both runners to pass between and through the circle.

Equipment: None

Objective: IT tries to tag the runner.

Switzerland is a small landlocked country of west central Europe that borders France, Germany, Austria, Liechtenstein, and Italy. The surface area of Switzerland is 15,941 square miles, roughly the size of Massachusetts, Connecticut, and Rhode Island combined.

Switzerland is probably best known for its mountain ranges (the Alps), watch and clock making, chocolates, and Lake Geneva.

Directions: As in *Cat and Mouse*, players form a double circle with the inside circle players standing in front of the outside circle players. (Make sure enough space is between the circle players for IT and the Runner to pass safely.) One set of players leaves the circle to become IT and the Runner.

Keeping the play area limited to just outside the double circles, IT chases the Runner in an attempt to tag her/him. During the chase, the Runner may save her-/himself from being tagged by passing inside the circle and stepping in front of the nearest set of couples facing the center. This forms a three-deep situation. The outside circle player then becomes the new Runner for IT to chase.

If IT tags the Runner, the roles exchange and the new IT turns around and tries to retag the previous IT. At anytime when IT becomes tired, she/he may step into the circle and form a three-deep situation. The outside circle player then becomes the new IT to chase the Runner.

Also See: *Tierce* (8-14)

Cat and Mouse (8-15)

Squirrel Up a Tree (8-17)

8-17. Squirrel Up a Tree

Country: Uruguay (South America)

Type of Game: Tag—One Runner/One Tagger—Exchange

Formation: Players stand in a double circle with circle players spread out enough to allow both runners to pass between and through the circle. Both the Cat and the Squirrel begin outside the circle.

Equipment: None

Objective: The Cat tries to catch the Squirrel.

Uruguay has a temperate climate. January and February temperatures average 71° F. and in June (the coldest month) the temperature averages 50° F. Frost is virtually unknown throughout most of the country.

Directions: This version of *Squirrel Up a Tree* calls for players of the inside circle to stand in front of the outside circle players. Space between sets of circle players should be enough to allow the Squirrel or the Cat to safely pass through.

The action begins when the Cat begins to chase the Squirrel. Going anywhere in the play area, the Squirrel may pass through the circle without interference from the circle. Anytime the Squirrel is tired, or feels threatened of being tagged, she/he may step in front of an inside circle player; the outside player of that group then becomes the new Squirrel.

When the Cat catches (tags) the Squirrel, roles change and the former Cat becomes the new Squirrel who is now being chased by the new Cat.

Also See: *Tierce* (8-14)

Cat and Mouse (8-15)

Drei-Mann Hock (8-16)

8-18. Go-Tag

Country: India/Pakistan (Asia)

Type of Game: Tag—One Runner/One Tagger—Exchange

Formation: Players form a straight line with players facing alternate directions. IT and the Runner begin at opposite ends of the line.

Equipment: None

Objective: IT tries to tag the Runner.

Roughly one-third the size of the United States, India covers 1,222,559 square miles. Located in southern Asia, India slowly became part of the British Empire in bits and pieces beginning around 1750. On August 15, 1947 India gained its independence from the British Empire.

Located in southern Asia, Pakistan is bordered by China, India, Afghanistan, and Iran. Pakistan has seaports on the Arabian Sea. Earning independence from British India in 1947, Pakistan was divided into two parcels—about 1,000 miles apart! In 1971 the eastern parcel seceded and became the country of Bangladesh. Pakistan is roughly the size of the state of Texas at 339,697 square miles.

Directions: Players squat in a straight line. Each player faces in an opposite direction. Players on the ends become IT and the Runner.

IT may chase after the Runner by traveling around the line of players in only one direction. When beginning to run, therefore, IT must carefully decide what direction around the line is better for her/him to catch the Runner. As IT runs around after the Runner, IT may step behind a line player, tapping her/him on the shoulder as a signal to have that player take IT's place. The new IT must then choose in which direction to run around the line.

IT and the line players work together in a cooperative effort to catch the Runner. For example, since the Runner can only run around the circle in one direction, IT can change places with a player in line who can step out of line and in front of the Runner and tag him or her. When IT tags the Runner, the two players exchange roles and the new Runner is to be chased.

Also See: *Kho-Kho (8-38)*

8-19. Hawk and Dove

Country: China (Far East, Asia)

Type of Game: Tag—One Runner/One Tagger—Exchange

Formation: Groups of three are scattered throughout the activity area.

Equipment: Playing area

Objective: The Hawk tries to tag the Dove.

China is located in East Asia and follows only Russia and Canada in total landmass at 3,696,100 square miles—slightly larger than the continental United States. Having almost one-quarter the world's population, China is the single most populous country.

Directions: Players are in groups of three: Player number one is the Chinese Child; player number two is the Hawk (who represents evil); and player number three is the Dove (who represents good). The Dove and the Hawk hold hands with the Chinese Child.

On the signal "Go!" from the Chinese Child, the Dove is allowed to run away. A count of "1 Mississippi, 2 Mississippi, 3 Mississippi" is called before the Hawk begins to chase the Dove. The Hawk runs after the Dove, trying to tag her/him before the Dove can tag the Chinese Child. The Chinese Child needs to remain stationary throughout the chase.

At the end of this turn, whether a tag is made or not, the three children change roles.

Also See: *Rabbit* (8-20)

Elbow Tag (8-21)

8-20. Rabbit

Country: Colonial America (North America)

Type of Game: Tag—One Runner/One Tagger—Exchange

Formation: Sets of partners are spread throughout the activity area to form Rabbit Holes by holding both hands.

Equipment: Playing area

Objective: IT tries to tag the Rabbit.

Many games have evolved while people watched animals play, chase, and survive. Rabbits have natural enemies that chase them. This game depicts one such unnamed enemy chasing a rabbit from one hiding place to another.

Directions: Partners stand together holding hands to form a Rabbit Hole. All groups of partners are scattered throughout the playing area. IT and the Rabbit are chosen from the groups of partners. As IT runs after the Rabbit, the Rabbit may enter a Rabbit Hole at any time for safety. The player at the Rabbit's back then becomes the new Rabbit to be chased.

When a tag is made, the players exchange roles and play continues.

Also See: *Tierce* (8-14)

Hawk and Dove (8-19)

Elbow Tag (8-21)

8-21. Elbow Tag

Country: Colonial America (North America)

Type of Game: Tag—One Runner/One Tagger—Exchange

Formation: Partners are scattered throughout the playing area with inside elbows hooked.

Equipment: Playing area

Objective: IT tries to tag the runner.

Played similar to Rabbit, *this game allows partners to hook elbows instead of holding hands.*

Directions: Partners stand together scattered throughout the play area. Hooking inside elbows together, partners wait for their turn to run. An IT and a Runner are chosen to begin.

IT runs after the Runner to try to tag her/him. While running away, the Runner dodges around and between the sets of partners in the area. At any time the Runner may hook elbows with any player to form a group of three. The other end player now becomes the new Runner for IT to chase.

When a tag is made, IT and the Runner exchange roles, with the new IT chasing the new Runner. Play is continued until all players have a turn to be IT or the Runner or both.

Also See: *Tierce* (8-14)

Hawk and Dove (8-19)

Rabbit (8-20)

8-22. Spain

Country: Spain (Europe)

Type of Game: Tag—One Runner/One Tagger

Formation: Players form two teams and stand on parallel lines that are 40–50 feet apart.

Equipment: Parallel lines

Objective: Each player chooses who is to chase her/him back to her/his own parallel line.

Forming the greater part of the Iberian Peninsula in southwest Europe, Spain has coastlines on the Bay of Biscay, the Mediterranean Sea, and the Atlantic Ocean. Spain shares land borders with Portugal, France, and Andorra. The Pyrenees mountain range forms the eastern border of Spain to France and the rest of Europe. Spain is 194,898 square miles, the size of Arizona and Utah combined.

Directions: In the game *Spain*, the teams are named after two cities or regions of the country. In this example, the two teams are named Barcelona and Seville.

Players on team Barcelona line up on one of the parallel lines and team Seville lines up on the other. The captain or leader of Barcelona chooses one of her/his players to go to Seville and challenge a player. The Seville players hold out their right hands, palm up at waist level. The Barcelona player goes up and down the line sliding her/his right hand over the palms of the Seville players. At any time the Barcelona player gently slaps the palm of a Seville player. This is the signal that the Barcelona player chooses this Seville player to chase her/him. The Barcelona player then runs back to her/his parallel line as the Seville player tries to tag her/him.

If the Seville player tags the Barcelona player before the Barcelona player reaches the safety line, Barcelona goes to the Seville side as a captive.

It is now time for Seville's team leader to choose a player to challenge someone from team Barcelona.

Variation: The game *Cuba* is played in the Caribbean Islands in the same way as *Spain*. The only difference is that in *Cuba*, the two teams are named Cuba and Spain.

8-23. Steal the Bacon

Country: United States (North America)

Type of Game: Tag—One Runner/One Runner

Formation: Players form two teams and stand on parallel lines about 20–30 feet apart.

Equipment: 1 beanbag

Objective: The player tries to grab the beanbag and return to her/his own team before being tagged.

The United States, including the District of Columbia, is 3,787,318 square miles in size.

Directions: Players are divided into two teams and stand on parallel lines. Beginning at opposite ends, the players count off and remember their numbers. A beanbag is placed in the center of the play area between the lines. (See Illustration 1.)

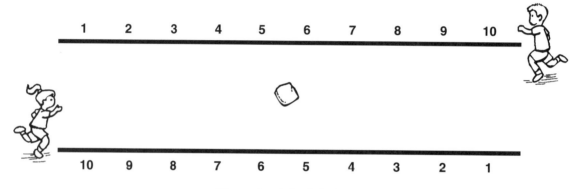

Illustration 1: *Steal the Bacon*

The leader calls out a number. The player from each team with that number runs out to try to be the first to grasp the beanbag ("the bacon") in the center and run back to her/his line before being tagged by the other team's player. If the player is able to "steal the bacon," one point is scored. If tagged, no points are scored. The beanbag is then replaced in the center of the play area and a new number is called.

Variations:

- Use letters of the alphabet instead of numbers.
- Use the names of animals (or other names related to subjects being taught in the classroom) instead of numbers.
- Use math problems for which the answers are their numbers.
- Call more than one number each time.

Also See: *Poison (8-13)*

8-24. Cat and Lynx

Country: Kalahari Desert in Botswana (Africa)

Type of Game: Tag—One Runner/One Tagger

Formation: Boundaries are formed with obstacles inside. Two teams spread out around the boundaries.

Equipment: Obstacles (indoors: chairs, boxes; outdoors: trees, bushes); playing area with boundaries

Objective: The Lynx tries to chase and tag the Cat.

The Kalahari Desert covers the western two-thirds of Botswana and areas of eastern Namibia and South Africa's Cape Province. Remnants of once an inland sea, the Kalahari Desert has isolated salt pans, Makgadikgadi Pans (an ancient drainage basin), and Lake Ngami. Rainfall ranges from 26 inches per year in the northeast to 6 inches in the southwest. Temperatures during the summer averages 68° F. to 86° F. but can reach 117° F. Winter temperature averages can drop below 40° F. and reach down to 8° F.

The Kalahari Desert covers 100,386 square miles and is sparsely populated by nomadic Khoikhoi, San (Bushmen), and Tswana people. The Bushmen of the Kalahari Desert mimic the actions of the Cat and Lynx in this game.

Directions: Two teams are formed: one represents the Cat; the other, the Lynx. The playing area is large and has obstacles throughout to be used to block the running paths and to dodge around.

One player from each team wanders out into the play area. As the Cat and the Lynx meet, they tell each other how one is better than the other in its abilities to chase and flee.

Finally, the Cat says, "Try to catch me!" The Cat, being the more cunning of the two, runs throughout the play area using the obstacles to block the pathway of the Lynx. The Lynx tries to tag the Cat while following the same pathway. The Lynx, being the faster of the two animals, tries to tag the Cat on the back, but is not allowed to reach over or around the obstacles.

Once the chase starts, the teammates of both the Cat and Lynx perform a 20-second countdown. If the Cat is tagged within this time, the Cat joins the Lynx team. If not, both go back to their own team and new members come out for their turns. The Cat team wins if all Cats are successful in not being tagged.

8-25. Tying the Sun to the Hitching Post

Country: Ancient Peru (South America)

Type of Game: Tag—One Runner/One Tagger

Formation: Players hold hands to form a semicircle. IT and the Sun stand apart and away from the other players.

Equipment: Playing area

Objective: IT tries to catch the Sun.

The Inca Indians were the rulers of the largest empire of Native Americans. With its beginnings in the Cuzco region of the Andes mountains of South America, the Inca empire expanded to include an estimated 12,000,000 people in today's countries of Peru, Ecuador, and large parts of Chile, Bolivia and Argentina.

The Inca religion was centered on the sun. The emperors were believed to be descendants from the Sun god and worshipped as divine beings. Gold was the symbol of the Sun god and mined for its rulers and elite, not for exchange and wealth, but for decorative and ritual purposes.

Believing in many spirits, which they felt aided them in everyday life, the Inca Indians had a huge sundial for their worship. They tried to catch the sun on this sundial with a net attached by hooks on the sides of the dial.

Directions: In this game IT chases the Sun. The remaining players join hands to form a semicircle (the net). While chasing the Sun throughout the play area, IT is allowed to pass between the semicircle players while the Sun cannot.

If the Sun is caught by IT, the net closes around the Sun for the capture. A new IT and Sun are then chosen for a new game. If the Sun is not caught after a predetermined amount of time, a new IT and Sun are chosen for a new game.

8-26. Badger and Sun

Country: Ancient Japan (Far East, Asia)

Type of Game: Tag—One Runner/One Tagger

Formation: Players form a spoke design radiating from a common center.

Equipment: None

Objective: The Badger tries to chase and catch the Sun.

The first human habitation of Japan is not known, but cultures have been identified as early as 8000 B.C. These Jomon people were hunters and gatherers who used stone and bone tools. The Yayoi people (3000 B.C.) introduced rice cultivation, primitive weaving, domesticated horses and cows, and simple iron tools. It is believed the Yayoi immigrated from continental Asia.

Legends, fables, and folk lore are very important to the Japanese. Here is one about the Badger and the Sun.

"Many years ago the Sun goddess was believed to hide in a cave from the Japanese people who were mean and wicked, leaving the world cold and dark. Being unable to get the Sun goddess to come out, the people asked the help of a Badger. The Badger, a great teaser, was delighted for this challenge. Standing at the entry way to the cave, the Badger was able to make the Sun goddess so mad that she came out of the cave to catch him. But she, herself, was the one captured by the people and put back into the sky—never to leave her place again due to ropes made of her sun rays."

Directions: The game is played with one Badger and one Sun. The remaining players form spokes of a wheel radiating from the Badger, being the centerpiece. The Sun stands outside the spokes. (See Illustration 1.)

The game begins with the Sun running between a pair of spokes towards the center where the Badger is standing. The Badger runs away while the Sun tries to catch the Badger by following her/him around the outside of the spokes or between them through the center. At no time is either the Badger or Sun allowed to pass between players who form a single line of a spoke.

Players forming the spokes call out directions for the Sun, but actually try to confuse the Sun. If the Sun catches the Badger, they hold hands and the children forming the spokes join their hands also. The Badger and all spoke players on her/his side face one direction. The Sun and all spoke players on her/his side face the other direction. (See Illustration 2.) When ready, the players run forward (and around) using the Badger and the Sun as the center point, until the players on the ends of the lines can't keep up with the speed and eventually let go and fall away.

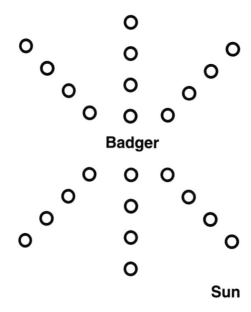

Illustration 1: *Badger and Sun*

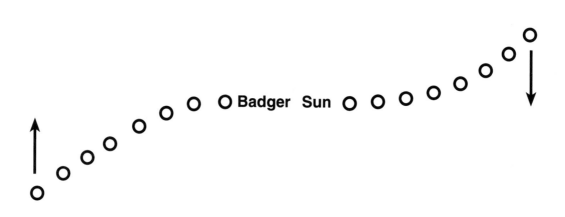

Illustration 2: *Badger and Sun*

One Tagger–Many Runners

Probably the most played form of tag today is one Tagger (IT) chasing many Runners. In the following 15 games of *Tag*, the formations change from the players scattered throughout the area and running in any direction, to having the players standing in certain formations and running to home bases where they may not be tagged.

8-27. Touch Iron, Touch Wood, Feet Off the Ground

Country: Colonial America (North America)

Type of Game: Tag—One Tagger/Many Runners

Formation: Players are scattered throughout the play area.

Equipment: Different objects for home bases; playing area

Objective: IT tries to tag runners who are not on safety bases.

Colonial children would use common items of the times as home places where a runner would be free from being tagged. These items might have included wooden buckets, axes, and churns.

Directions: Home bases are scattered throughout the playing area. These bases might be made of wood and iron, and a place where a runner must keep her/his feet off the ground by lifting them into the air or hanging from a tree or a bar. Players touching or standing on a home base cannot be tagged. Runners off a home base and tagged are eliminated from the game until a new game begins.

Also See: *Touch Pole Tag* (8-39)

Touch Wood

Touch Fence

Feet off the ground

8-28. Spot Tag

Country: Mexico (North America)

Type of Game: Tag—One Tagger/Many Runners

Formation: Players are scattered throughout the playing area.

Equipment: Playing area

Objective: IT tries to tag another player who becomes the new IT while performing a special challenge (placing a hand on tagged spot).

Mexico is the largest Spanish-speaking country and second largest Roman Catholic nation in the world. The United States borders Mexico to the north, and Guatemala and Belize border Mexico to the south. The Gulf of Mexico and the Caribbean Sea are on Mexico's eastern shoreline and the Pacific Ocean is on its western.

Directions: IT runs to tag any player she/he can. The tagged player becomes the new IT and runs to tag another player while placing one hand on the spot where she/he was tagged. The special spot is touched only until the player is able to tag another player.

8-29. Goellki

Country: Russia (Asia/Europe)

Type of Game: Tag—One Tagger/Many Runners

Formation: Players form a double-file line facing forward. IT stands behind the line.

Equipment: None

Objective: IT tries to tag one of two players running to the front of the line.

Russia runs the full length of Asia and continues into Europe.
Despite its size, Russia is located in an unfavorable location to major sea
lanes. Much of Russia is either too cold or too dry for agriculture.

Directions: Players stand in a double-file line facing the same direction. IT is a single player not in either of the lines, standing 3–5 feet behind the double-file lines and facing the players.

On the signal "Go!" from IT, the last couple separate and run to the outside of the double lines away from IT. IT runs and tries to tag one of these two runners before she/he can get to the front of one of the lines.

When IT tags a player who has not yet reached the front of the line, IT takes that player's place in line and the tagged player is the new IT.

Also See: *Gorelki* (8-30)

IT

Illustration 1: *Goellki*

8-30. Gorelki

Country: Russia (Asia/Europe)

Type of Game: Tag—One Tagger/Many Runners

Formation: Players form a double-file line facing forward. IT stands in front of the line. (See Illustration 1.)

Equipment: None

Objective: IT tries to tag one of two players running to the front of the line.

Russia is the largest nation in the world in landmass. It takes up one-ninth of the world's landmass.

Directions: Players stand in a double-file line facing the same direction. IT stands ten large steps in front of these lines of players, facing them.

On the signal "Go!" the last couple separate and run to the outside of the double lines to go to the front. In order to be free, the couple must join hands in front of the double line before IT is able to tag either runner. If IT tags one of the runners, IT takes that person's place and the game continues.

Also See: *Goellki (8-29)*

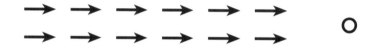

Illustration 1: *Gorelki*

8-31. Wolf! Wolf!

Country: Egypt (Middle East, Africa)

Type of Game: Tag—One Tagger/Many Runners

Formation: Players stand in a single circle. The Wolf stands in the center.

Equipment: Playing area

Objective: The Wolf tries to tag a running player.

Ninety-nine percent of Egypt's population lives on only 4% of its land!

Directions: The Wolf stands inside the circle of players. The circle players ask the Wolf what she/he is doing. The Wolf responds by saying an everyday performance ("Brushing my teeth," "Washing my hands," "Combing my hair," etc.). When the Wolf calls out "Chasing you!" the circle players run away from the Wolf while the Wolf runs to tag one of the circle players. The first circle player tagged becomes the new Wolf for a new game.

8-32. Fox and Geese

Country: Canada (North America)

Type of Game: Tag—One Tagger/Many Runners—Exchange

Formation: Players form a circle with spokes (lines) through the center marked in snow or on the ground.

Equipment: Marked spokes (lines)

Objective: The Fox tries to catch the Geese.

Canada is the world's second largest landmass country (only Russia is larger). From its easternmost point at Cape Spear, Newfoundland, to its westernmost point at Mount Elias in the Yukon Territory near the Alaskan border, Canada stretches 3,426 miles east to west covering six time zones.

Canada's southernmost tip is Middle Island in Lake Erie and its northernmost tip is Cape Columbia on Ellesmere Island 1,150 miles away, north of the Arctic Circle.

Directions: A pathway in the snow is walked off to form a circle with ruts cutting through representing spokes in a wheel.

The Fox stands at the center of the circle where the spokes come together. The Geese stand spread out on the outer wheel. A leader leads the Geese around and through the circle, trying to keep all away from the Fox. The Geese must remain in the pathways, but the sly Fox may run out of the ruts in order to snatch (tag) a Goose. A captured Goose becomes the new Fox and, if necessary, a new play area is made.

Adaptation: Lines may be marked on the ground to form the circle and spokes if you do not live in a snowy area.

Variation: Once the Fox begins to chase the Geese, the Geese can scatter (following separate lines) to run away from the Fox. The Geese still need to follow the lines while running away and the Fox will need to also follow the lines while chasing the Geese.

Also See: *Atya–Patya* (8-49)

Bell in the Steeple (8-50)

8-33. Water Sprite

Country: China (Far East, Asia)

Type of Game: Tag—One Tagger/Two Runners—Two teams

Formation: Players divide into two teams. Teams stand on opposite parallel lines 15–20 feet apart. The Water Sprite stands in the center between the lines.

Equipment: None

Objective: The Water Sprite tries to tag one of the two Runners exchanging places.

In the 1950s and 1960s the direction of education in China was to produce secondary school and college graduates. Students were required to spend half their time working on academic subjects and the other half learning practical skills in factories and in the fields.

Directions: Players are divided and lined up on two parallel lines 15–20 feet apart. The Water Sprite stands in the center area (the River).

The Water Sprite names a player, closes her/his eyes, and counts to ten. During this count, the chosen Runner silently signals a player on the other team and the two exchange places. On the count of ten, the Water Sprite opens her/his eyes and tries to tag one of the two Runners. If a Runner is tagged, that person is the new Water Sprite.

Variation: In the past, this Chinese game was traditionally played by girls. Play some games with only girls, some with only boys, and others with both girls and boys.

Also See: *January* (8-52)

8-34. What's the Time, Mr. Wolf?

Country: Great Britain (Europe)

Type of Game: Tag—One Tagger/Many Runners

Formation: Players are scattered behind Mr. Wolf. Two dens (home bases) are marked 30–35 feet apart.

Equipment: 2 dens (home bases); playing area

Objective: Mr. Wolf tries to tag Runners.

This game also became very popular in South Africa after Britain gained control of South Africa under provisions of the Congress of Vienna in 1814 following the Napoleonic Wars. Large-scale British settlement began in 1820.

Directions: Two dens are marked in the playing area. One is for Mr. Wolf; the other is a home base for the Runners.

Mr. Wolf walks through the playing area while the other players follow and call out "What's the time, Mr. Wolf?" Mr. Wolf turns around and calls back some time of the day, such as "One o'clock." After answering the question of the time, Mr. Wolf turns back around and continues to walk around.

The group of Runners again asks Mr. Wolf what the time is, and Mr. Wolf answers with some time of day. At some point when Mr. Wolf feels she/he has the advantage, she/he calls out "It's dinner time!" and proceeds to chase the Runners. The Runners rush back to their den to remain free. Any tagged Runners must go to the Wolf's den.

When Runners are either in their den or have been tagged, Mr. Wolf begins walking again being followed by untagged Runners. This continues until one or no Runners are left and a new Mr. Wolf begins the next game.

8-35. Puss in the Corner

Country: Colonial America (North America)

Type of Game: Tag—One Tagger/Many Runners

Formation: Three or four home bases are marked throughout the play area. Runners begin at a home base. The Puss stands anywhere in the play area.

Equipment: 3–4 home bases; playing area

Objective: The Runners try to move to different home bases without being tagged by the Puss.

The United States shares borders with only two countries—Canada to its north and Mexico to its south—for a total of 8,611 land miles. When the first colonists came to the New World, they of course did not know of the size and scope of the land!

Directions: Runners go from one home base to another while avoiding being tagged. When the Puss gets impatient, she/he may call "All Change!" and everyone must run to a new safe base while avoiding being tagged. Tagged players are eliminated until a new game begins.

Variations:

- An eliminated player is out only until the next player is tagged.
- Set a time limit per game. When time is up, a new Puss is chosen and a new game begins.
- Set a number limit. When a specified number of players are tagged, a new game begins.

Also See: *What's the Time, Mr. Wolf?* (8-34)

8-36. Kabaddi

Country: India (Asia)

Type of Game: Tag—One Tagger/Many Runners—Two teams

Formation: A center line is marked widthwise on a rectangular field. Players divide into two teams.

Equipment: Playing field; center line

Objective: One player tries to tag runners from the other team while saying "Kabaddi" repeatedly on a single breath.

Early evidence shows the game of **Kabaddi** *is 4,000 years old! Not restricted to the country of India,* **Kabaddi** *is played throughout Asia. The Kabaddi Federation of India was founded in 1950 and the Amateur Kabaddi Federation of India was founded in 1973.*

Directions: The play area boundaries are set up and divided in half by a center line. The boundaries need not make a large area. Staying within its own boundaries, Team One sends one player across the line into Team Two's boundaries. While trying to tag as many Team Two players as she/he can, Team One's tagger must repeat the word "Kabaddi" repeatedly on a single breath, and return to her/his side before taking the next breath. If this is done correctly, any Team Two player tagged is eliminated. If the Team One player waits too long to return and must take a second breath before returning to her/his side, she/he is eliminated. It's then Team Two's turn: At the same time Team One has a tagger running on Team Two's side, Team Two has a runner on Team One's side trying to tag Team One's players.

Also See: *Breath-Hold Tag (8-37)*

8-37. Breath-Hold Tag

Country: Northwest Coast Native Americans, United States (North America)

Type of Game: Tag—One Tagger/Many Runners

Formation: Players are scattered in a small playing area. One player is IT.

Equipment: Small playing area

Objective: IT tries to tag runners while everyone says "Tillikum" repeatedly on a single breath.

Native Americans needed to be able to control their actions and reserve their strength while hunting and fighting. Games were played to help children and young adults develop these skills.

Directions: This is a quick game of tag. All players including IT must repeat "Tillikum" over and over while the game goes on. Any player having to take a breath is eliminated. When IT needs to take a breath, the game stops and a new IT begins the next game.

Also See: *Kabaddi (8-36)*

8-38. Kho-Kho

Country: India (Asia)

Type of Game: Tag—One Tagger/Many Runners—Two teams

Formation: A center line is marked on a 50' x 100' rectangular field. The tagging team sits on the center line with players facing alternate directions.

Equipment: Playing field; center line

Objective: The tagging team tries to tag the runners in its half of the playing field.

In ancient times, Kho-Kho *was played in chariots and was known as* Rathera.

Directions: A large playing area is marked with a center line. Two teams are chosen—Runners and Taggers. The tagging team sits on the center line with the players facing alternate directions. (*Hint:* Count off the taggers, with odd-numbered taggers facing one side and even-numbered taggers facing the other side.) The direction each Tagger faces is the half of the playing area she/he is limited to run and chase the Runners. (See Illustration 1.)

Runners are allowed anywhere in the boundary lines. The Runners can change sides by running across the center line. Gaps between Taggers sitting on the center line are left open to allow Runners to safely pass through to the other side.

On the signal "Go!" the first Tagger gets up and begins chasing the Runners. As the Runners pass the center line into the area the Tagger is not allowed, the Tagger gives a *kho* to a teammate facing that area. (A *kho* is a simple touch signal to the new Tagger.) The new Tagger jumps up and begins chasing the Runners in her/his half of the playing area, facing the direction in which she/he entered the line from. The other Tagger sits in the vacated spot.

Tagged Runners leave the playing area.

Runners will divide themselves into both halves so *khos* can happen at any time. When Taggers change off frequently, the chance of tags being made increases. After all Runners are tagged, or a set time has expired, teams exchange duties and play begins again.

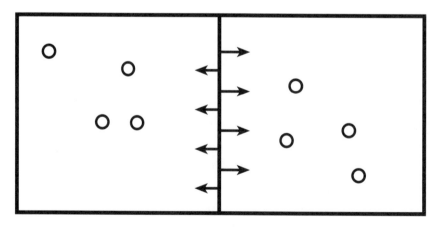

Illustration 1: *Kho-Kho*

Also See: *Go-Tag* (8-18)

8-39. Touch-Pole Tag

Country: Philippines (Asia)

Type of Game: Tag—One Tagger/Many Runners

Formation: Players are scattered throughout the playing area. A pole (or other marker) is at the center of the playing area.

Equipment: Pole (or other marker); playing area

Objective: The Farmer tries to tag the runners before they can touch the pole.

The Philippine Islands lie about 750 miles east of Vietnam. Separated from Taiwan by the Baski Channel, the Philippine Islands lie west of the Philippine Sea, north of the Celebes Sea, and east of the South China Sea.

Made up of about 7,100 separate islands covering a total of about 115,800 square miles, the Philippine Islands are slightly larger than the state of Arizona. Only about 460 islands are larger than one square mile in size and eleven are larger than 1,000 square miles in size.

Directions: This activity is based on a ceremony farmers used to help their harvest grow. A chant is used with appropriate actions to begin the game.

A pole or other marker is placed in the center of the playing area. The Farmer is at the marker at the start of the game. The other players are scattered.

FARMER: *"Would you know how the farmer plows?"*

RUNNERS: *"This is the way the farmer plows."* (Players mimic how the farmer plows a field using an ox-pulled plow.)

FARMER: *"Is that so?"*

RUNNERS: *"Yes, that's so."*

FARMER: *"Would you know what the farmer does when the plowing is done?"*

RUNNERS: *"This is what the farmer does when the plowing's done."* (Players bow towards the Farmer, turn facing away, and bow again.)

FARMER: *"Is that so?"*

RUNNERS: *"Yes, that's so."*

FARMER: *"Would you know what the farmer does when the work is done?"*

The Runners now run away from the Farmer, who runs after them trying to tag as many as she/he can. When a Runner is touching the pole, she/he cannot be tagged. The Runners can only stay a few seconds at the pole before they must leave the pole to be chased again.

Tagged players stand near a boundary line, waiting for the next game.

Also See: *Touch Iron, Touch Wood, Feet Off the Ground (8-27)*

8-40. Catching Fish in the Dark

Country: China (Far East, Asia)

Type of Game: Tag—One Tagger/Many Runners—Blindfold

Formation: Players are scattered. The Fisherman is blindfolded in the playing area.

Equipment: 1 blindfold

Objective: The Fisherman tries to tag the Fish, who in turn are trying to tag the Fisherman.

China's fishing industry is one of the world's largest fish producers.

Directions: Scattered throughout the playing area, the Fish try to tag the blindfolded Fisherman without being tagged themselves. When the Fisherman tags a Fish, the Fisherman tries to identify the player by carefully touching the player's face, hair, and shoulders. If successful, that Fish becomes the new Fisherman. If not successfully identified, the Fisherman tries to catch another fish.

Variation: The Fish scatter throughout the play area. The Fisherman is taken to the center of the area, blindfolded, and turned around three times. While the Fisherman is being turned around, the Fish move throughout the area. Once the Fisherman has stopped turning, the Fish must freeze in place.

On the signal "Go!" from the Fisherman, the Fish begin making noises for the Fisherman to try to locate and follow to find the Fish. Once a Fish is found, the Fisherman tries to identify the Fish. If successful, the Fish and Fisherman exchange places. If unsuccessful, the Fisherman tries to find a new Fish to catch.

8-41. Blind Man's Bluff

Country: Worldwide

Type of Game: Tag—One Tagger/Many Runners—Blindfold

Formation: Players are scattered in an open area. IT is blindfolded.

Equipment: 1 blindfold

Objective: IT tries to tag a player and identify her/him.

In medieval times men wore hoods attached to shirt collars. To play this game, IT would turn his hood around to cover his face. The other players would take off their hoods, put a knot in them, and hit IT with them until a player was caught.

Directions: Blindfolded, IT is turned around three times while the other players scatter throughout the area. When finished being spun around, IT tries to tag a player as the players move in and out of arms' reach of IT.

When a player is caught, IT carefully touches the player's face, hair, and shoulders to try to identify the caught player. If correct, the player is the new IT. If incorrect, IT remains blindfolded and must try to catch and identify another player.

Variation: See Section 1, "Blindfold Activities."

Multiple Taggers

The following 25 games of *Tag* may begin with one tagger and increase as players become tagged, or begin with more than one tagger.

8-42. Abumbutan (Falling Stick)

Country: Nigeria (Africa)

Type of Game: Tag—Multiple Taggers

Formation: A 10-inch stick is vertically stuck into a mound of sand with only 4–5 inches showing above the surface. Players squat or sit around the stick.

Equipment: Sand; stick; playing area

Objective: Players try to scoop away the sand without the stick falling.

Once a British colony, Nigeria gained its independence from Britain on October 1, 1960. Located on the Atlantic coast of West Africa, Nigeria shares land borders with Benin, Niger, Chad, and Cameroon.

Directions: The players decide in what order the players come to the sand pile and scoop away one handful of sand from around the stick. As the sand around the stick is almost gone, the players need to be careful. The player who takes away the handful of sand that allows the stick to fall will need to run away quickly because the other players will run and try to be the first to tag that runner. This scores a penalty point for the runner. When a player reaches a set number of penalty points, she/he is eliminated from the game.

Variations:

- Instead of running away to be tagged, the player who makes the stick fall may be required to perform some kind of stunt, activity, or exercise.

- Have a home base marked off. If the runner reaches this area before being tagged, a penalty point is not awarded and the player may rejoin the group for a new game.

8-43. Pebble Tag

Country: Greece (Europe)

Type of Game: Tag—Multiple Taggers

Formation: Players stand in a line with a goal line 30 feet away. IT stands in front of the players and holds a pebble.

Equipment: 1 small pebble; goal line

Objective: The player with the pebble tries to run to the goal line and back without being tagged.

Greece has a total landmass of 51,146 square miles. A peninsula in the Mediterranean Sea, Greece has 9,385 miles of coastline.

Directions: The players stand in line with their hands cupped together to form a hiding place for the pebble to be dropped into, but not seen. IT walks along from player to player, pretending to drop the pebble into a player's hands—and then actually putting it into one player's hands. The player receiving the pebble must try to run to the goal line and back without being tagged by the other players. If any other player tags the runner before she/he returns to the starting line, the tagging player becomes the new IT.

The player receiving the pebble can be sneaky and wait to run with the pebble. However, she/he must begin running before IT gets to the last player in the line. The players in line will be watching IT as she/he moves along the line and may miss an early player as she/he begins to run.

8-44. Baste the Bear

Country: Colonial America (North America)

Type of Game: Tag—Multiple Taggers

Formation: The Bear and the Keeper stand inside a small circle. The other players form a larger circle around the Bear and the Keeper.

Equipment: None

Objective: The circle taggers try to tag the Bear without being tagged themselves by the Bear or the Keeper.

In May 1607, Captain John Smith and 105 cavaliers in three ships landed on the Atlantic coast and started the first permanent English settlement in the New World at Jamestown, Virginia.

Directions: The Bear and the Keeper stand in a small circle. Neither the Bear nor the Keeper may leave their circle. All other players form a circle around the Bear and the Keeper out of arm's length.

When the Keeper calls out "My bear is free," the circle players try to tag the Bear without being tagged by either the Bear or the Keeper. If a tagger is tagged, she/he can no longer try to tag the Bear. If the Bear is tagged, the tagger becomes the new Bear, the Bear becomes the new Keeper, and the Keeper becomes a circle tagger for the next game.

8-45. North Wind and South Wind

Country: Sweden (Europe)

Type of Game: Tag—Multiple Taggers

Formation: Players are scattered throughout playing area. Two players are the North Wind and one player is the South Wind.

Equipment: Playing area

Objective: The North Wind tries to freeze (tag) runners, while the South Wind tries to thaw (tag) them.

With one-seventh of the Kingdom of Sweden above the Arctic Circle, the weather of Sweden is comparatively moderate. Influences from the Gulf Stream and warm winds from the relatively warm North Atlantic Ocean keep summers warm with temperatures ranging from 57° F. to 71° F. Winter temperatures are influenced from cold air masses coming from the east. Winter temperatures range from 6° F. to 34° F. High elevations and mountains in the north keep moderating marine influences from raising winter temperatures.

Directions: Two players are chosen to be Sweden's cold and dangerous North Wind. Any player tagged by either North Wind must freeze in a squatting or all-fours position. A third player is chosen to represent the warmer South Wind. The South Wind runs and tags as many frozen players as she/he can to thaw them. These players then rejoin the game and try to avoid being tagged again.

Play is stopped after a predetermined period of time. The South Wind wins the game if five or fewer players are still frozen. The North Wind wins if more than five players are frozen.

Also See: *Beware the Antelope (8-47)*

8-46. Lame Fox and Chickens

Country: Colonial America (North America)

Type of Game: Tag—Multiple Taggers—Increase

Formation: The Lame Fox begins in a fox den (home base). Other players (Chickens) are scattered throughout the playing area.

Equipment: Playing area

Objective: The Lame Fox tries to tag the Chickens.

Colonial games rarely used equipment because resources were so scarce.

Directions: The Lame Fox stands in a den (home base) somewhere inside the playing area. The other players (Chickens) are scattered throughout the area. The Lame Fox may leave her/his den at any time to chase the Chickens. The Chickens may run on both feet, but the Fox, being lame, must hop on only one foot. The Lame Fox may not put both feet down at the same time when outside the den, but is allowed to switch feet periodically when chasing the Chickens. The Fox may return to the den to place both feet down to rest. If the Fox puts both feet down when outside the den, she/he must return to the den before continuing the chase. Daredevil Chickens may run close to the Fox to challenge the Fox into chasing them. When the Lame Fox tags a Chicken, both return to the den where the Chicken becomes a Lame Fox to help the first.

The last remaining Chicken is the winner.

8-47. Beware the Antelope

Country: Congo Republic (Africa)

Type of Game: Tag—Multiple Taggers—Increase

Formation: Players are scattered within marked boundaries.

Equipment: Playing area; marked boundaries

Objective: The Antelope tries to tag runners.

Once a French colony, the Middle Congo gained its independence on August 15, 1960. (The Congo Republic is also known as Congo-Brazzaville. It should not be confused with Democratic Republic of the Congo [formerly Zaire], now commonly called Congo, and also known as Congo-Kinshasa.) Found with little coastline on the Atlantic Ocean, the Congo Republic shares land borders with Central African Republic, Cameroon, Democratic Republic of the Congo, Angola, and Gabon.

Directions: Antelopes are sure-footed animals that can run very fast and change directions quickly. This is necessary because in Africa many animals hunt the antelope for food.

The Luba Kasai children of the Congo Republic play a tag game that is played in an area having marked boundaries. One player begins the game as the Antelope and stands near one side of the play area. All the other players are grouped in the center.

In this game, the roles are reversed from real life: Here, the Antelope chases the runners. When the Antelope tags another player or can force another player to run out of the boundaries, that player becomes a second Antelope and begins to chase after other runners.

Games usually can end quickly with the last player tagged becoming the winner and the new Antelope for the next game.

Also See: *Lame Fox and Chickens (8-46)*

8-48. King Caesar

Country: Italy (Europe)

Type of Game: Tag—Multiple Taggers—Increase

Formation: King Caesar stands in the center of 2–3 home bases. Runners stand in one of the home bases.

Equipment: 2–3 home bases

Objective: The Runners try to change home bases without being tagged by King Caesar.

Italy is a long boot-shaped peninsula stretching into the Mediterranean Sea, with coastlines on the Ligurian Sea, Tyrrhenian Sea, Ionian Sea, and Adriatic Sea. Because of its lengthy reach into the Mediterranean Sea, Italy has the advantage of controlling sea traffic between the eastern and western basins of the Mediterranean Sea. Italy shares land borders with France, Switzerland, Austria, and Slovenia.

"Caesar" is the title of the emperor of Rome or of the Holy Roman Empire. Perhaps the most famous was Julius Caesar, dictator of the Roman Empire from 49–44 B.C.

Directions: Two or three safe bases are marked off and called "dens." King Caesar begins the game in the middle of the area. Players begin in a den of their choice and are safe as long as they are in a den. Players may leave one den to go to another whenever they feel they can make it safely.

When King Caesar calls "All out!" the players must leave their den and go to another den while avoiding being captured. To capture someone, King Caesar has to hold onto the player and count to ten out loud. Captured players then help King Caesar to capture more players.

If King Caesar can invade an empty den and call out "Crown the base, one, two, three," the players freeze in place. King Caesar names one player and tries to tag that player as they both try to run across into the invaded den. If safe, the player continues the game as a runner. If caught, the player helps King Caesar to capture more players.

8-49. Atya-Patya (Lines)

Country: India (Asia)

Type of Game: Tag—Many Taggers

Formation: Players form four teams on a tennis or basketball court.

Equipment: 2 home bases; tennis or basketball court

Objective: The Tagging Team tries to tag members of the Running Teams.

The seventh nation in land size, India ranks second in the world for population (behind China). Located in south Asia, India is 1,865 miles wide and has about 4,350 miles of coastline along the Bay of Bengal and the Arabian Sea. Land neighbors include Pakistan, China (mostly Tibet), Nepal, Bhutan, Bangladesh, and Myanmar (formerly Burma). The island of Sri Lanka (formerly Ceylon) is located off the southern tip in the Bay of Bengal.

Directions: The Runners must follow the connecting lines on the court. Two areas are marked off: one as a home base, the other as a holding pen. The players are divided into four teams: one being the Taggers, the others being the Runners.

On the signal "Go!" the Taggers chase after the Runners, trying to tag as many as possible. The Taggers and Runners must run on the lines at all times. If players leave the path of the lines in order to make a tag or avoid being tagged, they are sent to the holding pen for one minute. Runners who are tagged go to the holding pen and remain there until the end of the game.

Tired Runners may enter the home base; a Tagger may come to the base, however, call a Runner by name and count to five. The Runner must leave the home base by the count of five or be considered tagged.

Once all Runners are tagged, a new team is chosen to become the taggers. Play continues until all teams have been taggers.

Variations:

- Each team has identification markings (colors, arm bands, etc.). When a Runner from the yellow team is tagged, for example, and goes to the holding area, that Runner cannot leave until another Runner from her/his team is tagged and is in the holding area to take the first one's place. Only one Runner from each team is allowed in the holding area at a time.

- Set a time limit of play. At the end of the time limit, the Running Team with the least number of players in the holding area wins that round. Play four rounds so all teams will have three scores (teams cannot score when being the Tagging Team). The team with the lowest total score at the end of four rounds wins the game.

Also See: *Fox and Geese* (8-32)

8-50. Bell in the Steeple

Country: Russia (Asia/Europe)

Type of Game: Tag—Multiple Taggers

Formation: Playing field as shown in Illustration 1. The Guard stands inside the Steeple holding a small box. The Leader has a bell.

Equipment: Snow (or other markings); 1 small box; 1 bell

Objective: The Guard tries to tag the Bell Holder while being chased by the other runners.

The capital city of Moscow has many towers with bells. The winters are cold and long, with plenty of snowfall in which the children can play.

Directions: A small bell and small box are needed. If snow is not available, some other sort of markings on the ground are needed to form the playing field.

A Leader and a Guard are chosen from the players. The Guard stands inside the Steeple holding the small box. All other players line up on one of the outer boundary lines. The Guard closes her/his eyes and the Leader hands the bell to one of the players. The Leader then goes to one of the four outer corners.

The game is ready to begin. The Guard is told to open her/his eyes. The Leader begins leading the other players around the outer boundary lines, walking on the marked lines. As the players move around the area, the bell is rung and passed off to other players. The players must try to hide the bell from the Guard so the Guard does not know who has the bell.

After traveling around the outside boundary at least one complete time, the Leader may lead the players on the diagonal lines—with the bell still being passed from player to player up and down the line. At any time after the players have completed one complete trip around the outer boundary, the Guard claps her/his hands. The bell is silenced and all the players run to stand around the Guard.

The bell is dropped into the box in the Guard's hands and that player runs away. The Guard runs after this player while carrying the box and bell. The rest of the players chase after the Guard. When a tag is made—either the Guard tagging the runner or the other players tagging the Guard—a new game is begun with a new Guard and a new Leader.

If no tag has been made after several minutes of running, the Leader can run into the Steeple and stop the game at that point. The person with the bell becomes the new Guard, and the Guard becomes the new Leader.

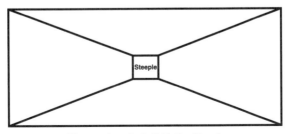

Illustration 1: *Bell in the Steeple*

Also See: *Fox and Geese* (8-32)

Atya Patya (8-49)

8-51. Blackberry

Country: Canada/United States (North America)

Type of Game: Tag—Multiple Taggers—Increase

Formation: Goal lines are drawn 20 feet apart. The Blackberries stand on one goal line; the Pickers stand at a center line between the two goal lines.

Equipment: Goal lines; center line

Objective: The Pickers try to pick (tag) as many Blackberries as possible.

Blackberries are members of the rose family. The purple or black fruit is edible and can be used in pies, crisps, and cobblers.

Directions: Blackberries begin by standing on one goal line. Pickers are chosen from the Blackberries and stand on the center line. The number of Pickers should be one Picker for every ten Blackberries.

Blackberries begin the game by chanting:

> *"Blackberries, blackberries, on the hill,*
>
> *How many pails can you fill?"*

The Pickers reply:

> *"Briars are thick and briars scratch,*
>
> *But will pick all the blackberries in the patch."*

At this point, the Blackberries try to run to the opposite goal line without being tagged by a Picker. If a Blackberry is tagged, she/he becomes a Picker and begins picking the next round.

The last Blackberry to be tagged is the leader for the Pickers in the next game. The leader is the Picker who makes sure all are ready and begins the chant.

Also See: *Water Sprite* (8-33)

January (8-52)

Catching Stars/Gathering Stars (8-53)

8-52. January

Country: Canada (North America)

Type of Game: Tag—Multiple Taggers—Increase

Formation: Goal lines are drawn 20 feet apart. Runners stand on both goal lines. Taggers stand on a center line between the goals.

Equipment: Goal lines; center line

Objective: Taggers try to tag Runners traveling to the opposite goal line.

Winter temperatures vary greatly throughout Canada. The Pacific coastal temperatures range from 32° F. to 39° F. due to Pacific marine influences. Interior plains have winter temperatures averaging –5° F. to 5° F. during the long cold winters. The Great Lakes, St. Lawrence Lowlands, and Appalachian Region have January averages of about 14° F. The Ontario peninsula winter temperatures average 25° F.

Directions: Goal lines are drawn, with Runners standing on both lines to begin the game. Taggers stand on a center line ready to tag Runners who try to run to the other line. There is one Tagger for every ten Runners. Runners cannot run until Taggers chant:

> *"January, January*
>
> *One, two, three.*
>
> *If you don't run now*
>
> *I'll catch you where you be."*

At this point Runners run to the opposite goal, trying not to be tagged and watching for oncoming Runners! Tagged Runners become Taggers with the next round.

Also See: *Water Sprite* (8-33)

Blackberry (8-51)

Catching Stars/Gathering Stars (8-53)

8-53. Catching Stars/ Gathering Stars

Country: Pygmy Tribes, Gabon (Africa)

Type of Game: Tag—Multiple Taggers—Increase

Formation: Goal lines are drawn 20 feet apart. Stars stand on one line. Star Catchers stand at a center line between the goal lines.

Equipment: Goal lines; center line

Objective: The Star Catchers try to gather (tag) the Stars.

Located on the West Coast of Africa, Gabon is bisected by the Equator. Its land neighbors are Republic of the Congo, Cameroon, and Equatorial Guinea. Due to the large number of people entering Gabon, large numbers of the Pygmy population have been displaced.

Directions: Stars stand on one goal line. Depending on the size of the play area and the number of Stars, either one-third or one-fourth of the Stars is chosen to stand on the center line. These are the Star Catchers.

The Star Catchers call out:

"Star light, star bright,

How many stars are out tonight?"

In response the Stars call out:

"More than you can catch!"

The Stars then try to run to the opposite goal line. The Star Catchers try to tag as many Stars as possible before the Stars reach the other goal line where they are safe. Tagged Stars become Star Catchers for the next round.

When there are no more Stars to catch, a new game begins with new Star Catchers.

Also See: *Blackberry* (8-51)

January (8-52)

8-54. Great Wall of China

Country: China (Far East, Asia)

Type of Game: Tag—Multiple Taggers—Increase

Formation: Goal lines are drawn 50–60 feet apart. The Great Wall (formed by a second set of parallel lines 10–12 feet apart) is in the center between the goal lines. (See Illustration 1.) Players stand on one goal line. The Guard stands on the Wall.

Equipment: Goal lines; center lines for Wall

Objective: The players try to run across the Great Wall of China without being tagged.

The Great Wall of China was originally a series of smaller walls of various states within China built as defenses against invaders. Shi Huangdi (Shih Huang-ti) of the Qin (Ch'in) dynasty (221–206 B.C.) created the original wall to unify the Chinese empire. The Great Wall of China extends along northern China and is 1,500 miles long, 15–30 feet high, and 12–20 feet wide. It can be seen from outer space!

Directions: All players begin on one outer line. The Guard stands on the Wall. On the signal "Go!" from the Guard, the runners rush the Wall, trying to cross without being tagged. Any player tagged becomes an extra Guard on the wall.

As runners cross the Wall without being tagged, they continue to the other goal line. When all players are at the other goal line, the original Guard calls again for them to run.

Begin the game again with a new Guard when all players have been caught.

Variation: Set up Guard Towers at the ends of the Wall. One player may be chosen to stand guard in each Tower. Although these players cannot leave the Tower, they have fleece balls, soft Nerf™, or sponge balls to throw at the players running across the Wall. Players hit by a ball are eliminated from the game and stand behind one of the Towers. Tagged players still become extra Guards.

```
Wall
```

Illustration 1: *Great Wall of China*

8-55. Red Lion

Country: United States (North America)

Type of Game: Tag—Multiple Taggers—Increase

Formation: Goal lines are drawn 20 feet apart. The Red Lion stands on one goal line (the Lion's Den) while the other players stand on a center line between the goals.

Equipment: Goal lines; center line

Objective: The Red Lion tries to tag as many players as possible before they reach the other goal line.

The United States is the third most populous country behind China and India.

Directions: Unlike other tag games using parallel goal lines, the players in this game stand between the goal lines while the Red Lion stands on a goal line (the Lion's Den). One runner is chosen to challenge the Red Lion by coming to the Lion's Den. The Red Lion remains in her/his den until the challenging player chants the rhyme:

> *"Red Lion, Red Lion,*
>
> *Come out of your den.*
>
> *Whoever you catch*
>
> *Will be your men."*

Anytime following this chant the Red Lion leaves the den and tries to tag as many players as possible before they reach the other goal line. Players tagged by the Red Lion still have a chance to be free. They must reach the far line before the Red Lion shouts "Red Lion" three times. Runners who do not make it safely become a Hunter and help the Red Lion the next time.

8-56. Last Couple in the Middle

Country: England/Scotland (Europe)

Type of Game: Tag—Stay Connected

Formation: A rectangular playing area is marked off into thirds. Players are connected to partners by holding hands.

Equipment: Playing area

Objective: The couple tries to tag a running couple.

This game was played to symbolize the war between England and Scotland. King Alexander II of Scotland (1214–1249) joined English barons against King John of England to determine who was to control Scotland: the overlords of Scotland or the Crown in England.

Directions: A rectangular playing area is divided into thirds. The center square is called the Middle. (See Illustration 1.)

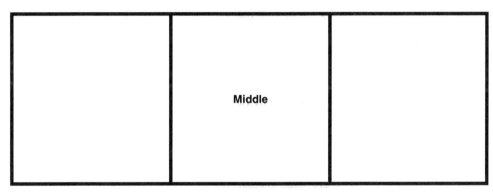

Illustration 1: *Last Couple in the Middle*

Two players who are IT hold hands in the Middle. The other couples are spread out in the two end squares. IT must enter one of the two end squares and try to drag a couple (who also hold hands) from an end square into the Middle. If IT is successful, that captured couple becomes the new IT.

Variation: Another way to play is to have only one person be IT and the other players run separately in either end square. Any captured players help IT to capture more players.

Also See: *Twin Tag (8-57)*

8-57. Twin Tag

Country: Native Americans, United States (North America)

Type of Game: Tag—Stay Connected

Formation: Partners are formed by tying near ankles together. Partners are scattered throughout the playing area.

Equipment: 30-inch strips of soft material; playing area

Objective: The IT couple tries to tag Runners.

Working together was vital to Native Americans. They knew that in order to survive they had to depend on each other.

Directions: One set of connected partners is chosen IT and begins chasing the other connected partners on the signal from the leader. The first set of runners tagged becomes the next IT.

Variations:

- Players may need to have inside legs tied at the ankles and knees for better control while running.

- Have the IT couple tag three or four sets of runners before a new IT is chosen.

- Runners continue to run until both partners have been tagged by IT.

Safety:

- Carefully select the playing surface due to the possibility of partners falling. A grassy flat playing field is the best.

Also See: *Last Couple in the Middle (8-56)*

8-58. El Gavilan, La Coneja, y Los Conejos (The Hawk and the Rabbits)

Country: El Salvador (Central America, North America)

Type of Game: Tag—Stay Connected

Formation: Players divide into two teams. One team begins in each half of a round playing area. Players form a single-file line and grasp the waist (or shoulders) of the player in front of them.

Equipment: Round playing area

Objective: The Mother (Father) Rabbit tries to protect the Baby Rabbits from the Hawk.

El Salvador is the most densely populated country of the Latin American countries. It is the smallest republic of the American Mainland, with only 8,124 square miles in landmass.

Directions: A play area is drawn on the ground as shown in Illustration 1. Two games can be going on at once, one in each half of the area. Two equal teams are formed, one in each half of the play area. Players form a single line on their half of the circle. This line may cross over into several marked sections. Players connect the line by placing hands on waist or shoulders of the person in front. The front player is the *Coneja* (Mother Rabbit). The other players in line are the *Conejos* (Rabbits).

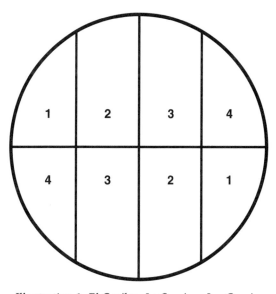

Illustration 1: *El Gavilan, La Coneja, y Los Conejos*

The *Gavilan* (Hawk) enters the circle and tries to tag the last *Conejos* in the line. The *Coneja* tries to remain face to face with the *Gavilan* as the *Conejos* stay behind her. When the *Gavilan* tags the last *Conejo* in line, the section number is noted where the tags took place. For example, if the *Conejo* is tagged in section 3, the last three *Conejos* are taken off the line from behind the *Coneja*.

After a specified time period, the next *Gavilan* is chosen from the remaining *Conejos*.

Variation: As a twist to this game, if the *Coneja*, whose hands are free, tags the *Gavilan*, any eliminated *Conejos* may reenter the game and the game begins again.

Also See: *Wolf's Tail* (8-59)

Eagle and Chicken (8-60)

Chase the Dragon's Tail (8-62)

8-59. Wolf's Tail

Country: Colonial America (North America)

Type of Game: Tag—Stay Connected

Formation: The Wolf stands in front of a connected line that forms the Geese. The front Goose has her/his hands free, while those behind have their hands on the waist of the player in front.

Equipment: None

Objective: The Wolf tries to tag a Goose behind the Mother or Father.

Although spare time was scarce, when their work was done, colonial children would get together and play simple games.

Directions: Holding on to the waist of the player in front of them, the Geese form a single line with the front player being the Mother Goose or Father Goose. The Wolf stands in front of the Mother/Father to begin the game.

The following dialogue may be used:

> WOLF: *"Geese, geese ganio."*
>
> GEESE: *"Wolf, wolf wannio."*
>
> WOLF: *"How many geese have you today?"*
>
> GEESE: *"More than you can catch and carry away."*

The Wolf tries to tag the Geese behind the Mother/Father. The Mother/Father's hands are free to try to block the Wolf, but she/he cannot grab or hold the Wolf. Once the Wolf tags a Goose, the Wolf takes the Goose to her/his den. Only one Goose at a time can be taken.

When the last Goose is taken from behind the Mother/Father, the Mother/Father runs away from the Wolf who then tries to tag her/him. A new Wolf and Mother/Father are chosen to start a new game.

Also See: *El Gavilan, La Coneja, y Los Conejos* (8-58)

Eagle and Chicken (8-60)

Hook-on Tag (8-61)

Chase the Dragon's Tail (8-62)

8-60. Eagle and Chickens

Country: (Asia)

Type of Game: Tag—Stay Connected

Formation: All but one player form a straight line and place their hands on the shoulders of the player in front. This line represents the Chicks with the front player being the Mother Hen. The one remaining player is the Eagle who stands about five feet in front and facing the line.

Equipment: None

Objective: The Eagle tries to tag the last Chick in line behind the Mother Hen.

Asia is the largest of the seven continents. It covers 17,159,995 square miles—about 33% of the world's total landmass.

Directions: The Chicks must remain in contact with each other and the Mother Hen as the line twists and turns away from the reaches of the Eagle. The Eagle tries to tag the last Chick in line. When tagged, the last Chick is eliminated and the Eagle tries to tag the new last Chick. The game is over when all Chicks behind the Mother Hen have been tagged.

Also See: *El Gavilan, La Coneja, y Los Conejos* (8-58)

Wolf's Tail (8-59)

Hook-on Tag (8-61)

Chase the Dragon's Tail (8-62)

8-61. Hook-On Tag

Country: Colonial America (North America)

Type of Game: Tag—Stay Connected

Formation: Players form groups of three or four. Standing in single file, players grasp the waist of the person in front. The front person leaves the line to become IT.

Equipment: Playing area

Objective: IT tries to attach her-/himself to the back of the line.

Colonial children would find a small clearing in which they could do a lot of running and moving around in a short period of time with this game.

Directions: IT stands in front of each group. On the signal "Go!" from the first person in line, IT tries to attach her-/himself to the end of the line of players in her/his group. When successful, the front player in line becomes the new IT and is released by the second player in line.

Safety: The groups of children must be careful not to run into each other.

Variations:

- IT may try to attach to any line of players.
- Have more than one IT.

Also See: *El Gavilan, La Coneja, y Los Conejos* (8-58)

　　　　　　　Wolf's Tail (8-59)

　　　　　　　Chase the Dragon's Tail (8-62)

8-62. Chase the Dragon's Tail

Country: China (Far East, Asia)

Type of Game: Tag—Stay Connected

Formation: Players form a single line and connect with the player in front.

Equipment: None

Objective: The first person in line tries to tag the last person.

This is a popular activity in Chinese communities around the world to celebrate the Chinese New Year.

Fire-breathing dragons are legends in China. These fearsome creatures were believed to carry off princesses and maidens, and destroy farmers' crops with fiery breaths. Paper dragons are a mainstay of Chinese celebrations.

Directions: All players form a single-file line and place their hands on the shoulders of the person in front. The first person in the line is the Head of the Dragon, and the last person is the Tail.

Maneuvering around the area, the Head of the Dragon tries to get into position to tag its Tail. The Dragon must stay together during this moving, so the Head needs to be careful as to how sharp are its turns and twists.

The line of players forms the Body of the Dragon and tries to prevent the Head from tagging its Tail. When the Tail gets tagged, the Head goes back to the Tail position, allowing the next person in line to become the new Head. The tagged Tail leaves the line, making it shorter.

The game ends when the Dragon is too short to allow enough bend for the Head to tag the Tail.

Also See: *El Gavilan, La Coneja, y Los Conjos* (8-58)

Wolf's Tail (8-59)

Hook-on Tag (8-61)

8-63. The Bear

Country: Russia (Asia)

Type of Game: Tag—Stay Connected

Formation: A square playing field is marked off with the Bear's den in one corner. The Bear stands in the den. The Runners are scattered throughout the playing area.

Equipment: Playing field

Objective: The Bear tries to tag the Runners.

The bear is the national symbol of Russia.

Directions: When leaving the den, the Bear (*Mevdisko*) calls out "The Bears are coming!" and begins chasing the others. When a player is tagged, the tagged player and the Bear return to the den, hold hands, and announce that "The Bears are coming!" They then run out to chase other players while still holding hands.

    Only one player can be tagged at a time before the Bears and tagged player return to the den. The original Bear is to always remain on one end and Bears must always stay connected.

Variation: If two players begin the game as the Bear, they enter the game from the den holding hands. The initial tagging of the first player is with the inside locked hands. Thereafter, all tagging is to be done with the outside hands.

Also See: *Boa Constrictor* (8-64)

8-64. Boa Constrictor

Country: Ghana/Togo (Africa)

Type of Game: Tag—Stay Connected

Formation: Players are scattered throughout the playing area. The Snake stands in a den.

Equipment: None

Objective: The Snake tries to grow by tagging Runners.

The boa constrictor is a nonvenomous snake noted for its great size and crushing powers.

Directions: One player begins the game as the Snake in the den. The other players are scattered throughout the play area. The Snake runs and tags other players who must then join the Snake by holding hands. As the Snake grows, it might come apart while chasing Runners. When this happens, the free players can tag the broken parts of the Snake, forcing the Snake to go back to its marked den to rejoin. (If the Snake can rejoin before any parts are tagged, it does not need to go back to its den.) The last Runner remaining wins.

Also See: *The Bear* (8-63)

8-65. A Fishing

Country: Ghana (Africa)

Type of Game: Tag—Stay Connected

Formation: Parallel lines are drawn 20–30 feet apart. The Net (four players holding a length of rope) stands between the lines. The Fish (players) stand on one of the parallel lines.

Equipment: Rope; parallel lines

Objective: The Net tries to catch the Fish.

Fishing is a large economic industry in Ghana. Its 1997 fish catch, for example, was 446,483 metric tons.

Directions: Parallel lines are drawn to represent the shoreline. Four players are chosen to be the Net and are given a piece of rope to catch fish. The rest of the players are Fish and swim between the shorelines as the Net runs to try to catch Fish by circling the rope around players.

Caught Fish are released on a shoreline. When all Fish are caught, four new players are chosen for the Net and a new game begins.

Variation: Begin a game by having the four Net players sing a fishing or water song (such as "Row, Row, Row Your Boat"). The chase for the Fish begins when the song ends.

Also See: *Fish Trap* (8-66)

8-66. Fish Trap

Country: Northwest Coastal Native Americans, United States (North America)

Type of Game: Tag—Stay Connected

Formation: Players are scattered throughout the playing area. The Net (4 or 5 players holding a rope) stands away from the Fish (players). There are several Nets.

Equipment: Rope; playing area

Objective: The Net tries to catch the Fish.

Northwest coastal Native American Indians lived near many rivers and streams and used many different tools to make their catches. Woven pole fences, called weirs, *let water flow through while keeping the fish, which could then be speared or netted. The huge long-handled nets used to scoop up the fish are known as* dipnets. *Fishing was the main source of meat for the people of the Northwest.*

Directions: Each Net tries to catch one Fish inside the net. To begin, each Fish has about a 20-foot head start before all the Nets begin the chase.

Staying within the boundaries, the Fish can double back, dodge, and weave about trying to get away. A catch is made when the two ends of the Net meet with the Fish inside. The Fish cannot break or dodge under the net. Two Nets cannot connect to trap a Fish.

Also See: *A Fishing* (8-65)

Teams

These next 11 games of *Tag* depend on one team going against another team to see which team can first tag the players of the other team.

8-67. New Orleans

Country: United States (North America)

Type of Game: Tag—Teams

Formation: Goal lines are drawn 20 feet apart. Players form two teams, each standing on opposite parallel lines.

Equipment: Goal lines

Objective: One team performs an action or activity, while the other team tries to guess it.

This game is also known as Lemonade.

Directions: Beginning on opposite goal lines, one team is the Acting Team and the other is the Guessing Team.

The Acting Team huddles to discuss what actions it is going to do. Possible actions can include eating an ice cream cone, flying a kite, mowing the lawn, or jump roping. Once decided, the Acting Team approaches the Guessing Team while saying this chant:

ACTING: *"Here we come."* [walking towards the Guessing Team]

GUESSING: *"Where you from?"*

ACTING: *"New Orleans."* [walking closer to the Guessing Team]

GUESSING: *"What's your trade?"*

ACTING: *"Lemonade."*

GUESSING: *"Show us something if you're not afraid."*

The Acting Team then performs the actions to help the Guessing Team guess what it is trying to be.

The Guessers must raise their hands and wait to be called before giving their answer. Both teams must be ready to run when a correct guess is made. (The Actors yell "Yes!") The Acting Team turns around and runs away from the Guessing Team, running back to its goal line. The Guessing Team tries to tag the Acting Team players. When a tag is made, the tagged Actor joins the Guessing Team. When time is called or no Actors remain, the original Guessing Team becomes the new Acting Team and makes plans of what to act out.

8-68. Four Chiefs

Country: Nigeria (Africa)

Type of Game: Tag—Teams

Formation: Four Chiefs are chosen, each sitting in different corners of the playing area. Each Chief has two Soldiers. Other players are scattered.

Equipment: A supply of ribbons in four different colors; playing field

Objective: The Soldiers try to tag as many Runners as possible for her/his Chief.

Different tribes of Africans controlled different areas of Nigeria. These tribes tried to capture invaders as captives for their Chiefs. Early cultures in Nigeria date back to at least 700 B.C.

Directions: Four Chiefs are chosen and assigned a color. They sit somewhere at the edge of the play area. Each Chief chooses two Soldiers who have a supply of colored ribbons matching the Chief's color.

On the signal "Go!" the Soldiers try to tag as many players as they can. When a player is tagged, the Soldier gives a colored ribbon to that player, who must then sit behind that particular Chief. At the end of a set time period or when all players have been tagged, the Chief with the most captured players wins.

Variations:

- The game ends when any Chief has a set number of captives; for example: six captives.

- When a player is tagged, the colored ribbon is given to the Chief and the player returns to the game. The game ends when one Chief has all her/his colored ribbons.

8-69. Saldu

Country: India (Asia)

Type of Game: Tag—Teams

Formation: Equal teams stand on opposite sides of a center line. Team One are the Defenders; Team Two are the Raiders.

Equipment: Center line

Objective: The Raiders try to tag Defenders on the Defenders' side of the center line and return to their own side without being tagged themselves.

This game is played in two halves by the Nicrobarese tribe in India. Teams have one turn as the Defenders and as the Raiders.

Directions: On the signal "Go!" Raiders enter the Defenders' area, attempt to tag a Defender, and return across the center line without being tagged themselves. If successful, the tagged Defender is eliminated and the Raiders score one point. If a Raider is tagged in the Defenders' area, the Raider is eliminated from the game and one point is scored for the Defenders.

When all players from either team are eliminated or time is called, the first half ends. Teams reverse roles and play the second half. At the end of the second half, the team with the greater accumulated score wins.

8-70. Catch Old Mother Winter and Throw Her in the River

Country: former Czechoslovakia (Europe)

Type of Game: Tag—Teams

Formation: Two teams start on opposite sides of a rectangular playing field. Old Mother Winter (a piece of cloth) is placed in one team's corner.

Equipment: 1 piece of cloth; playing area

Objective: One team tries to protect Mother Winter from capture.

Czechoslovakia split into two separate countries on January 1, 1993: the Czech Republic and Slovakia.

Directions: Players are divided into two teams. One team is the friend of Old Mother Winter (a piece of cloth); the other team is not. Teams begin at opposite ends of the playing area. The unfriendly team that wants to capture Old Mother Winter chants:

> *"We've come to get Old Mother Winter.*
>
> *It's time to throw her in the river."*

At this point, the friends of Mother Winter protect her by running and passing her off to others to keep her away. Once Mother Winter is touched by an unfriendly player, she is captured and given to the unfriendly team. The friends of Old Mother Winter then try to recapture her.

The game continues until players are tired, time is called, or a predetermined number of points (captures/recaptures) has been reached.

8-71. A Gecko and a Stag Beetle

Country: Australia

Type of Game: Tag—Teams

Formation: Two teams are scattered throughout the playing area. One team are the Geckos; the other players are the Beetles.

Equipment: 2 blocks of wood for each Gecko; playing area

Objective: The Geckos try to tag the Beetles.

The gecko is a lizard found in tropical and subtropical areas, including Australia. Children playing this game imitate the sound of the gecko by clapping together two pieces of wood. Beetles are a food source for geckos.

Directions: While clapping their blocks of wood, the Geckos run after and try to tag the Beetles. Tagged Beetles are eliminated and go to a marked-off area to wait for a new game.

The new game begins with the Beetles becoming the Geckos and the Geckos becoming the Beetles.

Safety: Tagging with the wood blocks is not allowed.

Variation: Time each game to see which team is quicker in tagging the other.

8-72. Getta-Chutt
(The King Ran Away)

Country: India (Asia)

Type of Game: Tag—Teams

Formation: Two teams are formed: the King's Team and the Defenders. Teams begin on opposite sides of the center line in the playing area. One member of the King's Team is chosen to be the King. The King stands behind the Defenders 70–80 feet from the center line (in the King's Chamber). Defenders spread throughout their side of the playing area.

Equipment: Marked-off playing area; center line

Objective: The King tries to return to her/his side without being tagged.

Variations of this game are played throughout the Indian state of Tripura.

Directions: Members of the King's Team enter the Defenders' area in an effort to reach the King. If tagged by a Defender, the player is eliminated from the game. If the King's Team can reach the King safely, players form a chain that reaches out of the King's Chamber and try to tag a Defender. Defenders tagged by the chain are eliminated from the game.

The King may at any time attempt to leave the King's Chamber and try to reach her/his side of the playing area. If tagged by a Defender before reaching her/his side, the King is dead and the half ends. If successful, the King's Team gets one point.

Teams change roles for the second half and repeat the game. After both teams have been the King's Team, the team whose King successfully escaped quicker wins. If one team's King is tagged and the second team's King is successful, the successful King's Team is the winner.

8-73. Prisoner's Base

Country: Colonial America (North America)

Type of Game: Tag—Teams

Formation: A large rectangular field has a center line dividing the area. Each area has a Prison and Base. (See Illustration 1.)

Equipment: Marked-off playing area

Objective: Each team tries to get into the other team's Base without being tagged.

This game was also popular in Great Britain at the time the colonies were settled.

Directions: Player A1 from Team A runs into Team B's area trying to get to Team B's base. Team B sends out player B1 to tag player A1 before she/he can reach Team B's base. While player B1 is chasing player A1, Team A sends out player A2 to chase player B1. Team B then sends out player B2 to chase player A2 who is chasing player B1 who is chasing player A1 who is trying to get to Team B's base. This process continues until all players from both teams are playing. Taggers can run after only one player, but they must be careful not to be caught by another tagger from the other team.

When a player is tagged, she/he goes to the other team's Prison being escorted by her/his captor. If the player you are chasing either tags someone else or gets back to her/his home Base, you must run back to your home Base.

Captured players may be freed by a teammate who can reach the Prison without first being tagged. Only one prisoner may be released and both players are immune from being tagged while walking back to the center line holding hands.

The game is over when all players from one team are captured or a time limit has been reached.

Illustration 1: *Prisoner's Base*

Also See: *Hurley Burley* (8-74)

Barley Break (8-75)

Stealing Sticks (8-76)

Capture the Flag (8-77)

8-74. Hurley Burley

Country: Uganda (Africa)

Type of Game: Tag—Teams

Formation: A playing field is marked off with a center line between each team's goal line. Team players are spread out on their half of the playing area.

Equipment: Soccer ball; playing field

Objective: Each team tries to get the ball across the opponent's goal line.

Despite being located along the equator, the temperature ranges from about 60° F. to 85° F. This is due to the fact that Uganda is at the relatively high altitude of 3,000–6,000 feet above sea level.

Directions: The referee tosses out a soccer ball (at the center line) that players scramble to get. Players try to get the ball across their opponent's goal line any way they can for a point. They are allowed to carry, pass, catch, throw, or kick it across.

Players on the other team try to tag the player with the ball. Once tagged, the ball is dropped. If it is not dropped, the referee gives the tagging team a free throw at the spot where the tag was made.

Also See: *Prisoner's Base* (8-73)

Barley Break (8-75)

Capture the Flag (8-77)

8-75. Barley Break

Country: Colonial America (North America)

Type of Game: Tag—Teams

Formation: A large rectangular field is divided in half with Goals and Prisons. Each team begins in its own half of the playing area. (See Illustration 1.)

Equipment: Marked-off playing area

Objective: Each team tries to run into the other team's Goal without being tagged.

This game was played by British and colonial children in barley fields following harvest. Stacks of barley were used as places to hide as players would sneak to the other team's area.

Directions: Teams begin on their half of the playing field. The object is for a member of either team to try to run into the opposing team's Goal without being tagged. Any runner who enters the other team's side of the field may be tagged by a defender and sent to Prison. The Prison is large enough for only one player to stand in it. Additional prisoners form a chain by linking to the prisoner in jail.

Prisoners can be freed if a teammate can tag any member of the chain without her-/himself being tagged first. Prisoners must return to their home field before attempting to go to the opposing team's Goal.

The game is over when a Goal is reached successfully by an opposing team's Player.

Illustration 1: *Barley Break*

Also See: *Prisoner's Base* (8-73)

Hurley Burley (8-74)

Stealing Sticks (8-76)

Capture the Flag (8-77)

8-76. Stealing Sticks

Country: Choctaw Native Americans, United States (North America)

Type of Game: Tag—Teams

Formation: Players divide into two teams. A playing field is marked off as shown in Illustration 1.

Equipment: Even number of sticks divided between teams; playing field

Objective: Each team tries to take the sticks from the other team's Mush Pot.

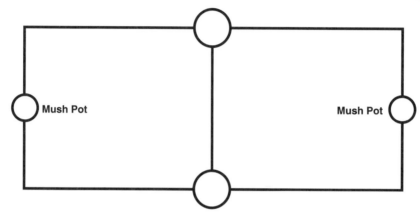

Illustration 1: *Stealing Sticks*

Native Americans held great respect for all of nature. They had special prayers and ceremonies to honor all living creatures. "Deer, I am sorry to hurt you, but the people are hungry."—Choctaw hunter's prayer

---

Directions: A field measuring 30' x 60' feet (or appropriate for the number and abilities of the players) is marked off with a center line. At the intersections where the center line meets the sidelines, circles are drawn large enough for all members of each team to be able to sit inside. On the end lines, smaller circles (called Mush Pots) are drawn and equal numbers of sticks are placed in each.

To begin, all players stand inside their team's side of the playing field. On the signal "Go!" each player tries to run to the opponent's Mush Pot, capture one stick, and bring it back to her/his team's own Mush Pot without being tagged. A tag can only occur while in the other team's area. Tagged players go to their own team's large circle at the center line and wait for the end of the game.

A game is over when all sticks of one team is captured, all opponents are captured, or time runs out.

Variation: Tagged players in the circle are free to rejoin the game if their team captures a stick.

Also See: *Prisoner's Base* (8-73)

Hurley Burley (8-74)

Barley Break (8-75)

Capture the Flag (8-77)

8-77. Capture the Flag

Country: England/Scotland (Europe)

Type of Game: Tag—Teams

Formation: A field divided in half with Flags and Jails. Teams begin in their own half of the playing area. (See Illustration 1.) Each team has one Jailer.

Equipment: 1 flag for each team; marked-off playing field; center line

Objective: Each team tries to run into the other team's area, grab its Flag, and return to own area without being caught.

Capture the Flag is believed to be based on territorial raids between England and Scotland, where raiding parties would enter the other's area, capture the reigning monarch, and return home.

Directions: Before play begins, each team gets together to make and coordinate plans. A leader is chosen to listen to suggestions and set plans as to how the raiding party can best capture the other team's Flag. Defense should also be discussed and planned as the best way to defend its Flag from being captured.

When the game starts, an attack may occur at any time. The defending team needs to be ready to repel and capture any attackers. Capturing an attacker of the raiding party involves holding the player and shouting "Caught, caught, caught!"

Captured players are escorted to Jail by either the defender who caught them or by another defensive player. An unescorted attacker can escape before getting to jail. Once in Jail the player must remain there until a teammate gets to the Jail, without being caught her-/himself and calls out "Freed, freed, freed!" Freed players have safe passage back to their own territory where they rejoin or reform raiding parties.

Decoy raiding parties can be used to distract defenders away from other raiding parties, looking for an opportunity to attack when the defense is down.

The game ends when one team successfully captures and brings back the other team's Flag to its own territory.

Illustration 1: *Capture the Flag*

Also See: *Prisoner's Base* (8-73)

Hurley Burley (8-74)

Barley Break (8-75)

Stealing Sticks (8-76)

Grabbing Flags

In the following four games of Tag, players wear flag football flags, handkerchiefs, or strips of cloth from belt loops, back pockets, or the waistlines. Instead of tagging a player, her/his flag must be pulled. The player being chased is not allowed to block a person from grabbing the flag by pushing the hand away or holding onto the flag that she/he is wearing. Wrapping or tying the flag around a belt or belt loop is also not allowed.

8-78. Tails

Country: Australia

Type of Game: Tag—Grabbing Flags

Formation: Players stand in a single circle with two players inside. All players have a handkerchief tucked in a back pocket.

Equipment: 1 handkerchief for each player

Objective: Players hop on one foot and try to grab the flag of the other player.

Oceania is the collective name for the approximately 25,000 islands in the South Sea having inhabitants with Asian ancestry. It is considered synonymous with Melanesia, Micronesia, and Polynesia. Although not truly part of Oceania, Australia and New Zealand are traditionally included.

Directions: Two players stand inside the circle on one foot. On the signal "Go!" both players hop around trying to grab the other player's handkerchief while protecting her/his own. Players must position their bodies to block opponents from grasping the handkerchiefs; players can't grasp or hit the other's hand away. If a player puts a foot down, she/he forfeits this flag and any previously won flags to her/his opponent. Individuals with the most flags at the end of play win.

When players finish their turns, they become part of the circle again as two new players enter.

Variation: Teams may be formed. Players compete against members of the other team. When play ends, the team with the most flags wins.

Also See: *Ribaki (Fishermen) (8-79)*

Catch Your Tail (8-80)

Western Round-up (8-81)

8-79. Ribaki (Fishermen)

Country: Russia (Asia/Europe)

Type of Game: Tag—Grabbing Flags

Formation: Players are spread throughout the playing area. Each player has a long string and a cardboard fish tied to one end. The other end of the string is tucked in the back of the player's pants or a pocket so the fish drags on the ground.

Equipment: 1 long string attached to a cardboard fish for each player

Objective: Each player tries to protect her/his own fish while stepping on other players' fish.

In 1997, Russia's total fish catch was 4.66 million metric tons.

Directions: When play begins, the players (Fishermen) run around and step on the other players' fish while trying to protect their own. Hands are only allowed to gather up the fish the player has caught. The first Fisherman to catch five fish wins.

Also See: *Tails* (8-78)

Catch Your Tails (8-80)

Western Round-up (8-81)

8-80. Catch Your Tail

Country: Nigeria (Africa)

Type of Game: Tag—Grabbing Flags

Formation: One partner stands behind the other and holds the front partner's waist. The back player has a flag tucked in the back pocket or back waistband.

Equipment: 1 flag for each player

Objective: Partners try to stay connected while trying to grab the flags of the other sets of partners.

Nigeria is easily the most populated country in Africa and one of the fastest growing on Earth. Inhabitants of Nigeria are divided into 250 different ethnic groups. Although English is the national language, each ethnic group speaks its own language.

Directions: On the signal "Go!" the partners must stay connected and move to protect the flag of the back partner while trying to grab the flag from another set of partners. When a flag is taken, those players must leave the game. When one set of partners has its back flag remaining, the game is over and that set of partners is the winner. The partners change positions and the front player now becomes the back player.

Variation: When the back partner has lost her/his flag, the two partners change places immediately. The game continues as described.

Also See: *Tails* (8-78)

   Ribaki (Fishermen) (8-79)

   Western Round-up (8-81)

8-81. Western Round-Up

Country: United States (North America)

Type of Game: Tag—Grabbing Flags

Formation: Players are divided into three groups: Cows, Horses, Cowgirls/Cowboys. Horses and Cowgirls/Cowboys become partners holding hands. Cows have tails tucked in the back of their pants or pockets and are scattered throughout the play area.

Equipment: 1 tail (5-foot rope with beanbag tied to one end) for each Cow; playing area

Objective: The Cowgirl/Cowboy tries to grab the tail of a Cow.

The number of heads of cattle on farms in the U.S. has risen through the years from 1900 to 1999. In 1900, there were 59,739,000; in 1999, there were 98,522,000. These numbers also include milk cows.

Directions: The Cows begin by wandering off, dragging their tails behind them, to graze in the pasture (playing area). When the leader calls out "Go!" the Horse and Cowgirl/Cowboy hold hands and run together after a Cow, trying to grab the tail. Only the Cowgirl/Cowboy is allowed to catch the tail, not the Horse. Play continues until all the Cows are caught. Then players change positions so everyone has a chance to be a Cow, Horse, and Cowgirl/Cowboy.

Adaptation: A small group might play until only the first Cow is caught.

Also See: *Tails (8-78)*

   Ribaki (fishermen) (8-79)

   Catch Your Tail (8-80)

Resources

Every effort has been made to include the proper sources for the activities described in this book.

Arnold, A. *The World Book of Children's Games.* Greenwich, CT: Fawcett Crest Books, 1972.

Barbarash, Lorraine *Multicultural Games.* Champaign, IL.: Human Kinetics, 1997.

Bernarde, A. *Games from Many Lands.* New York: Sayre Publishing, Inc., 1970.

Ide, E. *Lost Colonies Games: First English Games Brought to America.* Raleigh, NC: Sparks Press, 1984.

Koh, F. *Korean Games.* Minneapolis: East West Press, 1997.

Lankford, M. *Hopscotch Around the World.* New York: A Beach Tree Paperback Book, 1992.

——— *Jacks Around the World.* New York: A Beach Tree Paperback Book, 1996.

Macfarlan, Allen and Macfarlan, Paullette. *Handbook of American Indian Games.* Mineola, NY: Dover Publications, Inc. , 1985.

Maguire, J. *Hopscotch, Hangman, Hot Potato, and Ha Ha Ha—A Rulebook of Children's Games.* Englewood Cliffs, NJ: Prentice Hall, Inc., 1990.

Nelson, W. and Glass, H. *International Playtime—Classroom Games and Dances from Around the World.* New York: Fearon Teacher Aids, Simon and Schuster Education Group, 1992.

Newmann, Dana. *Native Americans Resource Library* (four-book series). West Nyack, NY: The Center for Applied Research in Education, 1995-1997.

Oakley, Ruth. *Games Children Play Around the World—Ball Games.* Tarrytown, NY: Marshall Cavendish Corporation, 1989.

——— *Games Children Play Around the World—Chasing Games.* Tarrytown, NY: Marshall Cavendish Corporation, 1989.

——— *Games Children Play Around the World—Games with Rope and String.* Tarrytown, NY: Marshall Cavendish Corporation, 1989.

——— *Games Children Play Around the World—Sticks, Stones and Shells.* Tarrytown, NY: Marshall Cavendish Corporation, 1989.

——— *Games Children Play Around the World—Games of Strength and Skill.* Tarrytown, NY: Marshall Cavendish Corporation, 1989.

Sernaque, V. *Classic Children's Games.* New York: Dell Press, 1988.

Stull, Elizabeth. *Multicultural Discovery Activities for the Elementary Grades.* West Nyack, NY: The Center for Applied Research in Education, 1995.

Wiswell, Phil. *Kids' Games.* New York: Doubleday, A division of Random House, 1987.

Notes

Notes

Notes

Notes

Notes

Notes

Notes

Notes

Notes

Notes

Notes